AGAINST THE ODDS

SURVIVAL ON THE RUSSIAN FRONT

1944 - 1945

JOHN STIEBER

First published in 1995 by
Poolbeg Press Ltd, Dublin, Ireland.
This 2nd edition published in 2016.

© John Stieber 1995

The moral right of the author has been asserted.
Reprinted with permission from the children of the author:
Anthony Stieber, Christine Cann, and Annette Kunigagon.

A catalogue record for this book is available from the British Library.

ISBN-13: 978-1523347360
ISBN-10: 1523347368

Original cover photograph of crest by Gillian Buckley
Original cover design by Poolbeg Group Services Ltd

2nd EDITION NOTES

Against the Odds was first published in 1995 by my grandfather, John Stieber. His book was read and his story shared by many. He passed away peacefully in the arms of his family on July 11, 2010. This reprinting finally happened in 2016 after many requests from friends and family members to make the book available again. It is our family's wish to share his story so that this piece of history is not forgotten.

Proceeds from this book will go to non-profit organizations near his home in Booterstown, Co. Dublin, Ireland.

This 2nd edition matches the text of the first with some changes from my grandfather. The original cover art was reused. Some minor corrections and edits were also made.

Marcel Stieber
Sunnyvale, California
January 2016

ACKNOWLEDGEMENTS

I want to thank my late wife, Hertha, for proof-reading all drafts and offering many constructive comments. My daughter, Christine Cann has given me much help in dealing with the typical quirks of modern word-processors and printing the first sets of the completed manuscript.

I am very grateful to Jonathan Williams, my agent, for all his help and advice and for doing over and above what I could have expected of him.

To all ESB colleagues many thanks for the encouragement they have given me and especially to Alf Kelly for the helpful and copious notes he compiled on the first completed draft.

Finally, I wish to express my appreciation to all friends both here and in Germany, who read the manuscript and made many valuable suggestions.

CONTENTS

AUTHOR'S NOTE

It is many years since I decided that someday I would write a book about my experiences and adventures on the Russian Front in the last year of the Second World War. I think it was as much as forty years ago when I started to keep a little notebook, recording names of people and places, which I still remembered. My jottings included references to incidents, the nature of the countryside and memories of my thoughts and sensations of sound and smell. Retirement brought me time and peace of mind to settle down to my task.

My biggest problem was getting background military information on the role of the Division Hermann-Göring, in which I served, since most of its military records were lost during the retreat. Painstaking research in Germany military archives and libraries rewarded me with some information on my division's activities. A soldier on the Front rarely knows exactly where he is, or even the date - so it is against the background of situations comparable to those I remember that I have set my narrative as well as I could.

Writing my story brought many memories flooding back to me, far more than would have been practical to include in my book. Strangely enough, I found it more scary writing about some of the particularly dicey situations I survived on the Front, than when I actually experienced them.

The past came back to me even more vividly in the summer of 1990. "The Wall" was down and I could again visit my old boarding-school, Haubinda, in East Germany. I had expected never to see it again and I gazed at it as if I could not believe my eyes. As I walked slowly up the avenue, pausing every now and then, every step brought back new memories to me. Sadly, I noted the absence of many lovely old trees and I was shaken by the sight of a stark memorial to the dead of the Second World War. Suddenly I felt myself jerked back to the harsh reality of tragic events that had taken the lives of many of my school-friends.

As I drew nearer to the main school buildings, the shabbiness of the once impeccably maintained exterior became evident. The school bell no longer hung in its prominent position on the front wall; only a rusty bracket remained to show where it had been. Once again I experienced the feeling of security that my school had given me in the early years of the war. Shielded from all, but the most peripheral effects of the National-Socialist doctrine, school life had continued with remarkable normality. What a contrast were the years that followed, when gunfire became my constant companion.

John Stieber
Blackrock, Dublin
April 1995

CHRONOLOGY

Late 1926	Arrival in England
Spring 1932	Move to Brünn, now in Czech Republic
Spring 1933	Move to Ireland
April 1939	At school in Eger
May 1939	At school in Gebesee
Nov. 1940	At school in Haubinda
22 Feb. 1943	I start serving with FLAK battery
15 Feb. 1944	I join Labour Service
1 May 1944	In Training with Division Hermann Göring
25 July 1944	Sent to the Russian Front, Warsaw area
8 Aug 1944	Division sent to Magnuszew Bridgehead
3 Sept. 1944	I join gun-group Trapp
19 Sept. 1944	Division returns to Warsaw area
7 Oct. 1944	Destruction of train to Radom
9 Oct. 1944	Division transferred to East-Prussia
10 Oct. 1944	I join a suicide squad
16 Oct. 1944	Russian onslaught towards East-Prussia
18 Oct. 1944	Division transferred to Gumbinnen
27 Oct. 1944	I join 37-millimetre gun-group
12 Jan. 1945	Russian offensive at Baranow Bridgehead
17 Jan. 1945	Division moves to Lodz
18 Jan 1945	I join the "Wandering Pocket"
10 Feb. 1945	Ambush of Division Göring
14 Feb. 1945	I join supplies unit at Lauban
17 Mar. 1945	Division sent to Neisse area
14 Apr. 1945	Division operating in Görlitz area
7 May 1945	End of hostilities
9 May 1945	Reunion with Erika
15 May 1945	Arrival in Rotenburg
4 May 1946	I return to Ireland

SKETCH MAPS

Map 1
Map of Germany and my escape route to safety.

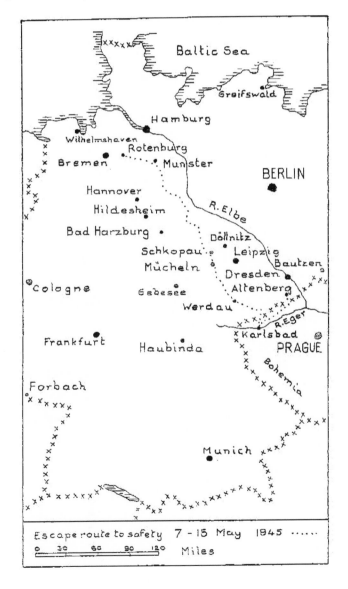

Escape route to safety   7 - 15 May   1945 ······

0   30   60   90   120   Miles

Map 2

Areas of deployment of Division (Later Panzer Corps) Hermann Göring on the Russian Front from July 1944 to closing stage of the war.

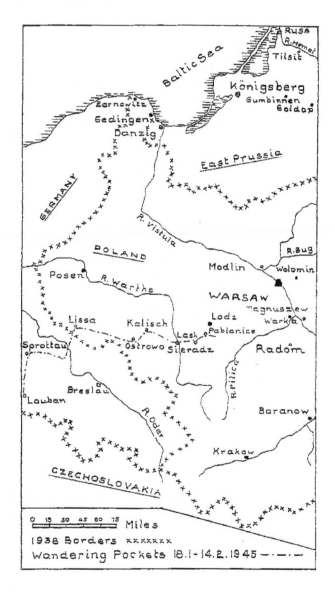

Map 3
Map showing sweeping advance of Russian forces between
March 1943 and July 1944.

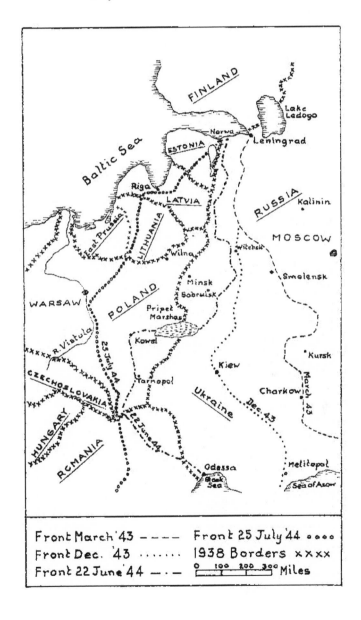

Me in uniform

My father in World War I

My mother in Brünn

x.62 15

On the beach in Woolacombe

My father and Erika in Alscott

Straw Hall Villa in Carlow

Erika and I in Carlow in 1938

My mother, Uncle Anton and Aunt Hella in Karlsbad in 1939

GEBESEE

The main building of my boarding school

Left to right: The headmaster, Dr Max Prüss, Frau Kieschke
and Herr Kieschle

Döllnitz in 1939

Frau Goedecke, Adolf, Georg and Hertha

Music with Madonna and Child and "Hitler"!

One of our lovely family houses

HOMELAND FLAK

My accommodation hut

Our bunk beds

Our jazz group, Gefreiter Rother is on the left

Soldiers and auxiliaries at the control module

MY FRIENDS IN MUSIC

Heinz Rücker

Günther Heinelt

PROLOGUE

My first sentry-duty on being posted for active service on the Russian Front was a two-hour stint on 27 July 1944 from midnight until two o'clock in the morning. Alone, in the stillness of the night, I felt a strong sense of unreality, while being conscious of the deadly earnestness of my situation.

My mind went back to my early years in England, Czechoslovakia and Ireland and to the carefree days in boarding-school in Germany. I thought of the good times that I had enjoyed and of how remote they now seemed. And how remote, too, was the chance of seeing my parents and my sister again. My thoughts moved on to the years when life became more hazardous and I served in the Homeland FLAK, the Labour Service and as a member of the occupation forces in Holland.

So, as I paced my beat in the darkness, with slivers of moonshine casting strange shadows before my feet, the past seemed no longer to be of any consequence and I felt that I had arrived at the watershed of my life. From now on, everything that happened was going to be of vital importance; my life was going to be in constant danger and in twenty-four hours I could be dead.

1

EARLY CHILDHOOD

Although I had been born in Czechoslovakia to parents of Austrian descent, my early childhood was mainly spent in an English-speaking environment and my first language was English. My father, who came from several generations of professional engineers, was a chemical engineer with Die Erste Brünner, a Czech company that manufactured and installed heavy industrial equipment.

In late 1926, when I was only a few months old, my father was sent with a team of engineers and technical back-up staff to Shropshire in England to build and operate a sugar factory for "English Sugar". My mother followed soon afterwards with me and my sister, Erika, who was almost four years old. We quickly settled down in the rural hamlet of Alscott, near Wellington, where we spent six very happy years.

My father was intensely dedicated to his profession. A man not given to many hobbies, he spent much of his spare time reading up technical literature and working out problems that had occurred in the factory. For relaxation he loved to read non-fiction, but I think that motoring through the countryside, and sightseeing, were what gave him the most pleasure. One other form of relaxation that he engaged in was the occasional game of tennis or badminton that he played with a lot of enthusiasm. I do not think he shared Erika's and my keenness for board and card-games, but he was always very good-natured about joining in whenever we asked him. One of his other characteristics that I well remember was his subtle sense of humour; it was always quick to surface and he never lost it. Then, of course, there was his typically Austrian courteous manner for which he was well-known and liked.

My mother was a very practical person and could turn her hand to almost anything. Apart from being a wonderful cook and hostess, she could sew and knit beautifully and was forever making something new for us. Her good taste was reflected in the clothes she wore and the attractive furnishing of our house which was always enhanced by a display of flowers in the rooms. It was she who was the gardener in the family and she was also the more pragmatic of my parents. My mother loved to socialise and also became a very keen tennis and badminton player.

Despite the effect of my parental home, my development was very much influenced by English people, rather than by the small colony of Germans and Czechs living in Alscott. Meeting English people and visiting their homes, I became conscious of how different my parents, and the other foreigners, were from our English neighbours. Perhaps it was the greater calmness and sense of humour of the English that impressed me and I felt myself drawn toward their lifestyle in a way that was at variance with my hereditary influences. In a strange way, my father's colleagues became the foreigners to me; my parents were half-foreign, whereas I felt as if I was an English child. One result of this was that, since then, Erika and I have always spoken to each other in English.

I have always felt that the effect of my dual-culture upbringing was to instil in me, from an early age, a tendency towards objectivity. It also gave me a sense of detachment and the confidence I needed in later years when I had to cope with increasingly difficult situations and did not have my parents to guide me.

During our time in England, my family formed many close friendships with English people. We came to love the countryside and also saw much of Wales and Scotland. I do not recollect ever being lonely in Alscott, even though Erika and I had no other children to play with. Our house stood inside the extensive grounds of the sugar factory which itself was situated in open countryside. Most of the few houses in the area were far apart and the people living in them had no children. However, Erika and I got on very well with each other and spent a lot of time playing together. At the same time we had no trouble keeping ourselves occupied individually.

Since we were surrounded by open countryside, there was unlimited space for rambling across the fields or flying a kite, but I also loved to play in our garden and look after my pet rabbits. When I became the proud owner of a tricycle, there was almost no limit to the distance I could travel on the traffic-free roads accompanied by Erika on her two-wheeled "Fairy" bicycle.

My earliest contacts with other children came mainly through friends of my parents or those they knew on a social basis in the Wellington/Shrewsbury area, but I did not meet them often enough at the various children's parties to enable me to form any close friendships. I had a lot more contact with grown-ups during the years in England than would have been usual for a child of my age and I must have benefitted from a greater mental maturity as a result of this.

My parents settled down very quickly in England and loved the English way of life. I think that my mother was much happier than she had been in Czechoslovakia, where she always felt more of a foreigner. My father also seemed to prefer the more relaxed atmosphere and a greater sense of freedom than he had previously experienced. Then again, working conditions in the sugar factory were definitely better than the twelve-hour shifts he had had to work during the beet-processing season in Czechoslovakia.

When I was five years old, I began to attend a kindergarten in Wellington which meant taking the train from our local railway-station in Admaston. Erika, on her "Fairy" bicycle, and I on my tricycle had to cycle the three-quarters of a mile to the station and after reaching Wellington we had to walk another half a mile to the school. Covering these distances was quite an undertaking, but I did not consider it a hardship; in fact I actually looked forward to each day as if I were setting out on a new adventure.

My parents' happiness in Alscott, and in England generally, was a confirmation of my own acceptance of the English lifestyle and we were all very sad when the time came for us to leave in the spring of 1932. By this time, the sugar factory was operating well and my father was recalled to the head office of his firm in Brünn.

Since my father did not expect to remain in Brünn for very long, our family moved into the house of my grandmother on my mother's side, who was a widow. There was plenty of room for us in her suburban villa which backed onto a fine wooded area overlooking the river Moldau. The only other occupant of the house was my mother's unmarried sister. Aunt Hella was a domestic science teacher and a woman of diverse accomplishments. In later years Erika and I were to form a very close relationship with her when she was married and we spent many happy school-holidays in her house.

In Brünn I was faced with adapting to a new, and very different, culture. People struck me as generally being more serious and formal and I missed the relaxed atmosphere to which I had been accustomed in England. My grandmother's house was a bit like an oasis in an alien land. She herself was a typical Viennese lady, very stout, a wonderful cook and full of good humour, so there was always fun and laughter in the house.

Our garden was quite large and very sheltered. I remember the lovely smell of peaches ripening in summer, the pungent aroma of box-hedges and the scent of the many roses that my grandmother lovingly cared for. Unfortunately, Erika and I were not allowed to play in the woodlands behind the house, so we went there only when accompanied by our parents. This usually meant going on somewhat formal walks and I sorely missed the unrestricted freedom to roam that I had enjoyed in Alscott.

I do not remember ever meeting my grandfather on my mother's side, since he died while I was a small child. Erika remembers him as being a very upright person and a man of great integrity, but she felt intimidated by him. My father's widowed mother also lived in Brünn. She had an apartment near the centre of the city and we regularly went to visit her. She was tall and thin and very serious. As a young woman she had been an accomplished violinist and, according to photographs, must have been extremely attractive. Although my grandfather on my father's side died when I was very young, I did meet him once when we went over to Brünn on a holiday from England. I remember him as being very tall with a long white beard. He often took me to a playground in a public park, the Spielberg, where I loved having a swing and getting a push from him.

In Brünn I went to a boy's school, known as a Gymnasium, and this took some getting used to. The boys in my class were truly a hard bunch and our teacher, Herr Zelinka, a huge terrifying man with a black beard, ruled the class with an iron fist. Although this was a German-speaking school, most of the boys were Czech in appearance and by nature and most of them also had Czech names. My father's Czech colleagues in England did not have any children, so this was my first contact with Czech children and I did not find it easy. It was not that I actually had any trouble from any of them but, with my English upbringing, I was so different from them that I found myself attending classes without achieving a personal relationship with the other boys.

My sister fared similarly in her girls' class in the Lyceum. One day she brought a box of sweets into class, which she shared with the other girls. When all the sweets had been eaten, the girls told her how stupid she was to have given them away when she could have eaten them all herself. How different this was from what we had experienced in England!

I remember going reluctantly on several outings to the countryside with my class. The boys' mothers invariably came along too, weighed down with huge rucksacks filled with food. It seemed that the purpose of these outings was to sit down and consume mountains of food, each mother setting herself up as a conveyor-belt between the rucksack and her offspring. There was no question of any games being played and when the rucksacks were finally empty, everybody went home.

Coping with these aspects of my new environment was not the only problem I was up against. I also had to learn to speak Czech, an immensely difficult language to learn and pronounce. Being already fluent in English and German, I managed to make reasonable progress, but it was not easy.

We stayed in Czechoslovakia for less than a year and I was not yet seven when we left. All in all, living there had been tough for me. At the same time my perception of people and the differences between nationalities had been further sharpened. I had also learned that excitable people have a tendency to say unreasonable things and to act in an uncontrolled manner and that people of one nationality grow up uncritical of their way of life if they have no means of comparing it with another. Though I was still only a child, I had already developed an ability to discriminate between people and between different ways of life.

When news came that my father's next posting was to be in Ireland, I felt quite glad, even though this meant yet another change. Although I had learned to cope with all that was foreign to me in Brünn, I never felt fully at home there and doubt if I would have become much happier over a longer period of time.

These brief notes on our family history in Brünn have a very sad ending. My father's mother died there before the end of the war and was lucky to be spared the terrible aftermath. However, my other grandmother was less fortunate and was evicted from her home at eighty-five years of age and told to pack a single bag and leave. Despite her advanced age, she took a neighbour's two orphaned children under her wing and set off on the road. The ordeal finally became too much for her and she died in a small town not far from Vienna, her place of birth.

My father had been appointed as assistant manager to the Carlow sugar factory, about fifty miles south of Dublin in Ireland, and we left Brünn for our new destination in the spring of 1933. I remember having an instant liking for our new home, the surrounding area and the town of Carlow. The house we lived in was one of the spacious Strawhall Villas, which the Sugar Company provided for its senior staff. It was situated on the Athy road within walking distance of the factory and about a mile outside the town. Surrounded by a large garden on three sides, and backing onto open fields and a small wood, it was in a perfect setting for young children who loved the outdoor life. To me it was like being back in England again, but now I had lots of children to play with. There was a large colony of factory employees living near us and most of them were not Irish. The foreigners were German, Czech, Dutch and French. They were mostly engineers, supervisors and specialist craftsmen.

When we moved to Carlow, I was not yet seven and faced going to school for the third time in a different country. My parents decided to engage a governess so that Erika and I would get off to a good start after spending almost a year in Czech schools. Our teacher, Miss Dorothy McMullen, lived about half a mile away and gave us several hours of lessons each day.

Our first playmates in Carlow were the children of other employees of the sugar factory. In time, other children were introduced to us through our parents' social contacts and, later again, it was in the local schools where I made more friends. What a change Carlow was from Brünn. Apart from enjoying the advantages of a rural environment, I was once again living in a country whose inhabitants were relaxed, full of good humour and, to my mind, well-adjusted.

Just as in England, I was acutely conscious of the differences in manner of our continental neighbours compared with the native population. That is not to say that there were no exceptions among them, but the general comparison was still valid. Once again, I categorised them as foreigners and felt as if I was "back with my own people". My parents continued our bilingual upbringing, but though I was fluent in German and enjoyed reading German books, I still felt more at home with English. I must also admit that, although our parents always spoke to us in German, unless English-speaking people were present, we almost invariably replied in English.

In 1934 my parents considered that Erika and I had received sufficient individual tuition and were ready to hold our own in a regular school. Erika was sent as a boarder to Alexandra College in Dublin, while I attended the local Methodist School run by Miss Dixon, a tall, thin lady who was a good teacher and a very kind person. I immediately felt at home in the Methodist School; the friendly atmosphere was so different from the impersonal relationship I had had with my classmates in Brünn!

Erika had been an avid reader for years and I developed the same passion as soon as I could read effortlessly. The county library, situated in the magnificent Carlow Court House, attracted me like a magnet. There were two rooms with floor to ceiling bookshelves presenting me with a huge selection from which to make my choice. Although I often went back several times a week to get new books, the librarian, Miss Iona McLeod, was always friendly and glad to help me find what I wanted.

I have always felt that the people of Carlow belonged to a particularly happy community. The thriving nature of the town was reflected in its tidy streets; the small industries it boasted, as well as the sugar factory, were all doing well. It was a constant hive of social activities and the big attractions in summer were the many tennis parties that were held at different venues. These were always organised as competitions in which the winners were given small prizes. There was no shortage of facilities and I used to practise enthusiastically with my friends on the courts, which the sugar factory provided for the residents of the local staff houses.

After I had attended the Methodist School for a year, my parents felt that the environment of a school under the direction of a male teacher would be better for my development and that I should transfer to the National School. I was quite happy about this change especially since some of my friends were going to make the same move.

Because of my fluency in two languages, and my past tussle with Czech, it was no great problem for me to learn Irish. In fact, I used to get top marks in class and was usually only beaten into second place by the son of one of the Czech workers in the sugar factory. This goes to prove that learning Irish was even then a problem for nationals in the early days of the State's existence.

My mother was the more strict of my parents, but they were both quite firm where a basic code of good behaviour was concerned. At the same time they placed great trust in me and I was allowed an inordinate amount of freedom. An example of this was that I could roam the fields for miles on my own or spend hours cycling. At ten years of age I was given a Diana air-gun and could sally forth armed with it and my catapult to engage in target practice wherever I wished, as long as I did not use them near people or houses. Taking pot shots at tin cans, or little targets that I set up as I went on my rambles, soon made me into a competent marksman, and handling my small weapons became second nature to me. The fact that I was always encouraged to acquire fresh dexterity and new skills was a demonstration by my parents of their trust in me. This must have instilled in me tremendous self-confidence which served me well in later years.

In 1936, Hitler began to feature more prominently in the news reports on radio and in the daily press. I remember my father sitting through Hitler's long speeches on our Pye valve-radio set, and being impressed by his eloquence. Although I normally obeyed my father, I was not happy to join him in listening to these speeches. From the start, I had no time for Hitler's ranting and considered him to be somewhat unbalanced. However, out of respect for my father, I sometimes compromised by sitting in the room with him, but I would read a book and, to humour him, occasionally listen for a few minutes to what Hitler was saying.

Erika's move to her new school meant that we became separated for long periods at a time, but we always made up for it in the holidays. In summer we even went so far as to set our alarm clocks at an unearthly hour so that we could go for long cycle rides together, before returning home for breakfast to tell our parents about all that we had seen and done. Another pre-breakfast activity of ours was doing physical exercises in the back garden under the direction of my father. We both enjoyed this somewhat unusual pastime and, to this day, I can get great satisfaction from early morning exercises.

As time went by I got more and more busy. I began to take violin lessons from Mrs Born, the wife of the German organist in the Catholic cathedral. Then I joined the Lifeboys, the junior section of the Boys' Brigade. Our weekly meetings took place in the gym room of the Town Hall and I used to cycle the mile and a half in and out, even on dark winter nights. Our uniform consisted of navy-blue shorts and pullover, and a flat, sailor-type cap with "Lifeboy" embossed in large letters on the front. It was all good fun and I enjoyed marching to music and playing games.

Early in 1937, my parents decided that I should go to a German school the following year for my second-level education. Since my Aunt Hella was now married and living in Karlsbad, the famous spa in the Sudetenland, it seemed an ideal solution to send me to the nearby town of Eger which had many excellent schools. I was to attend the Realgymnasium as a day boy and could live in a nearby home for students. The reason for not living with my relatives, who had no children, was that I would not become a burden to them. At the same time, they were near enough for me to visit them easily or be able to ask for advice about any problems that I might have.

Leaving school in Carlow meant that I would have to prepare intensively for a complete change of syllabus and in a different language. All studying was to be done at home and the teaching shared between my father and my mother. A syllabus was requested from the school in Eger; I was taken out of the National School and began to study, following a detailed curriculum that my parents had prepared for me.

My father taught me mathematics, German grammar and literature while my mother concentrated on geography, history and Czech. I had hoped to have seen the last of the Czech language, but here I was back again struggling with its difficult pronunciation and grammar. My parents must have gone to a lot of trouble taking on this onerous chore and I remember working very hard and spending long hours at my lessons. Life had certainly been a lot easier at the National School.

When 1938 arrived and I had successfully completed a year's study, my parents felt that they did not want to be parted from me so soon. It was then decided that I should stay at home for another year and that I would prepare for the next higher class. As I concentrated on my studies over the next months, a number of political developments concerning Czechoslovakia took place. On 24 May, Konrad Henlein, the leader of the Sudeten-German Party, called for autonomy for all Sudeten-Germans. On 20 June, partial mobilisation was introduced in Czechoslovakia and on 30 September, the fateful Munich Agreement on the acquisition of the Sudetenland by Germany was signed by Hitler, Mussolini, Chamberlain and Daladier.

I had no inkling about how portentous these developments were, and I never got the impression that my parents were worried. My studies continued, there was no change of plan and I went on enjoying my idyllic existence in Carlow. One result of the Sudetenland being taken over by Germany was that it was no longer compulsory for me to learn Czech and, to my great relief; it was dropped from the syllabus.

My father had kept up his love for motoring during our years in Carlow and we covered a large mileage every year. Most of our holidays were spent on the east coast, usually at Arklow or Ballymoney Strand and I always had a wonderful time. We slept in a four-berth caravan and had a ridge tent with table and chairs that was used as a dining room. A second ridge tent accommodated our live-in help, provisions and kitchen equipment. Cooking was done outside on an army-type stove and my mother continued to treat us to elaborate meals served on spotless linen in our dining tent. I was never keen on swimming, but the lovely beaches and holiday friends kept me happily occupied all day long.

At the beginning of 1939, my parents decided that my switch to the school in Eger should not be delayed any longer. For some time they had also spoken of sending Erika abroad to complete her schooling and it seemed to be a good idea that she and I should be within reasonable visiting distance of one another. It was arranged that I should enter my new school for the spring term. Erika was to go to a "finishing school" in Bad Harzburg, a spa in central Germany. To help us over the move, my mother was to accompany us and to remain until we had both settled down. I can give no clear reason why my parents sent us to school in Germany in the spring of 1939, of all times, apparently without any apprehension about the political storm gathering over Europe. They must have felt confident that Hitler would ensure that all German-speaking people in the Sudetenland would have full security. Since I had been geared up for the school in Eger, and had already been kept in Carlow longer than planned, it seemed that the move should be delayed no longer. It was probably assumed that Erika would be safe in Germany anyway. My parents might also have expected that we could get back home at short notice if necessary.

Whatever the reason was, we set off for Germany just after Easter. We were booked on the American cruise ship <u>Manhattan</u> from Cobh to Hamburg. Since the ship was too large to berth in the harbour of Cobh, all passengers had to go out to it by tender. My father came out onto the ship with us and there we said our goodbyes. We all put on a brave front at this, the first big parting in our life. Erika was now just over sixteen years of age and I was twelve.

2

STRANDED IN GERMANY

Our trip from Cobh to Hamburg took three days and included stops in Southampton and Le Havre. After swinging into the estuary of the river Elbe, the ship had to travel a further fifty miles before it reached the docking area in Hamburg. There was much to be seen and I spent the rest of the journey running from side to side of the ship so that I would miss nothing. Some two hours after entering the estuary, the *Manhattan* tied up at its berth. A new stage in my life had begun.

In due course, we set off by train for Karlsbad. My mother was to live in Aunt Hella's house while she went about getting me settled in Eger and Erika in Bad Harzburg. It was a long day's journey to Karlsbad, but Erica and I were used to travelling over much longer distances. Of course, the high standard of catering provided on continental main-line trains went a long way toward making tedious journeys more pleasant.

When we arrived in Karlsbad, my aunt was at the station and greeted us bubbling over with excitement. A surprise awaited us when got a taxi and I saw that it was not a motor car, but the customary horse-drawn carriage. Aunt Hella explained that all motorised traffic, including public transport, was banned from the centre of the town so that pollution and unnecessary noise were eliminated.

I was amazed at the quietness of our ride. The reason for this was that the roads were paved with wooden setts which muffled the sound of the horse's hooves. Soon I saw similar carriages, called Fiaker, everywhere, as they bowled along silently on their rubber-lined wheels while only the muted clip-clop of the horses' hooves could be heard.

Riding through Karlsbad, it struck me how beautifully the town was kept. Old buildings were perfectly preserved and window-boxes could be seen everywhere. My aunt lived in a detached villa in the suburb of Dönitz which bordered on extensive woodlands. I was delighted to discover that Uncle Anton was a man with a dry humour who always had a twinkle in his eye when he spoke. He had recently retired as professor of science in a third-level college in Eger.

The next day I packed all my essential belongings into a suitcase and left with my mother for Eger. Our first call there was to the students' hostel, the Morawetzer Schülerheim, a large and attractive building in the suburbs with a big garden at the front and a hard-surface playground behind. It had accommodation for 200 boys in ten dormitories. Half-board was provided during the week and full-board on weekends for those who required it. After meeting the director, my mother and I set off to visit my new school.

The Realgymnasium was not much more than half a mile away so we decided to walk. A pleasant downhill stroll to a bridge over the river Eger soon brought us to the somewhat forbidding-looking entrance of my school. The principal, a tall and pleasant man, showed us around some of the classrooms and then gave me instructions regarding the following morning, which was the start of the new school term. Our final task was to purchase a bicycle that I could use in Eger and for trips further afield. After my mother had taken the bus to Karlsbad, I felt sad over the parting, but this feeling soon gave way to an excited anticipation and a sense of freedom as I set off for the students' hostel on my bike.

That evening I had the unaccustomed experience of finding myself among a huge number of fellow-students. Shy by nature, I expected other boys to speak to me, but they all seemed to know each other and mainly ignored me. When I went to bed later on, the stark appearance of the dormitory did little to alleviate my sense of loneliness and the novelty of sleeping on an upper bunk-bed was the only diversion that captured my interest.

The following morning I awoke in a more optimistic frame of mind. It was a day of beautiful sunshine which made everything appear in a much more promising light and, as I cycled to school, I felt invigorated by the fresh morning air. During classes I had another boost to my self-assurance. I had no trouble following the lessons and felt grateful to my parents for preparing me so well. What immediately struck me about my fellow-students was how hard they worked and with what grim determination they applied themselves, as if their very life depended on it. After successfully completing my first day in school, I managed to get talking to some of my co-residents in the Morawetzer hostel, but my overtures were met with a cool indifference and I did not feel at home in their company.

Over the next few days I began to explore the town and neighbourhood by bicycle. Eger was a beautifully preserved mediaeval town of about 40,000 inhabitants and every building in the attractive town centre was of timber-frame construction. The town had a rich history, particularly in the days of General Wallenstein, a member of the Bohemian aristocracy, who figured prominently in the Thirty Years War. The magnificent castle in which Wallenstein had lived was just off my way to school; it had been perfectly restored and I was able to visit it on a few occasions.

Since the hostel was on the outskirts of Eger, it took me only minutes to reach the open countryside. The roads were smoothly paved with tarmacadam and, in the absence of much traffic, it was a joy to bowl along them on those mild spring evenings. I exulted in the feeling of freedom that my cycle rides gave me and they compensated me for the slight feelings of claustrophobia that I had experienced since arriving in Eger.

Although I had come to Eger without any preconceived notions, I soon found myself beginning to compare my fellow students with those in Brünn, even though there was an absence of Czech facial features or Czech-sounding names. However, there must have been some characteristic traits that I sensed as alien and, just as in Brünn, I felt that I did not belong there. The lack of social contact in school did not bother me as much as the fact that it was no better in the hostel. There was only one boy who displayed any friendliness towards me. His name was Horst Zain and he was in the habit of borrowing my bicycle, so I did not think that ours was a very sincere friendship.

After a few weeks I began to get worried, because I was experiencing a very near repeat of what I went through in Brünn. The prospect of spending several years working and living with boys who would probably remain strangers to me was alarming. My mother was very sympathetic about my worries when I discussed them with her on one of my weekend visits to Karlsbad and she promised to give the matter serious thought.

During my time in Eger I was not aware of any political unrest in Europe. It was certainly peaceful in this part of the Sudetenland and the only incident of note in Eger was a visit by Konrad Henlein. I remember seeing a procession of large state-cars, with mounted swastika flags, drive through crowd-lined roads, but it seemed to be a low-key affair. Come to think of it, this was the biggest public display of National-Socialist power at which I was ever present.

When I saw my mother a week later, she had good news for me. She had heard of a boarding-school in a small country town called Gebesee in central Germany that sounded ideal for me and she had already gone to visit it. My mother had immediately been won over by the relaxed and happy atmosphere and was told that the school aimed particularly at achieving a good social environment for the students. In addition, many sporting interests and a wide range of practical hobbies were catered for. All this seemed to be just what I wanted; friends and the opportunity to pursue a variety of interesting activities. It appeared that the director was prepared to accept me at short notice and I remember that I felt no hesitation in saying that I would like to go to that school. Of course, it would become impracticable to go to Karlsbad for weekends, but my mother was sure that the facilities offered by the school would ensure that I was neither bored nor lonely.

My departure from Eger was quickly arranged since my mother was due to return to Ireland and she wanted to see me settled in my new school before she left. My aunt and uncle in Karlsbad were very understanding and assured me that I could come and stay with them whenever I wanted to. I knew that the offer was sincere and that my enterprising Aunt Hella would love to be able to plan all sorts of wonderful holidays for Erika and me. I left Eger after being there just six weeks. There was much in the town and countryside that I would now not be able to explore, and this I regretted. However, I had made my choice and, once again, was on my way towards a new environment.

My new school was a two-hour train journey from Eger. Called Schloss Gebesee, it had previously been a castle in private ownership and had a park and a working farm attached to it. The main part of the school was a four-storey building with ancillary two-storey buildings enclosing a large cobbled yard. Of the 110 pupils, thirty were girls, but they were senior to the boys and in classes of their own.

After we arrived, my mother and I called on the headmaster, Dr Max Prüss, and his wife. They were a jovial couple who immediately gave me a hearty welcome and arranged for us to meet other members of the staff. One of the teachers, Herr Arnold Kieschke, and his wife Traute were given special responsibility for my welfare.

Gebesee was known as a Deutsches Landerziehungsheim, which literally translates as German Country Educational Home, and was one of a group of schools which had been founded by a gifted educationalist called Hermann Lietz. He had a novel approach when selecting locations for his schools. Together with fellow-teachers, whom he had hand-picked, he set off on his quest by cycling through Germany. It was usually an old castle with extensive land, which he found ideal for his purpose and over the years he acquired additional sites with the help of private donations and loans. In colloquial language the schools were called Hermann Lietz Schools and had been established at the turn of the century. Having gone through an extremely unhappy time during his secondary education, Hermann Lietz had resolved to become a teacher and to break away from established, conservative systems of teaching.

He was deeply opposed to methods which concentrated on filling pupils with knowledge, while neglecting basic pedagogic principles and the psychology of teaching. To him the person as a whole, with mental and physical attributes in harmony, was most important. The qualities which Hermann Lietz wanted to foster were a Christian outlook, honesty, integrity, freedom from bias (whether racial or social), friendship, helpfulness and an understanding of one's fellow man. In parallel with this, physical activities in sport, crafts and general handiwork were promoted, as well as a love of nature and an understanding of the arts. In order that students should receive good guidance at all times, they were divided into groups of about twelve, called families, each of which was headed by a teacher and his wife, who were known as family father and family mother.

The group of schools consisted of two junior, three intermediate and two senior schools of which one, Gebesee, was co-educational. Pupils usually progressed through all three grades and completed their secondary education by matriculating in one of the senior schools. A farm was attached to each of the schools and all students had to help out during periods of peak labour requirements. We also carried out manual work during the construction of new student facilities. This was considered by Hermann Lietz to be a very important aspect of our education.

Herr Kieschke, my family father, showed me around the school and introduced me to other students. Meeting them allayed any doubts I might still have had about my new school. The boys were so naturally friendly and open in their ways that I immediately took to them. There were eleven boys and three senior girls in my family and we boys slept in two dormitories in a third-storey wing of the main building.

I enjoyed the daily routine very much. Every morning the whole school went off on a pre-breakfast jog followed by a hot and cold shower. Lessons went up to lunchtime and the afternoons were devoted to the practice of "arts and crafts" for which a wide selection of training facilities was available. Among other things, one could do carpentry, sketching, build model gliders or learn to play a musical instrument. A different craft could be selected at the beginning of each term, but if a pupil had no interest in any of them, he was obliged to join the gardening guild and work in the fruit and vegetable garden

Prep was done after tea with the family father at hand and he would at any time during the week, or at weekends, give help with queries relating to the lessons no matter what the subject was. Of course, the teacher and his wife were also there to help us with whatever problems or wishes we might have. But, though we led a privileged existence, we were not pampered in any way and discipline, though not rigid, was strictly maintained.

Despite the emphasis on life within a family, the members did not become divorced from the main body of pupils. It was really during leisure hours that the practice of showing consideration for the other pupils in one's family arose. Since age-groups were purposely kept mixed, there was also an onus on the older boys to look after the younger ones. One boy in each family was termed "family representative." He had a disciplinary responsibility within the family, but was not allowed to beat the boys or make them do any personal chores for him.

I liked my fellow pupils very much and do not remember a single objectionable one among them. Our background was varied and a few of us had lived abroad. One important thing that the students had in common was that their family background was such that they would have been out of sympathy with the National-Socialist regime. I can honestly say that I never found it to be otherwise and was glad to be among schoolmates who shared my more independent way of thinking.

When I came to Gebesee, it was only about six weeks to the summer holidays. It so happened that the parents of two boys in school had told Dr Prüss that if any boy was not able to go home for his holidays, he was welcome to stay with them. As owners of a farm in Saxony they had plenty of room and a visitor would be company for their children. Dr Prüss immediately thought of me and asked me whether I would like to take up the offer. It sounded a great idea to me since I loved living in the country and also felt that it might be too soon to impose so long a stay on my aunt and uncle in Karlsbad. I hardly hesitated before accepting this kind offer, even though I barely knew the two boys, Adolf and Georg Goedecke.

At the end of the term we did not immediately leave for our holiday destinations. It was the practice that, after breaking up, the pupils of all Lietz schools met for the Summer Games at Schloss Ettersburg, one of the intermediate grade schools. This was a bit like an annual Mini-Olympic Games, except that all competitions were on three levels with schools of the same grade competing against each other. Events were held in athletics, field games and ball games. There were prizes, speeches, side-shows and plenty of food for everyone. It was certainly a wonderful occasion and, even though I was not a member of any team, I was thrilled during every moment of the proceedings.

Parents and relatives of the pupils arrived towards the end of the festivities to attend the final celebrations and to collect their children. Herr and Frau Goedecke picked up the three of us by car and brought us to their farm at Döllnitz, a large village near the town of Halle, about thirty miles from Schloss Ettersburg. There I met other members of the family and my schoolmates' sister, Hertha, who was several years younger than her brothers.

It was interesting for me to discover how farms are laid out in Germany. In Ireland it was usual on large farms to have the agricultural buildings tucked away discreetly out of sight from the residence. In Döllnitz, the residence overlooked the main farmyard with its stabling and ancillary buildings. All agricultural land was outside the village with adjoining fields comprising a single unit.

The next six weeks proved to be me one of my most memorable school holidays in which I learned a lot about farming. It was my good fortune to find myself on a farm known for its exemplary management and efficiency. It covered roughly 2,500 acres of fertile land, the greater part of which was used for grain crops while the rest was under grass. The farm manager regularly took lunch with us and I heard much of what was happening on the farm. There was normally quite a gathering at table since Frau Goedecke gave domestic science apprentices in-house training and they too ate with the family.

I also learnt a lot about horses during those holidays. To begin with, the boys and I had regular riding lessons from a professional teacher. These included instruction in the basic steps of the Spanish Riding School, and jumps over small fences. I was occasionally allowed to take the reins of the family single-harness dog-cart, a two-wheeled light carriage, and also to drive cart horses bringing in the harvest. The only difficulty I had was when driving the hay-tedder and I had to repeat my commands to the horse which had some difficulty understanding my Anglo-German accent! Of course, all this was a tremendous confidence booster to a thirteen-year-old and I was very grateful to my host for trusting me in these operations.

My schoolmates, Adolf and Georg, were wonderful company; our weeks together were crammed with activities, everything was tremendous fun and I gained many new experiences. Since Hertha was too young to accompany her brothers and me on our daily sprees, I did not see much of her. However, I remember helping her with her "Knitting Nancy" toy and also being at her birthday party, little thinking that many years later she would become my wife.

Quite frequently Herr Goedecke took me with him when he went off in his dog-cart to drive across the farmland, or to do some shooting. I never came away from these drives without having learned something new from him about nature, farming or other matters of general interest.

There seemed to be no end to all the exciting new ventures I engaged in, but all too soon it was time to go back to Gebesee. I must confess that having had such a wonderful time, I hardly missed my parents at all.

I had been back in school for only a few days when Dr Prüss called the school to a special assembly. He announced that the German army had marched into Poland and that Britain and France had issued an ultimatum that they would declare war if these troops were not immediately withdrawn. A day later we were informed that the ultimatum had not been met and that Germany was now at war with all three countries.

This news was heard in stunned silence, but I do not recollect any doomsday conversation afterwards. Maybe it was considered that the war would not last long and that some agreement would be reached. I certainly remember that the teachers seemed to play down the events and made us feel that our life would go on as before.

The fact that I would not be able to get back home in the foreseeable future did not immediately raise any feelings of fear in me. This could have been because I felt so secure and happy in my new school. I had my relatives in Karlsbad and Erika was also not far away. What probably helped me too was my recent holiday in Döllnitz and the feeling at the back of my mind that I had found a family that would offer me love and care if the need ever arose.

My father appointed an ex-colleague of his, Herr Oskar Soukal, to act as guardian for Erika and me and asked him to look after all financial matters. He had moved to Germany before the outbreak of the war and lived with his wife, Grete, in the small town of Mücheln, in central Germany, where he was manager of the Stöbnitz sugar factory. The Soukals were long-time friends of my parents and I always called them uncle and aunt.

At school none of the students had a radio of their own and we did not see any daily newspapers. Since the press was saturated with National-Socialist rhetoric, it looked to me like confirmation of the outlook in the school that these carriers of propaganda had no place with us. Our only information came from radio bulletins, which Dr Prüss read out to us on the state of the war - on some occasions the school met in the assembly hall to hear an announcement by Hitler over the radio. It was actually prescribed by law that one had to listen to all speeches by Hitler.

If it had not been for these news bulletins, I would not have noticed that there was a war on. Food did become rationed, but our diet was legitimately supplemented with vegetables, fruit and honey produced on the school farm so that nobody really felt the pinch. One factor that affected me personally was that all normal contact with Ireland by mail ceased when the war broke out. The only communication possible was via the Red Cross. A special form was used and I was permitted to write a maximum of only twenty-five words once a month. I came to bless the German language with its long, composite words, which sometimes allowed me to fit a whole comprehensible sentence into one or two words.

From the time I arrived at Gebesee I was obliged to become a member of the Jungvolk, the junior section of the Hitler Jugend (Hitler Youth), and I enjoyed the activities very much. One of the teachers, Dr Nahr, who held the rank of "Bannführer", was in charge of our unit and was therefore "one of us." Once an outside "Bannführer" came to inspect our unit, but we pelted him with snowballs and he never returned. We were certainly not typical of the average Jungvolk unit in Germany, of which many must have been led by people with strong National-Socialist views. However, I never saw anything objectionable in the basic Jungvolk pursuits of athletics in which we had to work up to specific standards, and I still remember the Morse Code that I mastered so long ago. We did have to memorise some dates concerning the rise of Hitler, but that was only a minor detail and, even if we did practise marching in formation, that was no different from what I had done with the Lifeboys in Carlow.

All in all, I stayed in Gebesee for only eighteen months. In that time I had learned carpentry and how to build model aeroplanes. I became a family representative, I helped out on the farm during peak harvesting and, generally, enjoyed every minute of my stay. I also had no difficulty passing my exams.

Each holiday offered me something special. In Karlsbad, I played tennis with my aunt and went to concerts and operas. In Harzburg, I was able to progress in the art of the Spanish Riding School. I spent more holidays with the Goedeckes and went skiing with them in Thuringia. Erika and I were usually together and we spent Christmas with our guardian in Mücheln.

It was no wonder that I was so unashamedly happy, and had not become downcast because the war seemed to be dragging on without an immediate end in sight. It was different for my parents and they suffered severely to be separated from Erika and me. It was not until after the war that I discovered how hard they had been hit and I felt guilty when remembering how happy I had been without thinking what the absence of their children must have meant to them.

In November 1940, my class transferred to Haubinda, the intermediate-grade school near the town of Hildburghausen in Thuringia, where a whole new range of interesting and exciting experiences was waiting for me.

Haubinda lay about sixty-five miles to the south of Gebesee and was beautifully situated in an elevated position at the edge of a long stretch of Thuringian woods. The main school building, of timber frame construction, rose to a height of four stories and was topped by a clock-tower that could be seen for miles. All classrooms and main function rooms were located there, as well as one family of boys. The accommodation for the main body of pupils must have been the most attractive of any provided in the Lietz Schools and was a specific idea of the founder himself. Dotted along the edge of the wood, but within a ten-minute walk of the school, were idyllically situated detached houses, one being provided for every family. Each house was different and all were of timber-frame construction. Twelve to fifteen pupils lived in each house together with their "family parents"; the younger boys usually slept two or three to a room while the senior boys had single rooms. There were one hundred and twenty boys in Haubinda, all between fourteen and sixteen years of age. The headmaster, Dr Willi Damm, was a small man, alert and enthusiastic in his ways. I think he was less strict than Dr Prüss, and always had a twinkle in his eye, but he was an excellent educationalist.

My family father, Herr von Papenhausen, was the teacher for gym and general sports. He was a wiry man who displayed a fantastic agility in the gymnasium. I was one of twelve boys who lived with him and his wife in the Kirschberg Haus (Cherry-Hill House) called after a nearby cherry orchard. Although my house was the furthest from the school, I did not mind, and loved to walk to my lessons along the pleasant woodland paths. In winter I sometimes used my skis to go back and forth, or maybe took time to make a detour if it was a particularly nice day. The crunch of hard snow under my boots or the swish of skis after a fresh, powdery fall were the only sounds that could be heard in the stillness of the snow-covered landscape.

Our daily routine was identical to the one we had in Gebesee, but in Haubinda we had the additional opportunity to learn pottery, and copper work in the "arts and Crafts" sessions. I joined the music guild, because I had not played the violin since leaving Ireland and was beginning to get rusty. Frau Zeilinger, the wife of one of the teachers, gave me lessons and soon brought me up to a standard at which I could join the school orchestra.

The facilities for sport were excellent. Apart from athletics grounds, we had a soccer pitch, a swimming pool, a rifle-range and a tennis court. There were several ponds on which we could skate in winter, and the hilly terrain gave excellent skiing and tobogganing opportunities. I thought ice-skating a bit dull until I managed to encourage other boys to start playing ice-hockey, but, to me, there was nothing to beat the exhilaration of a high speed ski-run down the side of a hill. In the woods at the back of our school we had natural bob-sleigh runs provided by the beds of small streams running down the hills. We turned snow into ice by spraying it with water and altered the shape of embankments to convert these into fast bends. The most popular toboggans in use were ridden by one person lying on his stomach and steering with movable runners at the front. We also used a large five-man toboggan with a steering wheel.

In Haubinda I gradually began to feel the pinch of food rationing. Being at an age when a boy's physical development is very fast, I was not getting enough food to still my hunger. Although the weekly ration of bread, at five and three quarter pounds, was satisfactory, I got only twelve ounces of meat and nine ounces of fat. This ration of fat also included that used in cooking. It is small wonder that I did not get enough calories to replace those burned off during all my activities. The farm provided us with plenty of potatoes, fruit and vegetables, which were healthy and filling, but barely lessened my gnawing hunger.

Game was not rationed and we were lucky occasionally to have our diet supplemented with venison, hare or wild fowl. Extra food allowances were available to special categories, but we did not qualify. These only applied to heavy labouring jobs, people on shift or working long hours, sick people, pregnant women or breast-feeding mothers. Men at the top of the scale got ten pounds of bread, 30 ounces of meat and 20 ounces of fat in a week.

Lack of adequate clothing was something else that gradually became a problem. Ration coupons for clothing were valid for one year and could be used for whatever one chose. However, the amount of goods to which I was entitled was limited and I often wore clothes that I had outgrown. Footwear could not be got for ration coupons. In this case, a detailed purchase application had to be made giving reasons and justification for one's need.

When I arrived at Haubinda, I was at an age when boys in the Jungvolk moved up into the Hitler Youth, but, just as it had been in Gebesee, we formed our own unit and had our own leaders. Of course, we still followed the prescribed routine and went through recommended tests, but it was all done as physical recreation without any propaganda creeping in.

Membership of the Hitler Youth had been mandatory in Germany for boys over fourteen years of age since 1933, and by 1939 the membership stood at 1,723,000. Total membership of all youth organisations, including the Jungvolk and the BDM (Bund Deutscher Mädchen - Association of German Girls), was about 8 million at that time and all were under the direction of Baldur von Schirach, who had been charged by

Hitler in 1933 with setting up these state-controlled organisations. There was something of interest for everybody. Besides an emphasis on athletics, there were camping and hiking trips that were thoroughly enjoyed by all the young people taking part.

I remember spending quite a lot of time in the Hitler Youth doing a form of orienteering and having to pass tests, which included map-reading, using a compass and rifle shooting. Although people have termed these activities pre-military training, I must say that I never saw any of our pursuits in that light and I know that I not only benefitted in some way from everything we did, but really enjoyed myself. Having had lots of practice with my air-gun in Carlow, I quickly got accustomed to rifle-shooting on the full-size range. It gave me great pride when I managed to win a medal for achieving the "sharp-shooter" standard.

All Lietz schools remained in private ownership right through the war, despite every effort by National-Socialist bodies to find a reason to have them nationalised. It was well-known that a liberal spirit existed and was fostered in the schools and, also, that pupils came from families who would not have been bracketed as loyal Party followers. At the same time, it appeared that the authorities were reluctant to take any action unless they could accuse the schools of unpatriotic practices or behaviour. This was a pleasure that every staff member and every pupil was determined to deny them.

The main credit for balking the authorities must go to Dr Alfred Andreesen, the director of the Lietz schools, who parried all attempts at cajoling him into giving up the schools' independence. In order to find a chink in Dr Andreesen's armour, each Lietz school was visited a couple of times a year by a group of six to eight National-Socialist inspectors, who spent a full day at a time attending all school activities. What happened was worthy of a comedy from the Ealing Film Studios. We invariably got a tip-off that the inspectors would be calling and everybody helped to spruce up the school.

31

When the big day arrived, we all turned out spotless - heels were clicked and "Heil Hitlers" resounded. Our voices suddenly lost their gentility and our answers in class were shouted out as if every teacher was stone deaf. It is hard to imagine anybody being so stupid as not to have seen through our act, but we could not be criticised for lack of discipline or for appearing to be perfect. And so, we were left in peace to resume our normal lifestyle until the next visit when the whole charade would start all over again.

In Haubinda we did not get much news of the outside world. Special speeches by Hitler were listened to communally, and Wehrmacht (Armed Forces) reports were read out in the assembly room. One or two national newspapers were displayed in our reading room, but not on a regular basis. I got the impression that all this was part of an act of putting up a pretence of political loyalty should questions be asked of any of us when we were away from school. Nobody paid much attention to the papers, but the army reports did interest us a lot.

Outstanding German military victories were heard communally over the radio in the assembly room. They were always ushered in by the rousing main theme from Franz Liszt's symphonic poem, Les Preludes, which was aimed to strike an emotional chord. Despite my aversion to military conflict, I could not but feel a sense of pride at being German at a moment like that.

Notwithstanding my dislike of Hitler, I did not altogether condemn Germany for having gone to war. I felt very strongly that the injustice of the Versailles treaty in 1919 had created the conditions under which "a Hitler" would come to power. I think I hoped that the demonstration of a strong nation would put it in a position in which a peace treaty could be negotiated which rectified some of the wrongs done to Germany.

Anybody in Haubinda who had a wireless was allowed to use it in his bedroom. I had a little "cats-whisker" crystal set which I had bought second-hand from a boy in my class. It could receive only one station, the Deutschland Sender, but reception was quite good and I sometimes listened to classical and middle-brow concerts.

Although I was able to attend church services during my holidays, the situation in Haubinda was different. It was the policy of Hermann Lietz that each school director gave an address with a religious theme during assembly on every Sunday morning. In this way members of all denominations were brought together and religious barriers were bridged. We were nearly all Protestants in Haubinda and when the time came to attend confirmation classes, a clergyman visited the school regularly to give us religious instruction. Special arrangements were made for us to travel to a church for the actual confirmation ceremony.

I thought the entertainment industry was very good during the war and I enjoyed going to the cinema in my school holidays. Although many Jews and liberals had left the country and films were often produced for propaganda purposes, some very prominent producers and actors remained. Among the best-known were Emil Jannings, Werner Kraus, Gustav Gründgens, and Lil Dagover.

The war dragged on and the chance of an early end became more remote than ever. Luckily, the rural location of the Lietz schools gave us immunity from the air-raids which were being increasingly launched on German cities. I never so much as heard a plane cross overhead. It was only during holidays in Döllnitz that I sometimes experienced air-raid alarms. The nearby Buna/Leuna chemical works attracted allied bomber attacks at night-time, but the massive vaulted cellars of the Goedecke's house provided us with complete protection.

I must admit that, despite the war, I continued to have wonderful holidays. I had a great rapport with my Aunt Hella in Karlsbad and we were always engaged in a whirl of activity. Going to the opera in the evening, or to concerts, was a cultural delight. In those days people still dressed up to go out. The ladies wore long evening gowns, and furs abounded, while the men put on evening dress. Bowling along to the opera house in the customary Fiaker, and walking up the double sweep of the magnificent marble staircase, has left me with the memory of an era which will never come back.

A number of my short holidays were spent with the Soukals in Mücheln. I recollect an interesting event concerning captured British soldiers who had accepted the option of working in the sugar factory rather than spending their time idly in a prisoner-of-war camp. When one of them died from an incurable illness, all German senior factory staff walked with the funeral cortege headed by the factory manager, Herr Rieper, who wore a silk top hat. I was much impressed by this show of respect for a prisoner-of-war who was also just one of hundreds of workers in the factory. When Herr Rieper died a few years later, the soldiers returned the honour by lining up at his funeral.

In 1942, our school orchestra began to give public performances in nearby towns. We usually played incidental music at small civic occasions in town halls or community centres. I liked going on these outings even though it was quite tiring. We were collected by horse and trap or, very often, with farm wagons and sometimes had to travel quite a distance. Our recitals were usually in the evening and in winter we were frozen stiff after our long journey. Having endured the trip, we had to play in an unheated hall and often put up with a piano affected by the cold. A redeeming feature of our trials and tribulations was that after each performance we were treated to mountains of open apple and plum tarts, a speciality in Thuringia, that were baked for us by a local unit of BDM girls.

During all the time I spent in Haubinda, the school gave me an immeasurable feeling of happiness and fulfilment. I also enjoyed an excellent rapport with my fellow students and some have remained lifelong friends. All this must have played a significant part in helping me cope with the continued separation from my parents. I naturally missed them, but I do not recall ever having been really homesick. The Red Cross letters that my parents sent me were a mixed blessing. On the one hand it was good to get them, but, on the other hand, there was something quite depressing about the terse lines that reached me on an impersonal form every month.

My stay in Haubinda came to an abrupt end in February of 1943 when my class was called on to staff an anti-aircraft battery in central Germany even though we were, on average, only sixteen years of age. My matriculation was still two and a half years away and, though an arrangement was being made that we would continue to receive our lessons, this did not sound at all like a practical idea. The only redeeming feature that I could see was that we were to be allotted in large groups to batteries and would still be with our friends.

However, for all practical purposes our schooldays were over and our idyllic existence in a protected environment was no more. As for me, the whole reason for years of preparation in Ireland, and my going to school in Germany had come to nothing.

3

AN END TO SCHOOLDAYS

Anti-aircraft batteries in Germany were manned by an arm of the Luftwaffe which was known as the Heimat FLAK (Home Ak Ak). On 22 February, 1943, I became a Luftwaffen Helfer, which means an auxiliary of the Luftwaffe. The purpose of establishing these units of schoolboys was to be able to release regular soldiers for service in the Front-lines. As a result, anti-aircraft batteries retained all officers and NCOs, but only a skeleton crew of rank and file soldiers. It was recommended that seventy soldiers should be released for every one hundred auxiliaries called up. A total of 100,000 schoolboys became auxiliaries between the beginning of 1943 and the end of the war.

All boys in my year had been called up, with the exception of a few who were older than the rest of us and had already been conscripted to the Labour Service. Our Classics teacher, Dr Reichler, was detailed to go with us and to give us our lessons in all required subjects.

After bringing my belongings to my guardian's house in Mücheln, I set off for the town of Schkopau, eleven miles to the north-east. My battery was stationed nearby in open country which put it about halfway between Halle to the north and the giant Buna/Leuna chemical works to the south. It formed part of a protective ring around these two vital production areas and also had to prevent bomber formations from flying further east to attack other targets. The battery consisted of four 105-millimetre anti-aircraft guns, radar equipment, a computer control module and a data conversion section. There were twenty-one of us auxiliaries and we were allotted in groups to the different sections of the battery, but not to the guns, apparently because we would have been exposed to greater danger.

The rules and conditions under which schoolboys were called up were very comprehensive and stringent; all civil laws governing the protection of youths were to be observed. Auxiliaries had to receive a minimum of eighteen hours of school classes a week and they were not allowed to carry out any manual labour. Strict rules applied to the accommodation provided and an officer in each battery was given special responsibility for their well-being and to ensure that they were not exploited. These, among a host of further guidelines, showed that the well-being of the auxiliaries was being taken seriously. In my group the conditions were generally met, with the exception of one rule which stated that all auxiliaries must get a minimum of ten hours' sleep a night, or be compensated with extra sleep during the daytime. As Allied bombing raids were stepped up, there was no practical way of meeting these requirements.

Our accommodation in Schkopau consisted of timber huts which had a floor area of some twenty by twenty feet, and were placed about four feet below ground level. Each was surrounded by a protective mound of soil about five feet high so that only the shallow roof of the building was visible. Since each group of seven auxiliaries had a hut to itself, there was plenty of room and, though furnishings were sparse, it was clean and adequate. We slept in two-tier bunk beds and each of us had a steel locker and chair. A table and an army stove completed the equipment. Spartan as it was, and though the beds were not comfortable, nobody groused and we took it all in our stride.

Our personal equipment was standard army issue, but the uniform was based on the design of the Hitler Jugend dress. As a distinguishing feature, we wore a wide band with a swastika on the upper left arm of our jackets. For normal daytime activities we wore light-coloured army fatigues.

The food we got was mediocre, unlike the meals we had been given in the Lietz schools. We were often served a kind of goulash, and sometimes the potatoes had suffered frost damage, but we got some very good milk puddings. Since by this time the war had been going on for over four years, I suppose we could not complain too much and we got enough to fill our bellies. A large hut served as a canteen and we used it as a recreation hall in the evenings after we had done our homework.

We generally had very little contact with the army personnel during leisure hours and even less contact with NCOs and officers. Maybe they had been instructed to keep it that way. One exception was a young, outgoing lieutenant, who often sat with us philosophising for many an hour.

Our daily routine began at 6.30, that is, if we had not been up half the night. After washing, making our beds and tidying up the hut, we ate breakfast and then had school classes up to lunchtime in one of the huts especially reserved for this purpose. The afternoons were devoted to instruction in our respective sections of the battery and we also had physical fitness training, as well as marching drill. We did our homework in the evenings and could then relax, provided there was no air-raid alert.

I was very impressed by the high degree of automation with which our heavy FLAK-battery operated. Approaching aircraft were picked up, either by our radar-disc or by an optical range-finder. All data relevant to the movements of the aircraft were fed into a control-module, a technical marvel that could best be described as a mechanical/electrical computer. This equipment made all ballistic calculations for the guns and positioned them correctly by remote control, so that they were set and ready to fire. We auxiliaries had only light work to do; it was just a case of watching dial-gauges and adjusting small hand wheels. The only heavy work was done by the loaders of the guns, who had to lift and thrust a four-stone shell into the breech of each gun every three to four seconds.

My own job was in the data conversion unit. The purpose of this unit was to enable the battery to fire at approaching aircraft, even if we had not picked them up optically, or on our radar disc. Using headphones, we received data from neighbouring batteries who had locked onto aircraft. Our equipment immediately converted this data and fed it direct to our control module.

During a typical air-raid alert an alarm had us tumbling out of our bunks while attacking aircraft were still far away. After a while we heard data being transmitted through our headphones which allowed us to pre-set our equipment. Next, the rumble of anti-aircraft guns could be made out, distant at first, but quickly getting nearer. We were left in no doubt when our own battery began firing, even though we got no warning. I must confess that I was always thrilled by the heavy crash of our four big guns opening fire, as a wave of uncharacteristic patriotism swept over me.

Our morning classes were largely disastrous. Although we probably ended up with the prescribed eighteen hours a week, often we were too tired to concentrate. There was an air- raid alert almost every night and we had to be ready even if the bomber formations were still a long way off. It could happen that the planes dropped their bombs before getting near us or that they changed direction. Even when they were well outside the range of our guns, we were busy tracking the flight path so that we could open fire as soon as the planes got near enough. Whether we opened fire or not, we were usually hauled out of bed about midnight and did not get back until a few hours later. There were many times when we had to get up twice in the same night.

Getting a couple of extra hours in bed did not help very much after our sleep had been ruined, and so the droning voice of our teacher failed to hold our attention. Army activities dominated our minds to such an extent that academic studies became unrealistic, if not farcical. When the time came for us to move up a class, nobody failed his exams.

We all got uniformly medium marks, probably by design, because it would not have been practical to fail anybody and so split the class.

Dr Reichler was very unhappy in his difficult job and I am afraid we did not make his life any easier. Our lack of support for him made me feel guilty, but we were young and had been put in an impossible position. We all felt happy that we were doing our bit in the war. Whatever its merits and demerits, if German cities were being bombed and we could help to save civilians' lives, we thought that we must be doing something worthwhile.

Our canteen boasted a good-sized billiard table and I often played against other auxiliaries in the evenings if I was not writing letters or reading. We were lucky to have a professional musician, Gefreiter Rothe, among the soldiers in the battery. He was said to be from Hungary and was a fantastic gypsy violinist. It was not long before those of us who had been members of the school orchestra teamed up with him and began to entertain the battery staff with popular light music and jazz. Heinz Rücker played on the canteen piano, Wolf Bredemeyer was the cellist, Claus Günther played on a set of drums and I was the second violinist.

Rothe managed to get sheet music since we boys were not experienced in extemporising, but we soon got the hang of it. Thanks to his musical leadership, our quintet developed great dash and we were much in demand. Heinz Rücker, who was by nature a very gifted piano player, later used his acquired skill in playing jazz to earn money for his upkeep when he was a student.

One of the few sinister aspects of my life in war-time Germany was that I had to be very careful about what I said unless I was in the company of intimate friends. Even when staying with the Soukals, we avoided speaking about the war or political matters in case the maid should overhear us. On the other hand, I invariably spoke English with Erika in public without ever getting a reaction from anyone, not even the police or members of the SS.

Although I knew of the GESTAPO and was vaguely aware of some sinister connotations, I do not have any personal memories of them. I think the only time I saw any members of that organisation was when I happened to be in a town and I recognised them by their uniform.

In the early summer of 1943, our battery moved near to the village of Schotterey, six miles further west, so we were still protecting the same industrial belt. I was fascinated to see how our equipment was dismantled, transported and reassembled. We auxiliaries took no part in this, but were allowed to watch as long as we kept out of the way. I was particularly impressed by the huge tracked transporters that were used to pull the heavy guns out of their dug-in locations and reposition them at the new site.

We now lived in converted railway carriages that were placed at ground level without any protective bank of earth around them. I suppose the thinking was that if there was an air-raid alert, we would be in our protected stations anyway.

Life went on as before; we still did not get sufficient sleep and the classroom situation was no better. I used to cut slices of bread into narrow strips and toast them on our army stove during the daytime. Then, when we had to sit up during air-raid alerts at night, I chewed them slowly to pass the time and counteract pangs of hunger.

I was able to continue my twenty-five words-a-month correspondence with my parents, but naturally mentioned nothing about my changed circumstances. Since the forms that were used still went through a central collection office of the Red Cross, there was nothing on them to show my current address and my parents thought I was still in Haubinda.

Some friction occasionally arose among the auxiliaries, but that was understandable in view of the strain caused by lack of sleep and our confined living conditions. Luckily, I had no problems and got on very well with my group. Being able to continue playing my music also went a long way toward compensating me for the hardships I was enduring.

After spending almost one year to the day with the FLAK, I was among the first to move on when I was conscripted to the Labour Service in February 1944. I was very sad to be parting from my school chums, many of whom I had known for four and a half years. Of course, it was not just that I was losing my friends; I was now severing my connection with what little had been left of a normal lifestyle.

On 15 February, 1944, I handed in all clothing and equipment and was given back my civilian clothes. My instructions were to report for service at a labour camp near the small town of Zarnowitz in East Pomerania. The camp was only a few miles inland from the Baltic Sea and about 45 miles north-west of the town of Danzig - now Gdansk.

It was a long journey by train. When we later crossed West-Prussia, I saw a part of Germany that was new to me. The landscape was very flat, with a few small hills, but it was good agricultural land and I saw many beautiful lakes and extensive woodlands. After Danzig, the train travelled to Zoppot on the Baltic Coast and then on to Gedingen, now Gdynia, the home of Lech Walesa, the Polish president. Gedingen was an important base of the German Navy and I was thrilled when I caught sight of many warships anchored in the harbour.

At Gedingen I had to change trains for the tedious, last part of my journey. As we crawled along in the gathering dusk, the countryside became increasingly bleak and relatively uninhabited. After a while, the woods closed in all around and the snow, so attractive in daylight, now only made everything look more desolate.

At my destination, a village called Krokow, I saw other young men, who were obviously fellow-conscripts get off the train. A man in Labour-Service uniform was waiting for us and led us on a forty-minute walk to the camp. It was a relief to walk through the snow after being cooped up all day in a railway carriage and I was looking forward to a hot meal. By the time we arrived and had our meal in the canteen, it was almost time for lights out. Chequered blue-and-white linen, the standard army issue, was already laid out on the two-tiered bunks and as soon I had settled in I was glad to go to bed.

The following morning I was able to take stock of my new surroundings. The encampment was situated on a flat clearing in a dense wood. There were seven large timber huts, five of which provided sleeping accommodation; another contained the kitchen, canteen and washrooms, while the last was the general store and first-aid centre, with a small ward. The accommodation huts contained two dormitories, sleeping twenty men each, and a medium-sized dayroom. The NCOs slept in our huts, but they had a section to themselves.

After breakfast we were issued with our new clothing and equipment. The formal uniform, which was worn only on parade and all leave of absence, was of an attractive chocolate-brown colour. It was made of high quality, felt-like, material and the dress hat that went with it had a stiff, conspicuously high dome. For labouring work and military drill, we were given light-coloured fatigues and a peaked cap to match.

The Labour Service, known as the RAD (Reichsarbeits-Dienst), was prescribed by decree of 6 September, 1936, and covered every able-bodied citizen of the Third Reich. All German men between nineteen and twenty-five had to work in labour camps. Most were assigned to farms where they worked in accordance with a strict disciplinary code under responsible leadership. During the war, men were drafted into the Labour Service at eighteen, and later at seventeen, years of age, so that they would have completed their stint when they were conscripted to the army. As the concept developed, men were employed in road building and other civil engineering projects and wherever a large pool of unskilled labourers was required. When the RAD was first established, men had to work in it for six months, but during the war the period was reduced to three months so that men could be released sooner to the armed services.

The RAD made no distinction; intellectuals, labourers, artisans and peasants were all subjected to common tasks. A cheap labour pool was thus set up and unemployment was reduced at the same time. Another aim of the RAD was to achieve a mix of people from the whole of Germany. Since there can be quite a difference in the characteristics of people living in different regions, it was considered essential to encourage a greater understanding of all one's fellow countrymen.

German girls had to do a spell of twelve months in the Labour Service during their three years in the BDM, between eighteen and twenty-one years of age. They usually spent the year on farms, helping in the house and the fields.

My sister, Erika, did her Labour Service in Austria while I was still in Haubinda. She worked on a farm in the beautiful Tyrolean valley of the river Stubai and was very happy there. Since then, Erika's life had not been without its hazards. After attending an interpreter's school in Leipzig, she was called up for service in an important naval communication centre in Wilhelmshaven. This city was a major warship base and was repeatedly hit by Allied air-raids. When the town was badly destroyed in 1943, the communication centre moved to the inland town of Hildesheim, south of Hannover. Then Hildesheim itself was levelled by air-strikes in 1944, so Erika's unit moved to the town of Werdau, not far from the northern border of Bohemia. Here, at last, she was out of danger.

In my labour camp we had to work as lumberjacks in the vast coniferous woods around us. Although I spent less than three months in the RAD, I remember it as a very satisfying period in my life. Working or marching, it was all healthy exercise in beautiful surroundings where the snow lay heavy on the ground and on the trees. It never seemed to rain and my memories are of blue skies and the sun bathing the landscape in brilliant light. The purity of the air is something else I vividly remember, especially after the pollution around the FLAK battery.

I got on well with the others in the hut and we had a relaxed relationship with the NCOs. Strict discipline was maintained in the camp, but there was nothing autocratic about it.

In the weeks ahead I acquired an important skill, which was to serve me well in the army and also in later life. I was taught how to lift and carry heavy loads safely and efficiently. Shifting weighty logs on my own and long tree-trunks in a gang of men, sometimes over a considerable distance, became routine as my technique improved.

When working in the woods, we became so much part of the scenery that animals accepted our presence fearlessly. Families of wild boar or deer would often amble past, sometimes just fifteen yards away.

Every day we did marching exercises similar to those done by regular army recruits, with one important difference; we did not train with rifles. All drill exercises were carried out with spades which meant that, though the manipulation had to be slightly different, the same effect was achieved. Going through the exercises in brilliant sunshine on the parade ground actually looked far more striking than if we had been using rifles. The flash of light reflected from hundreds of polished spade heads as they were smartly swung, or angled, in perfect unison was most spectacular.

The spade used in the RAD was just a standard digging implement. What made ours different was the care it was given. Only a person, who has gone through this knows how much painstaking work is necessary to prepare a spade that must pass a sergeant-major's eagle eye. I remember often being pulled up, even when I honestly knew that I had covered every square millimetre of mine and brought it to the condition of a highly polished jewel.

One of the first things I did after joining the RAD was to apply to join the elite Paratroop and Tank Division Hermann Göring, which was looking for volunteers. I was in no way motivated to becoming a soldier and must admit that, if the choice had been mine, I would have remained a civilian throughout the war. The whole idea of my going to Germany had been to continue my education there and not to get my head blown off fighting for Hitler. As it was, I knew that I would be conscripted in three months time and there were two important reasons for having a say in the matter:

Firstly, it was known that many young men were currently being drafted into the Waffen SS (the military arm of the political SS) and that certain SS units were called on to commit acts of questionable legality. I reasoned that if the Division Göring had already accepted me, I could not be drafted into the Waffen SS.

Secondly, if I had to be a soldier, I wanted to have the best possible training, and this I would get in an elite division. Although the primary motive for my wish must have been self-preservation, I also felt that I was too valuable to be sent into a trench with scant training, and for the sole purpose of pulling a trigger. Besides, my father had been an officer in the renowned Austrian Kaiserjäger (Mountain Troops) in World War I and I think that I may have been also motivated by sub-conscious ambition.

I had been in the camp for only a week when I made a discovery that was to transform my existence there. One day, I got into conversation with two RAD men from another hut that had an exceptional interest in the humanities. They were twin brothers, Heinz and Günther Heinelt, from the town of Greifswald on the Baltic Coast. In contrast to their six-footer frames, they were soft-spoken and of a gentle disposition.

Both were very keen violin players and, when they heard that I had played the violin for many years, they suggested that we get together in our free time to make music. None of us had an instrument with us, but that turned out to be no problem. When we approached our senior officers for permission to bring forward our first short leave to the end of the following week, and gave the explanation, permission was immediately granted. One reason for this cooperation was that an officer called Jablonski, who was an enthusiastic trumpet player, wanted to join our group.

I picked up my violin in Mücheln and Heinz Heinelt fetched the twins' violins in Greifswald - then practising began in earnest. Jablonski had meanwhile managed to get sheet music, which cannot have been easy. We were only interested in serious music and suitable scoring for our combination would have been unusual. Jablonski turned out to be an eager musician and used to get quite carried away. What his playing lacked in accuracy, he more than made up for in enthusiasm. On a number of occasions I had to laud our trumpeter's sense of priorities when he got the twins and me excused from our duties so that we could play the music of Mozart, Bach or Haydn.

Leading a healthy life, having good friends and playing music all gave me great satisfaction, especially since there was not an excessive amount of military drill. The food seemed to be especially good - certainly much better than it had been in the FLAK battery.

One day I got word that I was to go to Danzig and attend an interview for the Division Göring. When I reported to the recruiting centre, I was given a thorough medical examination and then was asked the usual questions about illnesses in my family. After that there was an oral test, which included some simple maths and questions obviously intended to establish my IQ. The whole matter took about half-an-hour, but I unfortunately did not have time to explore the historic Hanse town so well-known for its beautiful old buildings.

I had been back from Danzig only a few days when a serious epidemic of diphtheria broke out. Many of us went down with a severe infection and the small sick ward was crowded. All leave was cancelled and we had to remain in quarantine for three weeks before the camp was finally given a clean bill of health. Sadly, one of the men died and it was touch and go with several others. I remember visiting the man not long before his death, to chat and try to take his mind off his suffering. Standing well away from him, I was shocked to see his throat, as if ready to burst, ballooning beyond his chin with a bluish transparency - already he must have been near to asphyxiation.

Life in the camp gradually returned to normal. Luckily, the Heinelts and Jablonski escaped infection and our music-making continued uninterrupted. The twins and I often walked in the woods during our free time, talking about life and our families. Heinz and Günther loved to quote from the writings of Goethe and Schiller. They were romantics at heart and seemed to come under a spell as they recited, walking slowly, their minds occupied on a higher plane.

I had been in the camp for just over two months when I heard that the Division Göring had accepted me. The date of my conscription was 1 May, 1944, just three weeks away. I was to be allowed a few days off before reporting for duty at the division's main training establishment in Utrecht, about thirty miles south-east of Amsterdam in Holland. Naturally, I was sad to be exchanging a happy and safe environment for the grim uncertainty of life in the army, and that I would be leaving the Heinelt twins behind. To my regret at parting from those exceptionally good companions were added feelings of apprehension when I remembered that soon they too they would be conscripted. How would these gentle people cope with what lay ahead and how, since it was contrary to the rules that twins be conscripted to the same unit, would they endure being parted from each other?

The last days in camp passed quickly and on 27 April I said goodbye to Heinz and Günther and my other comrades. There was a touch of spring in the air when I took my last walk through the woods to Krokow to start the long train journey back to Mücheln. I had already written to Aunt Grete and she was expecting me that evening.

During my three days in Mücheln, I wrote letters and visited acquaintances. On the evening before I left for Holland, Aunt Grete's sister-in-law, who happened to be staying in the house said good-bye to me, mouthing a silent prayer as she made the sign of the cross on my forehead. I knew that her son had been killed in action a year before and, though I was deeply touched by her gesture, I could not but think that she would have done the same for him, yet now he was dead.

4

THE ARMY

My last day as a civilian had arrived and I got up in good time to catch an early morning train to Halle. My fellow-passengers were a mixture of civilians and military personnel, but there was little conversation except between people who were obviously travelling together. It must be remembered that soldiers were expressly warned about chance remarks they might make in conversation with strangers. Notices bearing the legend, "Feind hört mit!" (The Enemy overhears you) could be seen everywhere and civilians took care not to mention mail from relatives in uniform, recent air-raids, rationing, or many other things which could somehow be of use to a listener in foreign pay. This tended to put a damper on talk between strangers and I did not get into conversation with anybody in my carriage.

After reading a magazine that I had brought with me, my thoughts turned to idle speculation on what might lie ahead of me. I was aware of past spectacular successes of the Division Göring, but it was only when writing this book that I discovered that the division had twice before been almost completely wiped out in action. The first time was on the Russian Front in February of 1942, and the second time was as a member of the German Afrika-Corps in May, 1943. A new division was raised over the next two months and went into action in Italy. The Division Göring was involved in bitter fighting on the retreat in Tuscany, even as I was on my way to its training base in Holland.

When the train reached Holland I became very interested in the Dutch countryside and the architecture. I liked the neatness of houses and fields, and the abundance of canals and picturesque windmills. The rest of the train journey passed quickly and I arrived in Utrecht on time. For a trip of some 400 miles this was a remarkable example of the efficiency of the railway system in wartime Germany. After reporting to a staff sergeant in the military section of the station's administration building, I joined a group of other young recruits with whom I was driven to the barracks by army bus.

The barracks turned out to be a large complex of three-storey buildings surrounding a huge parade-ground and encompassing a number of other open spaces. It had once been a garrison for the Dutch army and was generously laid out. My dormitory was bright and pleasant with a high ceiling. It contained only sixteen beds which made it look sociable, but it was still rather spartan. Apart from a locker beside each bed, the room was furnished with only four tables and chairs. A small notice-board had a timetable pinned to it listing the following day's activities.

We had a quick wash and went off to the canteen, sitting together since we felt self-conscious in our "civvies" among the soldiers in uniform. The meal was hot and wholesome, if a little plain and for dessert there was fruit preserves and "ersatz" coffee. At this stage conversation began to flow more freely and I was able to get to know a little about my new colleagues.

About one-third of them had been Luftwaffen-auxiliaries before doing Labour Service, so they would have been secondary schoolboys like me. The others were barely out of their basic apprenticeships in technical crafts and other trades. All were cheerful and nobody betrayed any sign of the downheartedness that, I thought, must be lurking somewhere.

I became very conscious that my civilian clothes were now the last tenuous connection with my past. By the next morning I would be in uniform, a faceless number, a nobody, cut off from all my relatives and friends. It was as if I would suddenly become powerless, just as my relatives would lose all power to help me.

That night I slept like a log until I was woken by a shrill bell at seven o'clock. Breakfast consisted of two thick slices of the standard black army bread with a pat of butter, some corned beef and jam as well as "ersatz" coffee. Strangely enough, even though "ersatz" coffee was the standard beverage right through the war and I never really liked it, I also never got tired of it. Maybe it was just its comforting heat that my body appreciated, but this coffee, made of roasted barley, was a far more healthy drink than the real thing.

After breakfast, our corporal, called Berg, marched us to the store to collect our uniforms and kit. The store was an impressive sight; all shelves piled high with every possible item. There was nothing to indicate that this was the fifth year of war, with industries continually being the target of bombing raids and Germany staring defeat in the face on every front.

After the last of us had been fitted out, we were allowed to sling the rifle over our shoulder, pick up our heap and march back to the dormitory under the command of our corporal. This turned out to be very much the pattern of all future activities. Whatever we did, wherever we went, we always seemed to be marching, but this meant that all movements were carried out neatly and efficiently. There was, of course, method behind this, a psychological conditioning to conformity and discipline. A quick change into our uniforms was now required because we were due to assemble on the main parade-ground to hear an address by the garrison commander.

The commander, Colonel von Ludwig, had the reputation of being strict, but he was also just and humane. He did not treat us to a long address. After welcoming us he said that our training would be very tough and rigorous but, as members of the elite Paratroop and Panzer Division Hermann Göring, we must be able to meet higher demands than would be expected of other units. Colonel von Ludwig went on to refer to the past gallant action of our comrades in Russia and in Africa and how they were even now holding their own in Italy despite being outnumbered by British and American forces. When the colonel had finished his address, we marched off to our first class session.

Our lecturer, a lieutenant, explained the training programme to us: it would cover basic practical training, theoretical subjects, training on firearms and, at a later stage, intensive training in a special skill, and in practical manoeuvres. We would also have daily physical fitness sessions.

Basic practical training covered the care of clothing and equipment, and also drill on the parade-ground as well as camouflaged movement over open territory. Theoretical subjects dealt with discipline, ethics, hygiene, codes of behaviour and a whole range of skills required on active service. Training on firearms covered the care and handling of the army rifle, machine-gun and machine-pistol as well as target practice. Training in a special skill could be on heavier weaponry or as a sapper (construction of pontoon bridges, dynamiting and flame-throwing) or in communications. Finally, we would put our learning to the test in large-scale territorial exercises.

After a couple of short breaks in the class-sessions, and time allowed for us to ask questions, we were given a talk on the background of the division's training schools.

Our lunch break was a full hour. The meal consisted of a kind of Brown-Windsor soup, stew with boiled potatoes and vegetables, followed by tapioca pudding with stewed apples. There was no coffee. Warm meals never varied very much in the army, but the food was always well-prepared and cooked under hygienic conditions. The only complaints I ever had came later when I was on the Russian Front and the food was cold or non-existent, but that was always due to external circumstances.

The afternoon was mainly taken up with some very basic drill on the parade-ground. There was nothing new to me in the marching-in-formation exercises, or rifle-handling, but a much higher standard of perfection was demanded than I had known heretofore.

In our last session we were given more details of the forthcoming training during the rest of the week and we also got a strict lecture on behaviour, deportment, general discipline and matters of personal hygiene.

It had been a long first day and we were all pretty exhausted at the end of it. During this, the second evening in barracks, there was a tendency to split up into groups depending on individual interests. Everybody avoided talking about the war itself and nobody stood out to say that Germany was going to win or that the war must now be seen to be lost. It must have been patently obvious to all of us that, barring a miracle, the tide of fortune could no longer be turned. I could only hope that the war would soon come to an end with a minimum of human suffering and that I would be lucky enough to escape alive.

It was fortunate that everybody was interested in playing cards, which was also a great barrier-breaker. Since we invariably played Skat, a complicated form of Whist, and this only involved three people, it led to good mixing because there were always some two people looking for a third man to join in. I myself never tired of the intricacies of the game.

It seemed strange to me to be sitting there just like any other soldier when I really felt quite out of place in these surroundings. However, I never made any reference to my Anglo-Irish background and spoke only of my previous years in Germany. Actually, right through my army service, I never found out how much my superior officers knew about my earlier life outside Germany or what personal information was kept on the official records.

That evening, our corporal issued us with our identity discs. These were small, oval-shaped, made of light metal and simply bore a letter and a number without any further reference to the owner. A light, strong chord was attached to them and they were worn around the neck. In the case of one's death, this was the only confirmation of identity and survivors had the gruesome task of taking the discs off their fallen comrades so that the next of kin could be officially notified.

I had one final chore which meant parcelling up my civilian clothes, and all other items that I did not need, for posting back to Mücheln. With that I would be severing the last link with my past life. On impulse I kept a paperback edition of <u>Lord Emsworth and Others,</u> by P. G. Wodehouse, which I had brought along with other reading material. Although my reading days were obviously over for the present, I thought I might as well take along this small book and get enjoyment from it for as long as possible.

Our routine over the next days followed a standard pattern. Outdoor activities and classroom lectures were well mixed to counteract tedium setting in, and on each day we had a forty-five-minute session of physical fitness training, jogging and open-air gymnastics.

The common denominator of all our training could best be described as a ruthless grind to perfection. Nowhere was this more obvious or exasperating than in domestic tidiness. Beds had to look as if they had just come out of a fresh mould, while laundry in the lockers was expected to display virtually razor-sharp edges defying all physical laws. At the daily inspection of quarters, a sergeant-major would hold a ruler along the front edge of the folded laundry and if anything was a fraction out of line, the recruit got a roasting; he was lucky if he did not get the contents of his locker tipped onto the floor. Many a time we had murder in our hearts at such seemingly senseless provocation, but nobody ever demurred and expressions of rage were never vented within earshot of our superiors.

However, this seemed to be standard international practice; the higher the level of training, the higher the degree of this form of human torture. It was as if a soldier's sense of freedom was being systematically eroded so that he would become fatalistic about all suffering and even death.

I noticed that there was a clear difference between instructors who had seen active service and those who had not. The seasoned campaigners were hard, but humane, and they knew no pettiness. Maybe their approach was at variance with the official line, but it was they who earned our greatest respect.

Towards the end of my training in Holland, I did get indirect confirmation from an officer that I had not lost my pride and I must confess to having cherished the memory of this occurrence with some self-satisfaction. An officer once upbraided me, saying, "You know, Stieber, you salute your superior officers the way an English lord greets his underlings." He obviously exaggerated, but I do know that I fully intended to hold on to my self-respect while also being committed to becoming a good soldier.

The crotchety behaviour of our instructors did make a lot of sense in the matter of footwear. I recall many a time being exhausted after spending an hour kneading boot-grease into the leather and belabouring my boots with a bottle, in order to make them soft and supple. When he was inspecting our boots, the NCO would drop a sharpened pencil from a height of about two feet onto the front of each boot. If the point of the pencil did not make a clear indentation in the leather, the recruit was in trouble. Of course, the condition of one's footwear made all the difference between getting blisters or not on long, forced marches and on that could hinge survival. In later months I was often grateful for the skill I had acquired during this long and gruelling drudgery.

During classroom sessions we were lectured in great detail on various aspects of integrity, loyalty, decency, courage and other codes of behaviour, including hygiene. We were expected to be fully committed to the aims and aspirations of the fatherland and to display courage so that we would not let our comrades down.

Getting injured could lead to a court-martial if there was any suspicion that one had done something purposely in order to get out of the combat zone. (A court-martial was a court set up for the trial of military offenders and was composed of officers, none of whom could be of inferior rank to the prisoner). A court-martial also applied if anybody was caught looting, no matter where or how insignificant the items taken or what excuse was given. Theft from the army or from one's comrades was treated similarly.

Personal hygiene was of paramount importance. To become infested with lice was severely punishable, unless the first signs had been reported to the medical orderly. No excuse for getting VD was accepted, including the claim that one had got it from a public toilet. The penalty for this was a court-martial, because it was considered as serious a charge as that of desertion.

According to statistics of the allied armies, VD put more men into hospital than did combat with figures ranging from 6.1% in Europe to 10.2% in Burma.

The training that I enjoyed most was the handling of arms, and target practice. It was not the fighting connotation that attracted me, but the fact that here was a case where skill, and skill alone, counted. An air-gun owner since the age of ten, I had become a very good shot and had collected prizes and marksman badges during my boarding-school days. Heretofore I had handled only air-guns and .22 rifles, but a heavy army rifle was a different thing altogether and we had to shoot over a distance of more than two hundred metres without telescopic sights. The target was usually a cardboard ringed silhouette of the life-size head and shoulders of a soldier in a steel helmet. We also trained on the army pistol, machine-gun and machine-pistol. Of them all, I found the army pistol to be, by far, the most difficult to master. One of the exercises I liked most was the replacing of machine-gun parts. This was a speed exercise and a stop-watch was used on each of us as we performed the different actions.

Another form of target practice involved throwing dummy hand-grenades and "Mills" grenades onto a target area from three positions; standing, kneeling and lying down. I was surprised that we were never taught bayonet-work, although we did carry bayonets and kept them in spotless condition.

After twelve days in Utrecht, we were moved to Amersfoort, a much smaller town of 40,000 inhabitants and lying about ten miles further east. The garrison there had originally been a Dutch monastery and was not ideally suited for military requirements. The accommodation was adequate, although the grounds were small and we had to use a truck to get to some of our training sessions. The training programme continued along similar lines, except that we now had an additional classroom subject; skills on the Front-line. This dealt with observation-training; recognition of planes, tanks and other armoured vehicles, making out reports, the use of a compass, map-reading and guidelines on survival.

After only two weeks in Amersfoort, we were again transferred. This time our destination was the town of Apeldoorn, about 35 miles to the east with the somewhat larger population of some 70,000 people. This was a very welcome change. We had seen hardly anything of Utrecht or Amersfoort, because we had not been given town passes, but from now on we would be less restricted in our movements. I think it was out of concern for a good relationship between the German army and the Dutch population that young recruits were not allowed to leave barracks until good discipline had been drummed into them.

About fifty of us new recruits out of several hundred had been moved to Apeldoorn; the rest were sent to other parts of Holland. Our accommodation now consisted of a group of detached suburban houses on the outskirts of the town. These were four to five-bedroom houses which had been requisitioned because of their location and suitability. All original furnishing had been removed apart from the bathroom and kitchen equipment, but we still got our meals from a nearby field-kitchen. The same standards for the care of our accommodation were applied as in the barracks and penalties for neglect were enforced just as strictly. We were told that the houses would be returned to their owners after the war and there should be no adverse reflection on us occupants.

In Apeldoorn I got my first taste of a new responsibility given to us. Our accommodation had no perimeter protection, so one man in rotation was put on the tedious chore of round-the-clock guard duty.

Our training continued with undiminished vigour, but there were now few classroom sessions and most of our time was spent on a nearby scrubland area toughening ourselves with increasingly demanding exercises. Marching exercises, arms drill and target practice also took place every day as standards were relentlessly pushed higher. We used to march in formation to and from the scrubland, but the customary singing of marching-songs was always dropped when we passed through the suburbs of Apeldoorn. The intention was to avoid giving anybody unnecessary offence.

How did the Dutch population react to us? Since we were not allowed to fraternise, all social contact with the townspeople was out of the question anyway. We had strict instructions to treat civilians with respect, and this applied especially to females. Anybody who threatened or abused members of the population could expect to be severely punished.

My one regular contact with the local people was a fruit-vendor who visited us daily, his cart piled high with baskets of luscious and inexpensive fruit.

Walking through Apeldoorn I received neither friendly nor unfriendly looks; it was as if the citizens were intentionally ignoring me. It was widely known that the Dutch people very much resented having their country occupied by a foreign power and we were told that lone sentries had been shot or had dogs set on them. Since we were now doing guard duty, we were warned accordingly, but I never had any unpleasant experience during my remaining two months in Holland.   I had one encounter with Dutch people that caused me much embarrassment. I wanted to buy something to read and so I went to one of the larger book-shops in the town centre and asked if they had any English books. The frightened look on the assistant's face, and her vehement denials, made me realise how naive I had been. Trying to correct my mistake, I quickly told her, and an elderly gentleman who had come forward, that I wanted it only for my own use. I told them that I had grown up in England and Ireland and wanted to keep up my English. The gentleman said that he would have a look and disappeared into the back of the shop with his assistant. They were away quite a long time, probably discussing whether to trust me or whether this was just a ruse to catch them out.

They finally came back and offered me an English book about horses. I paid quickly and left, still feeling very sorry for having given them such a fright. After all the trouble the book had caused me, it turned out to be very disappointing. It was incredibly dull, so perhaps the Dutchman had decided to play safe by giving me a book whose contents could never be construed as evidence against him.

D-Day, the landing of the allied armies in Normandy, occurred on 6 June, while I was still in Apeldoorn. Apparently the German High Command had considered it highly unlikely that the Allies would land on that particular stretch of the coastline and had left it unfortified. The strength of the invading forces was enormous: almost 15,000 planes and 7,000 ships took part, including 115 warships. On the German side there were only 350 planes and 3 warships, apart from 34 speed-boats. Even after the Luftwaffe sent reinforcements to Normandy, the ratio of Allied to German planes was still 25 to 1.

We received very little information on the landings, but gathered that they were on a huge scale. There was no indication that we would be rushed to the front and our training continued uninterrupted. However, three days later we were unexpectedly moved away from Apeldoorn.

Our next location was at the town of Alkmaar, about thirty miles north-west of Amsterdam and just a few miles from the Dutch coast. Alkmaar was a beautiful town about the size of Amersfoort, and was known as the flower-town of Holland. The reason was obvious as I could see by the proliferation of window-boxes, flowers and shrubs. We again lived in a housing estate, but this time a much larger area had been taken over by the German army and many more units were accommodated there. The houses were in a lovely wooded district which must have been chosen because it was close to a mixed expanse of sand-dunes, woodlands and open countryside, an ideal training ground on which large-scale army manoeuvres could take place.

We had now reached the last phase of our training programme and at this point started our training in a special skill. We had to practise running cables cross-country for field-telephones. This was carried out by teams of two men, one of whom carried a heavy cable-drum strapped on his back like a rucksack. The second man carried a light, ten-foot pole which had a brass fitting at one end.

Having firmly fixed the free end of the cable to a point at the start of the run, the man carrying the drum would jog along the route where the cable had to be laid while the drum rotated and the cable unwound automatically. The second man slipped the fitting of his pole over the cable and, jogging after his mate, made use of the length of the pole to run the cable from tree to tree or across other suitable locating points. The cable had to be run as high as possible so that it was protected from damage by army vehicles or passing troops. It was essential that the cable should not work its way loose and drop down while at the same time not be liable to get damaged by the movement of branches.

The essence of our training was learning to operate at speed. In a combat zone there was no question of taking cover and we would have to operate fully exposed to sniper fire.

A major event that took place while I was in Alkmaar was the gigantic Russian onslaught against the German lines on 22 June, but we had no knowledge of this or of the catastrophic consequences it had for the German armies that were overrun. Our attention was on the happenings in France and we thought that we might be sent there, or maybe the Allies would follow up with an attempted landing on the Dutch coast. We had neither radios, nor newspapers, and information from the outside world reached us only as special announcements by our officer in charge.

In the course of our training there was one sickening exercise that we had to go through, related to gas-warfare. We first had to learn technical details of the common poison-gases which we might encounter and how to recognise them. Since the filters on gas-masks can provide protection only for specific periods, we had to practise changing filters in a gas-laden atmosphere. Having mastered the steps in normal air, and still wearing our gas-masks, we had to enter a hut in which a poison-gas cylinder was then discharged. The procedure was to start taking ever-increasing deep breaths and finally, with our lungs almost bursting, to hold our breath while loosening the filter with one hand and holding the replacement filter in the other hand. The filter was then quickly unscrewed while exhaling to counteract gas seeping past the seals and into the mask. As soon as the filter came away, leaving a large opening, we had to exhale explosively while slapping the new filter into place and quickly screwing it home. In this way, most of the poison-gas, although never all of it, could be expelled from inside the mask.

This "live" exercise was carried out only once because of the harmful effects repetitions would have on the human system.

The reason why it was even done once was to bring home to soldiers the horrific effect of carrying out this exercise inefficiently. I felt that I had accomplished a very slick exchange of filters and yet I experienced an unpleasant irritation of the throat and a choking sensation for several hours afterwards. The gas we had been subjected to, code name "Gelb Kreuz" (yellow cross), was a form of mustard gas. However, we all survived the exercise. In fact, during our whole three-month training period nobody ever went sick, collapsed or cracked up in any way. Probably the schedule was so excellently prepared that our gradual physical build-up enabled us to stand up to inhuman physical demands without suffering damage.

One day when we were going through our training exercises in the sand-dunes, a minor incident occurred which was to critically affect my life a few months later. We had been told that a group of officers would be coming to watch us in operation and that we should give a good account of ourselves. I was in a foxhole when they arrived and one of the officers happened to come my way and stop beside me. He questioned me about some aspects of our exercise and I replied as respectfully as was possible from my cramped position. I seemed to have an instant rapport with the officer and my intuition suggested that he was a highly educated person to whom army life did not come naturally.

Of all the conditions under which our training in Holland was carried out, there had been nothing compared to what we now faced in the sand-dunes of Alkmaar. Although the coast was six miles away, the sand was similar to that found on soft beaches. It was not that we were being trained for desert warfare, but that our physical stamina could here be best put to the ultimate test.

As if marching, sprinting and crawling across fields and scrubland was not bad enough, doing all this in soft sand seemed to be more than I could endure. To me, the peak was reached when we carried out manoeuvres in these hated dunes wearing not only full battle-dress, including the heavy steel helmet, carrying a rifle and machine-gun ammunition, but also wearing our gas-masks!

If anybody puts on a military gas-mask in a cool room and just stands there doing nothing, he will not find it easy to breathe freely and will quickly feel claustrophobic. How I felt on those warm days in June/July of 1944 I cannot adequately describe. I suppose that I can only be grateful for the training that I had previously received, which enabled me to outlive those days and also the months to come on the Russian Front.

On 20 July, we were told by our commanding officer that an assassination attempt had been made on Hitler. He read out the official announcement which actually began with the statement that Providence had protected Hitler from the dastardly action of a group of traitors and that these would be brought to justice and dealt with ruthlessly. This information was taken in by us without any reaction apart from some suppressed whistles of surprise, but I cannot recollect that even afterwards there was any discussion about it. This again followed the standard pattern whereby nobody could suicidally stick out his neck and denounce Hitler, except in privacy with intimate friends, but neither did anybody break out into any patriotic utterances.

I have very pleasant memories of Alkmaar. I loved the beauty of the town and the variety and multitude of blooms everywhere. Alkmaar, like all other towns that I passed through in Holland, showed no signs of war-damage and gave an illusory impression that the world was at peace. Of course, the war with Holland had only lasted for four days and it was mainly in Rotterdam where a lot of damage had occurred. An air-raid had been carried out on 15 May 1940 but, incredibly, the city was short of water-supplies and German fire equipment was brought from as far away as the Ruhr to effectively deal with the fires.

We were to remain in Alkmaar for just a month after the start of the major Russian offensive on 22 June. On 22 July, we were told that we were going to the Russian Front and would be leaving Alkmaar that same afternoon. We travelled by military train, but then made an overnight stop in Hengelo, a town near the German border. Since this was the school holiday period, a girls' secondary school had been requisitioned temporarily so that we could spend the night sleeping rough in the classrooms. It could have been a dull evening, but I found it very interesting to browse through various books and class-material that I found there.

Whiling away my time, I wrote the first lines of an Irish poem by Thomas Moore on the blackboard and put my name and address in Ireland below it:

There is not in this wide world a valley so sweet,
As the vale in whose bosom the bright waters meet,
O, the last rays of feeling and life must depart,
Ere the bloom of that valley,
Shall fade from my heart.

John Stieber,
Milford Villa, Mallow, Co. Cork, Ireland

It so happened that my writing was still there when the class returned for the autumn term and prompted a lively discussion among the girls. Defying the opinion of the rest of the class, one of the girls, Betty Ros, decided to write to the address in Ireland as soon as the retreat of the German army from Holland made this possible. My parents had not heard from me for several months and only then guessed that I must have become a soldier. Since joining the army I had not been able to correspond through the Red Cross and was restricted to using the regular army-mail service, which operated with Germany only. My parents were now living in Mallow. My father had been appointed manager of the Tuam sugar factory in June 1939 and manager of the Mallow sugar factory in January of 1943.

After the war, Betty and I wrote to each other for some time, but, as the reader already knows, my romantic future lay elsewhere. Many years later, after Betty and I were both married, our families met when we visited them in Holland. Betty was now Mrs Jan Kooiker, with a large family and married to the organist of the catholic church in Vlijmen.

Our night in Hengelo was a short one. At four o'clock in the morning we were aboard our train and heading towards a very uncertain future.

5

ON THE RUSSIAN FRONT

For our journey east we were accommodated in the relative comfort of railway-carriages, rather than in goods-wagons which were normally used for the transport of troops. Dawn had already broken when we left Hengelo, but it was easy to doze off undisturbed by the gentle rocking of the train.

During the day we travelled in brilliant sunshine through Osnabrück, Hannover, Berlin and Frankfurt-on-Oder. I was glad to have the opportunity to see something of the north German landscape with its flat, fertile plains. It was quite a contrast to the hills and woods of central Germany and the Sudetenland which I knew so well. I thought the distinctive farmhouses in the area south of Hamburg and Bremen, with their deeply sloping roofs, to be particularly attractive.

As the day wore on, the inevitable pack of cards emerged and we all became relaxed and cheerful. In later years when I looked back on that train journey, which must surely have been an odds-on one-way ticket, I was surprised at my lack of fear or even trepidation. Although army training sets out to instil in its recruits an unquestioning acceptance of whatever may come, perhaps I was just a typical case of the optimism of so many young people who cannot imagine their own death. I have often wondered what my feelings would really have been like if I had known the horrific extent of the catastrophe that had just befallen the German armies on the Russian Front.

I really knew very little about the state of the war as we made our way eastwards. At the time, propagandist news reports spoke about the heroic acts of German forces engaging the Western Allies in France and Italy, and the Russians in the east. Retreats were admitted, but played down, and the expression "victorious in retreat" was frequently used. While it was obvious to me and to the German population at large, that the war was gradually being lost on all Fronts, it was only many years later that I learned the full truth of what had really happened. At the Front to which we were heading, it was not a retreat or even a rout that had taken place, but one of the most colossal defeats of the German army in the entire war.

The prelude to the sweeping Russian victory in the summer of 1944 can be considered to have started when they re-took Stalingrad in February 1943. There German forces had suffered 100,000 dead and 34,000 wounded, on top of which 85,000 men had been taken prisoner. In major battles along the Russian Front, German armies suffered further defeats and by the end of 1943 Russian forces were approaching the Polish-Romanian border. After making more large territorial gains they took a breathing space in May 1944. Although it was obvious that the Russian forces were being built up for an enormous onslaught, Hitler stubbornly refused to allow a shortening of the Front-line and this was to have catastrophic consequences. Hitler's obstinacy resulted ultimately in the reckless and unnecessary sacrifice of the lives of countless German soldiers.

The ratio of the awesome power of the Russians compared with the strength of the German forces deserves mention. Apart from benefitting from an average 6:1 superiority in manpower, the ratio of equipment was even greater. It was 6.5:1 for aeroplanes, 7:1 for tanks and 16:1 for artillery. In fact, at breaching sections they deployed 600 guns per mile of front line giving them a superiority of 35:1 over German artillery, while manpower reached a superiority of 16:1. In the final two days leading up to the onslaught, 143,000 Polish guerrillas carried out 10,500 separate acts of sabotage behind the German lines on 21 and 22 June 1944, thus seriously affecting their supply routes.

The Russian onslaught came on 22 June, 1944. On 28 June, General Field Marshal Model took over the German Army-

Group Middle. He was a master of "firebrigade action," stopping up gaps and keeping the Front-lines reasonably intact. To him must be given credit for gradually stabilising a hopeless situation and restoring an orderly line of resistance. He prevented the even greater encirclement and destruction of the retreating German troops. The Front finally stabilised on 20 July, 1944, when it stretched from Narwa in the north through Warsaw to Bucharest in the south.

It was little wonder that within 12 days 350,000 German troops had been effectively wiped out. 200,000 soldiers were dead, 65,000 had been injured and 85,000 were taken prisoner. Many people know of the horrors of Stalingrad, but the huge losses of the German army (when casualties were twice as high in only a matter of days), quite apart from horrendous losses the Russians must have suffered, seems to have escaped general attention.   On 25 July, my division Göring joined the Army-Group Middle.

That was the general position on the Russian Front as I headed east; a breathing space had been won, but the situation was highly fragile and, if anything, more critical than it had been on 22 June. The number of reserve troops to replace the 350,000 soldiers lost to active service could be only very limited, and many of these would lack Front-line experience. Meanwhile, the Russians had been able to make up their losses and were back to a complement of 2.5 million troops on the Middle-Front.

After an uneventful journey through north Germany, the train stopped in the late afternoon on a siding in a small town close to the old border between Germany and Poland. We were not allowed to leave the train, but a field-kitchen provided us with a warm meal and the train then continued on its way.

When it was time for sleep, we settled down in the carriage as well as we could. Since we would all have spent many a night in over-crowded trains, sleeping in the luggage-racks or on the seats of the carriage, it was no trouble to us to drop off in these positions.

It was still dark when we were woken by an NCO and we saw that the train had come to a stop in a flat area surrounded by fields. We disembarked and marched along a narrow winding road for half an hour, until we reached a group of wooden army barracks, which were to be our temporary accommodation.

We now heard that we were near the western outskirts of Warsaw. Dawn was breaking as we sat down for a bite to eat. Soon I heard the ominous rumble of distant guns opening fire. The main Front-line was about ten miles to the south-east but, as yet, I had not learned to gauge the distance of the noise of warfare. We were told that what we heard was mainly Russian artillery shooting at the Warsaw-West railway goods-station, a major unloading point for German troops and equipment.

Moments later I heard the more familiar sound of German 88-millimetre anti-aircraft guns in action and could just make out a formation of medium-sized planes attacking a ground target to the north-east. Although the gunfire sounded menacing, I was not thinking of Russians out there who could kill me, but rather felt comforted by the presence of German guns.

We had assembled in the barracks to wait for the main body of our division which was due to arrive from Italy that same evening. The division had been in action in Italy between the rivers Tiber and Arno since 15 July and was then ordered to prepare for transfer to the Russian Front. All men and their equipment, including the administration company, butchery, bakery and clothing maintenance units, had been loaded onto 72 trains bound for the Brenner Pass and then Warsaw.

We remained confined to our barracks during the morning and spent the time going over our equipment. After lunch we were divided into groups, each of which was addressed by an officer who told us what our lot was to be. All those in my group were to join self-propelled anti-aircraft batteries, mostly at the rate of one man per unit of four guns. Since we would be the most junior of each gun-crew, our job was purely menial. Training for higher-level work would be given when a suitable opportunity arose. Apart from that, it was up to each of us to adapt to the new conditions, to learn quickly and to make the best use of our training.

The batteries to which we had been assigned were expected to arrive at nightfall when they would drive straight to their designated areas. There they would dig in and camouflage their guns in readiness for action the following morning. Some hours later, trucks picked us up and drove us about 20 miles to our batteries in the Wolomin area north-east of Warsaw.

The officer in charge of my battery, Hauptmann Borchard, was in his early forties and a serious person with a somewhat curt manner. He was in charge of twelve self-propelled 20-millimetre guns, divided into three groups of four guns each. One of the gun-groups was commanded by a lieutenant, who acted as deputy battery-chief, while the three other groups were under NCOs. I was handed over to my group-chief, Haupt-Wachtmeister Henning, a friendly man in his mid-twenties, who introduced me to my immediate superior, Obergefreiter Hans Schlemm, and to the rest of the crew. Schlemm was a typical Friesian with his reticence and his pale, blond hair, but he had quite a wry sense of humour.

My main task in action was to keep up a supply of full shell-magazines for the gun-crew. Each magazine held twenty shells and could be refilled by pushing fresh shells sideways into a slot in the magazine and against the spring pressure of a receiving mechanism. Although each gun carried a quantity of spare magazines, its high firing rate of 180 to 220 rounds per minute meant that I had to refill the magazines very quickly. Apart from this, I was a general dogsbody and would have to take my turn at guard duty.

The men in my unit were all young; none were much over twenty. All were very friendly, and we used our surname and the informal "you" form when speaking to each other. The officers and NCOs used our surname and the polite "you" form.

It was now time to get some sleep, especially since I was due for guard-duty from midnight to two o'clock in the morning. The July night was pleasantly warm and I simply lay down on my ground-sheet close to the gun and covered myself with a woollen rug.

All too soon I was woken by a tug on my shoulder from the man finishing his spell of guard-duty. Since I was now sleeping in the Front-line manner, with all my clothes on, getting prepared took only seconds. Putting on my steel helmet and slinging my rifle onto my shoulder, I was ready to take over.

In the stillness of the night a strange feeling came over me while I slowly paced to and fro. What was I doing here, and could all this be true? As I contemplated the outline of the guns which I was guarding and saw the glint of moonshine reflected by their barrels, I was struck by the contrast between menacing weaponry and the tranquillity of the night.

One thing that I never overcame was my aversion to guard-duty at night-time. As a nature lover I enjoyed the stillness of the night, the silvery beams of moonshine and the shadows and outline of trees against the sky. However, the utter tedium of time dragging on and almost coming to a standstill was highly frustrating. When I did my first night-time guard-duty in Holland, which was for just an hour, I was advised not to keep looking at my watch because this only increased one's impatience. With great willpower, I had kept my eye off my watch until I was sure the hour's stint must be up. To my horror, only ten minutes had passed. After waiting for another "fifty minutes," I had still covered only half-an-hour. By the time I got to the end of the full hour, I felt as if I had been up the whole night. Guard-duty on the Russian Front was always for two-hour periods, so my experience in Holland gave me a good breaking-in. Gradually I got to the stage where my estimation of time improved to the extent that, with my first glance at my watch, I had managed to get within fifteen minutes of my allotted time.

The following morning I was able to take stock of my surroundings. The battery was positioned in flat country. Further east, the terrain was slightly more elevated, but again flat without any hills or mountain ranges. Our guns were positioned about two-and-a-half feet below ground-level and surrounded on three sides by embankments of soil piled up to three feet high. Embankments and gun-carriers were camouflaged with branches and other greenery.

Our self-propelled guns were a cross between an open truck and a tank. They had ordinary road wheels at the front, but the driving force consisted of eight wheels on each side linked by caterpillar tracks, just like a tank. The gun was mounted on a steel platform behind the driver's cab and had a low metal shield on three sides. Self-propelled guns had very good traction in soft ground and higher road speeds than tanks, while being able to operate on much lower fuel consumption. As against stationery artillery their advantage was to be able to change position rapidly and to continue firing while travelling.

Compared with the technical complexity of my 105-millimetre battery when I was a Luftwaffen-auxiliary, the situation on the Front was very different. Our 20-millimetre guns, categorised as light Flak, were mainly used against low-flying aircraft. They had a maximum ceiling of just over two thirds of a mile and a horizontal range of three miles. Special steel-piercing shells were used against armoured vehicles, and fragmentation shells against infantry. Sometimes luminous shells were used, because they could be seen in flight and gave a very good indication of how accurate the shooting was. A special sighting device was used to aim the gun. Each self-propelled gun had its own small two-wheeled trailer for transporting boxes of spare shells.

Five men were associated with each gun, the key man being the first gunner; he lined up the gun with the target and operated the firing-control. Then there was the loader, who kept feeding fresh shell-magazines into the gun-breach from the left side. The dogsbody refilled the magazines with fresh shells from ammunition-boxes as soon as they were empty. The driver of the unit normally remained in his cab, in case a fast pull-out from the position was needed and the co-driver acted as a stand-in or look-out, using binoculars to pick out approaching aircraft or other army movements.

It was not long before I experienced my first action when formations of Russian fighter-bombers appeared and swept down at a target quite close to our position. Our first-gunner, Schlemm, despite being a chunky little fellow, was amazingly agile about the gun. I was astonished at the speed with which our gun followed the movements of an aeroplane even though this had to be done manually by the operation of two handwheels. Schlemm sat on a seat attached to the gun, which was fixed to a swivelling base. With one handwheel in his right hand he could turn the gun through a full horizontal circle. He used the handwheel in his left hand to adjust the lift of the gun-barrel, which could travel through a range from pointing straight up in the air to a bit below the horizontal. The firing-mechanism was activated by a foot-pedal. Tremendous co-ordination of the gunner's actions was needed to keep a plane in his gunsight, while accurately controlling all gun movements with his handwheels, a veritable one-man show.

This time the Russian planes came so close that Schlemm dispensed with the visually sighting instrument and used magazines with luminous shells. It struck me that it was like a man holding a high-pressure garden-hose and trying to hit a hare zigzagging past him. Having picked one plane as a target, Schlemm would open fire and violently swing the gun so that he was firing ahead of the plane and trying to make it fly into the hail of shells. Since the plane's pilot could see the path of luminous shells almost as well as Schlemm could, he would suddenly veer away and Schlemm had to attempt to again sling his shells ahead of the plane. The violent swings of the gun gave the shells a curved flight-path which was why the comparison with the jet of water from a swinging hosepipe seemed so apt.

Since Schlemm had to concentrate on his target, it was up to the loader and me, as well as the lookout man, to keep clear of the swivelling gun-barrel which could swing through 180-degrees in little more than a second. This was not so difficult for the loader or the lookout but, crouching to refill the magazines, I sometimes needed eyes in the back of my head to avoid injury.

The honours in this encounter with the Russian planes seemed to be evenly distributed. The concentrated fire from anti-aircraft batteries caused some of the attacking planes to turn off, but a number of them got through and I could hear the explosion of bombs and the crackle from cannons as they strafed their target. Two of the Russian planes were hit. I saw the pilot of one plane bale out. It looked as if the second plane just managed to limp back behind the Russian lines.

I was struck by the distinctive sound of different weapons and my ability to recognize each sound amid a cacophony of other noises became very important for my survival in the months to come. Our 20-millimetre guns spat like wild cats, whereas the cannons of Russian planes made a crackling noise. The most common German machine-gun, the Model-42, hummed like a dynamo, which was why the Allies nicknamed it "The Sewing-Machine."

We spent the next two days beating off Russian aircraft swooping down to strike at units lying close to us. They seldom attacked us directly because they were fairly vulnerable to our concentrated fire from behind the partial protection of the earth embankments. Hits on a plane were more effective than hits scored on our base.

For tactical reasons we moved our position each night. After being up at the crack of dawn and engaging Russian aircraft with our fire throughout the day, we had to pull out of our position after dark, which meant near midnight. We usually did not travel far, but by the time the new base was prepared for action, and I had maybe been caught for guard-duty, I was lucky to get three hours of sleep.

After the stabilising of the Russian Front on 20 July, the Russians had concentrated on bringing forward fresh supplies of troops and equipment. Now they began to renew their attacks in earnest. The 9th Army, to which my division belonged, was defending the area between the river Bug, north of Warsaw, and the town of Radom to the south of the capital.

On 29 July, strong Russian forces tried to cross the river Vistula, but we and other German units beat them back. My battery's role now changed. We did not occupy dug-in positions over the following days, but made use of our in-built mobility to dart from point to point. This time the Russian fighter-bombers began to attack us directly, even though they never came too close.

Between 31 July and 8 August, my division found itself in the thick of what came to be named "The Battle for Warsaw." Three Russian tank-corps had the task of achieving a crossing of the rivers Bug and Narew. They attacked in a northerly and westerly direction along a 10-mile front, but then suddenly came to a halt on 1 August. General Bor-Komorowski, the leader of the secret Polish resistance army, the "Armia Krajowa," took this as a sign that the Russian tank-corps were about to launch an attack to free the city of German occupation and he ordered his troops to start a revolt. However, there was no Russian attack and it seemed to suit Russian government policy not to come to the aid of the general. There was a strong nationalist element in Poland which was as much opposed to the Russians as it was to the Germans, and the Russians were satisfied to see it crushed and to save themselves the trouble at a later date.

This explains my surprise when, stationed within ten miles of Warsaw, I heard the explosions in the city behind me, while all was quiet at the Russian lines in front of me. Only the day before, we had been pounded incessantly. On 2 October, 1944, General Bor-Komorowski finally surrendered.

The commander of the German 9th Army had correctly interpreted the reason for the lull in the Russian attacks and saw an opportunity to encircle the three Russian tank corps west of Warsaw. On 2 August, my division went into action north of the railway-line between Warsaw and Wolomin, while two other German panzer divisions joined us in completing the pincer movements. By 6 August, all three Russian tank corps had been destroyed.

My own recollections of those days are just a blur of noise and groping to reload magazines on a gun-carrier bucking across uneven terrain. I found it very difficult to retain any sense of direction and sometimes wondered how anybody could make head or tail of the situation.

Despite the many skirmishes we had with the Russians, all members of my battery escaped injury and, thanks to the great skill of the drivers, none of the guns got stuck in the punishing terrain. I began to feel appreciative of my association with a vehicle that had delivered me unscathed from the bedlam of warfare. Of course, I had been on the Russian Front for only a few days and was lucky to have escaped all the shrapnel flying about my ears. Though the war was probably lost, it could continue for many months and I had to expect far worse situations ahead of me.

6

UNDER PROLONGED SHELLFIRE

With the destruction of the three tank corps, the Russians also lost 192 of their most modern tanks, and the pressure on the German forces decreased considerably. Then an alarming situation arose about thirty miles south-east of Warsaw. On 28 July, the Russians had been able to cross the river Vistula and three days later had established a bridgehead on the river at Magnuszew. The 19th Panzer Division, with which the Division Göring had fought side by side at Warsaw, had already been transferred to that hotspot on 4 August and the Division Göring was to follow four days later. The two divisions became the "fire-brigade" of Army-Group Middle, racing to plug gaps wherever they occurred, or blunting Russian attacks before they could get underway.

I remember the next weeks as a sleepless period during which we dug in our guns at a new position almost every night. However, it was not just the lack of sleep that was exhausting; it was the physical work of each time having to dig pits measuring about 20 feet by 10 feet by 2.5 feet deep. Added to this, a slope had to be made for every pit to give access for the self-propelled guns. The excavated soil was used to build a protective embankment along three sides. When this was done, the guns were camouflaged with branches or netting. All excavation was carried out using ordinary spades and pick-axes. The soil was frequently wet, sticky clay and almost impossible to dislodge. My spade head seemed to weigh a ton and I often felt a blind rage when trying to dig up this sticky substance. At just eighteen years of age, I was the youngest man on the crew and, though toughened by my training in Holland, my slight build put me at a disadvantage when brute force was called for. My companions, being three or four years older, were physically more developed and able to cope much better. Our driver, at about thirty-two, the oldest man on the gun-crew, was very powerfully built and always undeterred by the task. When he saw me struggling, he would often move over and loosen a section of clay so that I could cope better with it.

Our almost nightly back-breaking drudgery seemed to have no end. We counted ourselves lucky if we stayed two nights in the same place. If there were lulls in the action, we did jobs on our equipment and clothing, in particular on our boots. The soles and heels were made of leather and were covered with rows of domed steel studs to prevent them wearing out. These studs were almost indestructible, but they did work loose and we were always hammering them back home or knocking in new ones.

My fellow-soldiers seemed to be generally in good spirits. Nobody was unusually cheerful or morose. There were no bad feelings, no arguments, everybody was helpful and pulled his weight. Maybe our subconscious told us that we could not afford any unnecessary drain on our physical or mental reserves and that our lives depended on cooperating fully with each other.

Despite being thrown so closely together, there was little scope for a social relationship with my fellow soldiers. One obvious reason was that there was no such thing as common living accommodation. Everyone had his own shelter. Whenever we moved into a new position and had fixed up our self-propelled guns in their pits, we each dug our own "hole in the ground." This was roughly six feet by two feet by thirty inches deep. Then we had to find some boards or branches and lay them across the top of the hole covering about two-thirds of it. A mound of soil was then put on the roofing and, finally, the bottom was given a layer of greenery, if available. If not, one just put one's groundsheet on it.

The idea of this shelter was to have a place where one was safe from shrapnel and everything else except a direct hit. It was essential to have this protection against Russian artillery fire, which would often come from guns well outside our own range. If there were simultaneous attacks by Russian planes, we had to leave our shelters to man the guns. We slept with the upper part of our bodies protected by the mound of soil, while our feet were at the uncovered end through which we scrambled in and out. Our belongings were put at the head-end and we used some of them as a pillow.

Retiring to my shelter always gave me such feelings of incredible bliss as if I was lying on a sumptuous spring mattress. Suddenly everything would go quiet; there was no longer any wind and I could luxuriously stretch out my tired limbs. The hardness of the ground did not seem to matter. It became unpleasant only when it rained a lot. Drops of rain sometimes worked their way through the soil over my head and muddy drips would land unerringly on my neck or face. The sides of the shelter could also get streaming wet and, if I turned over, looking for a more comfortable sleeping position, I might get a muddy smear on the back of my hand. I used to find it intriguing that I could apparently face gunfire with equanimity and yet be put out by a harmless bit of mud when I was resting.

We always slept in our clothes. At night-time I undid my belt-buckle, took off my boots and covered myself with my army-coat. Socks were not worn in the army. Instead, we wore what literally translates as "foot-cloths," square pieces of flannel-like cloth, a bit bigger than an ordinary duster. It took a bit of practice to develop some skill in wrapping them around the feet, but it was said that, if the foot-cloths were properly worn, there was less likelihood of getting blisters than with socks. Probably the theory was correct because I never did get blisters, despite being on some very long treks.

Underwear was sent to the clothing maintenance-unit for washing and mending, but our own washing facilities were haphazard. We normally saved the last bit of our coffee so that we could clean our teeth, although this sometimes just became a matter of running the index finger along them. We were told to wash our feet regularly, but not to wash them on the evening before a long march. This was thought to soften them and to make them more prone to blisters.

One supplies truck was associated with each gun group. This was used to carry our digging implements, spares, small arms and our shoulder packs, as well as a host of various pieces of equipment. The confined space on our self-propelled guns obviously could not be used to carry these items.

Our rations of bread, butter, tins of meat, fish or jam were handed out every couple of days and it was up to the individual to spread his food over as many meals as he liked. Warm meals were provided by a mobile field-kitchen which was brought near to the gun batteries every evening whenever possible. The design of our metal canteens and flasks was such that one man could usually carry the meals of two to four men at a time.

A typical warm meal was made up of two ounces of meat in a stew, boiled potatoes and five ounces of beans, carrots or other vegetables. In warm weather we got half a tin of fruit preserves; if it was cold, we got thick soup instead. For the other meals we were given black bread and butter or dripping, as well as corned beef or sardines. Sometimes we got jam.

We had a ration of six cigarettes a day. Although I had bartered my cigarettes for food when I was in the Labour Service and in training in Holland, I could not bring myself to do the same on the Russian Front where a man's survival depended on his physical stamina. I preferred to give away my cigarettes.

Usually we had to make do with about a pint and a half of "ersatz" coffee a day which was not very much. During all my army days, rations were adequate. Of course, there were some periods when sabotage by guerrillas or Russian action prevented supplies getting through to us. At such times, or when I later came to be separated from my unit, I had to go for days with very little or nothing at all to eat.

During my first weeks on the Russian Front I had experienced a continued sharpening of my sense of sight, hearing and smell to all the influences impinging on me. With growing confidence, my mind learned to register the throbbing of different truck engines, the distinctive rumble-and-squeal of various tanks, the characteristic flying patterns of aircraft, the many sounds of weaponry and the whistle of approaching shells. I was now less confused about what was going on around me and better able to recognise the strategy with which army units were deployed.

It did not take me long to learn to judge, by the pitch of the sound of shells flying in my direction, whether I was in danger or not. I remember how I automatically drew my head between my shoulders, or ducked, when I first heard shells whistling towards me, as if that would have saved me. Very soon, when experience took over, it was a case of becoming more blasé and I knew exactly when there was danger of a direct hit and had to dive for cover. However, it was trickier when facing a barrage of fire because the cacophony camouflaged individual sounds. In these situations it was sometimes a matter of just hoping that fate was on my side.

Near the end of August 1944, when I had been a "war veteran" of just over a month, I had to face a big ordeal on my own. My battery had been positioned close to the end of a slightly elevated plateau. There was a small wood of low trees to the east and, beyond that, the Russian lines were about a mile away on the other side of a valley. There had been no action on the Russian side for twenty-four hours.

Our commanding officer announced that a forward observation post was to be manned during the next day in order to keep watch on Russian movements. There was a vantage point several hundred yards east of our line of trees which was ideal for the purpose. A generous and well-camouflaged foxhole was dug under cover of darkness and the first soldier took up his post. Since access to and from the foxhole, even by crawling all the way, meant risk of detection by an alert Russian look-out, our man was to remain at his post until he was relieved at two in the afternoon.

I was instructed to take over at that time and to remain there until I, in turn, was relieved, unless special developments justified my deciding to get back to my unit. When it was time to go, I slung my rifle onto my back, passing the strap over my head and shoulders so that I could crawl freely and move as unobtrusively as possible.

When I reached my comrade, he gave me a brief run-down on what he had seen of Russian troop movements and advised me to watch out for a build-up of forces. He also warned me that he thought the Russians had become suspicious because several times over the last hour he had noticed soldiers looking directly his way through binoculars.

I was now left on my own on a tedious stint that could easily last until nightfall. The foxhole was very deep, so I had to carry out all observations standing up. The only redeeming feature was the almost idyllic location. A narrow stream between me and the Russians meandered through the small valley and behind it the rising ground was lightly wooded. It was also pleasantly warm; there was a light breeze with clouds scudding across the sky. If the view had not been spoilt by the military array, it would have been perfect. I could see no human habitations and, if any work was being done in the fields or the woods, the Polish workers were keeping well out of sight.

Most of the Russian forces were assembled near the bottom of the valley, so I had a very good view of what was going on and would be able to make reasonably accurate estimates of numbers of troops and their equipment. The exercise ahead of me was going to be tiring, but relaxed vigilance might mean missing something important. I had some food with me and would, at least, not go hungry.

Standing in a foxhole in no-man's land was a new experience. It was as if I was suspended in limbo between two worlds and I felt disturbingly vulnerable. I had enough room to move around and could lean comfortably against the edge of the foxhole while observing the Russians, but peering through the camouflage greenery was tiring and I began to get cross-eyed.

However, I was not alone in my vigil. Lying contentedly just a few yards away was a cow. She never moved from the spot, as she lay there chewing her cud and looking at me with her huge eyes betraying just a hint of dolefulness. I could not tell if she was hurt, or why she never moved, but felt glad that her presence was helping to alleviate any suspicions the Russian may have had of a German soldier being nearby. At the same time I was concerned that "Daisybell," as I had now fondly christened her, might decide to move and block my view. It could turn out very hard to shift her without alerting the Russians to what was going on. That I called the cow "Daisybell" was just another example of the fact that I was still doing some of my thinking in English.

An hour passed while I made notes on Russian tanks, armoured vehicles, trucks and troop numbers, but then came a jarring development. I heard the whistle of a shell coming in my direction and knew it was going to hit the ground not very far from my foxhole. I ducked well down as it exploded about a hundred yards behind me. I was wondering whether the shell was meant to hit my battery or me, when more shells came whistling over, and they were getting closer.

It was now obvious that I was their target. Possibly they had seen either my mate or me as we crawled to or from the foxhole. The Russian fire continued over the next two hours, but I was puzzled by their method. The average firing rate was two to three shells a minute, with occasional short breaks in the firing. Although this was a low rate, it still added up to more than two hundred shells over the two-hour period. Surely a short and heavy barrage, using more guns, would have been a lot more effective and less wasteful of ammunition in the long run?

Despite the haphazard nature of the firing and the fact that the Russians had still not been able to score a direct hit, I was in a very sticky position. There I was, a sitting target, confined to my foxhole and without the option of taking alternative cover. There had been increased activity among the Russian units over the last two hours, so it was important that I keep up my observation.

Although my estimates of the strength of the Russian units did not indicate that there had been any increase, I was sure that a larger build-up of forces was taking place nearby. The sound of new arrivals could have been masked by the noise made by the running engines of vehicles within my field of vision.

Darkness was still a long time away and I foresaw my harrowing experience continuing for many more hours. Time passed and the Russians began to step up their rate of fire. Gradually their accuracy also improved and I found myself occasionally being showered with soil thrown up from small craters that began to appear around me. Then the situation began to get desperate.

The sudden, short whistle of a shell warned me that I was in for a direct hit and I flung myself down onto the bottom of my foxhole. The next moment there was a deafening crash as a shell exploded right beside me. I felt numbed and dizzy as my breath was whipped away by a blast of dust and fumes when one wall of the foxhole was blown in.

I was buried under a mound of soil until I groggily managed to force my body back up through it. Desperately gasping for breath, I began to choke when all I got was air still laden with dust and cordite fumes. Before I had fully recovered, I was urgently re-excavating my protective foxhole, now reduced to a shallow crater. Using my short army spade I worked as quickly as I could and then replaced the camouflage.

I could not believe my eyes when I suddenly noticed "Daisybell." There she lay, as if nothing had happened, the expression on her large face quite unchanged. I myself was still numb and my ears had not stopped ringing, while I felt a claustrophobic helplessness, restricted as I was, to just a hole in the ground.

Over the next few hours the pattern of events was repeated without change. The Russians continued to fire in fits and bursts; I had more occasions to dig myself free after near-misses and "Daisybell" also survived, as inscrutable as ever. Amazing as it was that I had not been killed, it was an even greater miracle that my cow was unhurt and seemed to be immune to the shells exploding around her. She did not even utter one single Mooh! of complaint.

As it grew late, things became quiet and, with dusk approaching, I began to feel rage that nobody had come to relieve me. Eventually darkness began to fall and I decided to make my way back to the battery.

I had barely come to this decision when I heard the din of fierce fighting suddenly erupt from the direction of my battery. The sound of machine-gun and rifle fire mingled with heavy explosions and I could hear the hard revving of the engines of our self-propelled guns. The next moment I was sprinting for all I was worth across the churned-up ground towards the battle-scene.

When I got to the small wood, I slowed down in case I ran smack into any Russians. I thought it best to make a quick circuitous movement to the west of the scene of action and so have a better chance of joining up with my comrades. As I moved between the trees, I became suddenly aware of other soldiers around me who were walking in almost the same direction. To my horror, I realised that they were Russians! Even now, sixty-four years later, I have a clear picture in my mind of the outline of the trees and the spectral shapes of the Russians as I made my heart-stopping way among them.

There was no question of suddenly stopping or diving to the ground; I had to keep on moving and do nothing which could attract their attention. Slowing down slightly, I took advantage of a broad tree to whip off my steel helmet - its distinctive outline could easily betray me. As I concentrated on following the deepest shadows I gradually managed to work my way out of the group, praying that nobody would decide to speak to me. Once clear of the soldiers, I stopped to take stock of the situation.

The noise of fighting, which now included the rapid fire of our 20-millimetre guns, had moved further away and I seemed to be alone. Hurrying to where our guns had been stationed I saw that one of them was still there, but nobody was around. The gun had been badly damaged, but whether by Russian bazookas or disabled by the gun's own crew I could not tell.

Moments later I could hear our surviving self-propelled guns roaring away into the distance. I was now truly on my own and, to cap it all, there were Russian soldiers in the wood around me. My immediate guess was that a special Russian task-force had sneaked up to the gun-group under cover of darkness and had launched a surprise-attack, knocking out one of our guns with bazookas or magnetic mines. Since it would not have been possible to see the attackers in the darkness, the loss of more guns could not be risked and a fast retreat was required.

I could not feel sore at having been left behind. To stay and search for me would have been suicidal and we all knew that, in a situation like this, whoever was unfortunate enough to get separated from the rest, would have to fend for himself.

What was I to do? Mental and physical exhaustion gave way to a sense of urgency. I had to get away as quickly as possible and not rest until I had put many miles behind me before the sun rose again. With no compass to guide me, I could only hope that some stars would become visible. Setting off in what I hoped was a south-westerly direction to try to avoid meeting the Russians again, I decided to keep going for one hour and then change to a westerly direction. I would keep walking until one o'clock in the morning and then find a hiding place for a two-hour sleep. I thought it essential not to get overtired and to be reasonably fresh to make a rational decision at daybreak.

As I walked through the darkness, I felt my mental energy sagging; rather too much had happened in one day. Sometimes my mind wandered to my home in Ireland and I thought how strange it was that my parents would soon be fast asleep in bed, while I was stumbling along some god-forsaken track in Poland in the middle of the night.

7

ALONE IN NO MAN'S LAND

Soon I was no longer sure that I was going in the right direction. Running into the Russians had made me doubly cautious about my movements and I found myself continually changing direction in order to make the best use of the terrain ahead of me.

Trying to cover too much ground turned out to be a major mistake, because I had completely ignored how much the shelling might have affected me. Looking at my watch later on I realised that I could not remember anything I had done over the previous two hours. I must have walked in a zombie-like daze as a result of a delayed shock reaction. It was incredible that I had not fallen or come to any other harm in the meantime and my mind was jolted by the realisation that I could have been walking exactly opposite to my intended direction.

An ominous warning had been given to me, so I looked around for a suitable hiding place where I could rest and also safely hole-up on the following day, if necessary. I found a good spot in some undergrowth among the trees from which there would be a good view of my surroundings when daylight came. As I dropped to the ground and stretched out my weary limbs I breathed a sigh of relief. Slowly, my mind began to relax.

After a while, I established what food I had with me. It amounted to three and a half slices of bread and some dripping. I also had just half a flask of coffee. Not knowing how long this would have to last, I decided to eat only one slice per day because this would give me some sustenance for three walking days. I then ate half a slice with a trace of dripping and drank some coffee before crawling deep into the undergrowth. The ground was soft and dry and I needed no mattress to help me fall into a deep sleep.

My body-clock served me well and I awoke soon after three a.m. I felt refreshed and the befogged state of my mind seemed to have gone. The coldest part of night always precedes sunrise and so, despite the relative comfort of my hide-out, I had woken up feeling stiff from the cold that had gradually seeped through my body. I stood up and set about getting my circulation going again while I avoided making any unnecessary noise. After slowly chewing my half slice of bread and drinking some of my remaining coffee I was ready to go.

The light from sunrise gave me a good east-west bearing and I decided to move off westwards and cover as much ground as possible while looking out for anything that might guide me back to the German lines. Despite my scare in having encountered Russians in a wood, I had to avoid all open areas where possible. I could be easily recognised as a German soldier at quite a distance and I did not have the faintest idea where there might be any Russians. In addition, there was the constant danger of coming up against Polish partisans. After an hour's march I came to the end of the wood and was afforded a good long-distance view. What I saw was an undulating landscape with quite an amount of woodlands, which was comforting. I could see a group of small farmsteads in the distance, but these were well away from the woods and I saw no towns or villages.

My next step was to pick a route that would give me reasonable cover. At the same time I had to memorise alternative routes in case I found an impassable obstacle in my way. My immediate worry was an open stretch of about half a mile that I had to cross before reaching a continuous expanse of woods. It was still early in the morning and, if I did not want to make an extensive time-consuming detour, I would have to take a chance and cross it now.

I held my helmet close to my body in the hope that only somebody with binoculars could recognize me as a German soldier, and set off quickly. I must have got to within 200 yards of safety when I heard a bullet hit a bush close to me. From the vibration of a branch and the sound of a rifle I knew that it had not come from ahead of me. It had to be from behind me and somewhere to the right and seemed to come from a sniper fairly far away.

Anticipating that there would already be a second bullet in the air and a third one just leaving the sniper's rifle, I automatically dropped to the ground and began to crawl swiftly to my left; hoping that the sniper had lost sight of me when I dropped down. I waited for the third shot and then sprang up and ran for a few seconds in the direction of the wood before dropping down again. Once more, I crawled to one side waiting for the next few shots to be fired and then leapt up for another sprint. This time I could keep my run shorter as I managed to reach an area covered with ferns about two feet high. I was now able to cover the last stretch by crawling, but had to be careful not to disturb the ferns too much, because the sniper was still taking the odd pot-shot at me. Having safely entered the edge of the wood I did not stop for a breather, but immediately hurried on. I decided to make a slight detour, although I did not think the sniper could alert anybody to try to intercept me.

At this point I jettisoned my steel helmet and gas mask. Their weight did not bother me, but they affected my freedom of movement. A soldier's first priority is to retain his means of protection and for this reason I had started off with my rifle, spare ammunition, steel helmet and gas mask. But I was now in an abnormal situation. I had begun to feel like an animal that could be hunted down and my first concern became territorial skill where anything affecting maximum progress had to be abandoned. The rifle could never be discarded since it gave me the means of protection if my life was threatened. My bread was in a canvas bag. Both it and the drinking flask were neatly attached to my belt with clips and were no hindrance to me.

In the course of the day I could hear the distant noise of action to the north and south of me and it seemed to move westwards indicating a gradual retreat by German units. I clearly had to push on as fast as possible to avoid falling behind the advancing Russians. There was still a lot of good cover, but at times it was too good and progress among the trees became laborious and even painful as I anxiously squeezed past prickly branches of fir-trees. In the evening I sat down to eat another half slice of bread onto which I scraped my last dripping.

Although I had been walking all day, except for the odd short break, it had often been in zig-zag fashion and I also had to double back several times to look for a safer route. My straight-line progress had probably not been many miles, so I decided to push on for a couple of hours after dark since I would be able to recognize my planned route fairly well.

Soon I experienced a bad hold up when I had to cross a main road and could hear a convoy of trucks approaching. They were driving on full headlights, so I knew they were Russian vehicles. Luckily for me, this Russian habit made it easier to gauge the speed and density of approaching traffic than if I had only the sound of the engines to go by. The string of headlights told me that I was in for a long wait, so I picked a suitable spot where I could take a breather and watch developments. Unfortunately, the road was almost dead straight for as far as I could make out. Had there been a bend nearby I could have used the seconds of momentary darkness, before a vehicle came round the corner, to make a quick dash across the road. It was the best part of an hour before all danger had passed and it was safe to sprint to the other side. I kept on walking for another half an hour until I reached a higher elevation and then picked a safe spot to settle down for a sip of coffee and some sleep. My growing hunger was no problem, but the coffee was getting more and more tasteless after repeated topping up with water from little streams that I came across. Moments later I was fast asleep in the second night of my lone trek.

I awoke with a general feeling of dampness having slept through a fall of rain. The rain had cleared, but the trees had not given me much shelter and my uniform was fairly sodden. I took stock of the dwindling supply of food which would now last me for only another two days. There was no way of knowing how far it was back to the German lines and how correct my decision had been to space my bread over three days. It might even take me much longer and it would be far too risky to look for food at any habitation. Strangely, I had not seen any edible wild berries. Thirst was not presenting a problem and I expected to be able to keep on topping up my flask with water on the way. Soon I would have to make do with liquid only.

It was only after setting off that I realised I was in added trouble; finding my way was going to be far more difficult than I had thought. Although I could roughly make out a westerly direction, I had no overview of the landscape and the woods around me were thicker than ever. Since I did not have a map with me I could be in a very extensive forest without knowing it and, although that meant being relatively safe from the Russians, I could end up lost and collapsing from hunger. A moment of panic overcame me with the feeling that I had stupidly relied on the size of woods following a similar pattern as before, but there was no reason why they should. My fears subsided when I told myself that I had a reasonable chance of getting back to where I had entered the present woodland and, at worst, I would have lost about six hours of walking. I was lucky not to know the full extent of my predicament. Huge woods covered the region where I was lost and there was widespread swampland further south in the direction of the river Radomka. Had I blundered into that area my prospects would have been even more hopeless.

I decided to climb a tree in the hope of getting new bearings. The task did not daunt me because I had become an expert climber during my boyhood years in Carlow. Even the mature beech trees in our back garden had been no problem to me after I managed to overcome the more difficult sections. Since the rifle would get in my way, I first hid it in some bushes. The chance of anybody coming along and finding it was surely nil, but there was no point in taking any risk and advertising my presence. I then picked the highest fir tree which was standing slightly away from its neighbours. Having got near the top I tried to look out between the branches in a westerly direction. This was frustratingly difficult and when I finally managed to unblock some of the view, all I could see was trees, trees and nothing but trees.

I could have shouted with exasperation. The exertion of climbing, and the disappointment, had so sapped my strength that I had to sit down on a branch for a while to recover. With a sinking feeling I forced myself to make another attempt. If I could only see a break in this damned forest, even if it was in the wrong direction, I would have been satisfied.

For the next ten minutes I struggled with the tree, often precariously balanced on a branch until I was finally rewarded with a glimpse of what looked like a break to the south-west. It was not much, but I would have to be satisfied. I got down the tree and took a short rest while recovering from the exertions. The supposed break was about two miles away and I had no option but to go for it, memorising the stages on the way. If I missed the break, more tree-climbing would be called for. If the break turned out to be no good, I might still have to make my way back to this starting point, but the prospect of having to do that did not bear thinking about.

My route turned out to be much more difficult than I had anticipated. Some sections seemed impenetrable and if I could not get through I had to find a way around them. It was early afternoon before I reached the edge of the wood, but it was clearly not the same place I had been aiming at. I was certainly very lucky not to have ended up in the depths of another part of the wood and I was scared to think how little control I had over the direction I had taken. It would have been so easy to keep going round in circles.

I was mentally and physically exhausted at this stage and sat down for half an hour to recover and to collect my wits. I would have to be more careful in future, but how could I find a better way of making progress? For the moment I would have to stay just inside the wood and keep going in a south-westerly direction.

Not wishing to continue in the darkness, since I was not sure of my bearings, I decided to look for a spot to spend the night. Eating half-a-slice of bread did little to pacify my grumbling stomach and I felt sure it would betray me if ever I had to hide close to any Russians.

The third morning of my lone trek dawned. It was obviously going to be a sunny and cloudless day, a matter not at all to my liking because I could be more easily seen. Having had my morning bite I was able to set off in a more westerly direction; it seemed reasonably safe to do so since the wood was not nearly as dense as it had been. After walking for an hour I caught a glimpse of wide stretches of open country to my right. I quickly headed in that direction and was soon rewarded by a good view into the far distance. At last I could get some fresh bearings.

Before I had gone much further my hopes were again cruelly dashed. Approaching the edge of the wood I saw massive Russian forces spread out over the adjoining fields. There were tanks, armoured troop-carriers, trucks and other assorted vehicles as well as any amount of soldiers. Luckily, I was still too far away to have been seen by any look-out, so I immediately retreated and managed to find a good vantage point half a mile away and hid behind some thick bushes, where I could safely watch what the Russians were doing while I checked out the landscape. There was at least three miles of very open country between me and the next wood to the west with no way of getting across safely during daylight. A detour was not practical and it looked like a whole day was going to be wasted while I waited for darkness. The good news was that I could see a number of compact woods stretching towards the horizon and it would be easier to walk westwards without seriously losing my way.

Very little activity was going on among the Russians. Within a short while, a motor-cycle dispatch rider arrived at the site and left soon after. I wondered whether this would signal an early departure of the troops, but nothing further happened and peace reigned supreme. My reasoning suggested that the Front-lines were not far away and that the Russian forces were being held in readiness to go into action. If this was correct it was good news, but it also meant that my time to reach the German lines was limited. From now on I could take only brief rests and I would have to keep walking as fast as my strength allowed. As the day wore on it became quite warm and I started to get drowsy. I hid away in a cooler spot in the wood where I could safely rest lying down and still hear if the Russians began to pull out.

It was late in the evening before I heard engines start up. Going back to my vantage point, I saw the troops preparing to leave. An hour later the site was deserted. I waited until it was almost dark and then set off cautiously. I was able to reach the first wood safely and then quickly set off westwards. Since I had rested for most of the day, I decided to eat nothing for a few hours and to keep walking till I got tired. At midnight I finished off the last slice of bread and settled down for an hour's sleep.

On this, the fourth day of my trek, I awoke feeling refreshed, but very hungry and there was not even a scrap of food left. Sipping from my drinking flask gave me little relief. In an attempt to fool my body that it was getting some nourishment, I decided to take a mouthful every hour even though all I got was a stale taste from my flask.

Visibility was poor when I set off and sometimes my progress was painfully slow due to the changing nature of the wood. I walked for two hours and then stopped for a breather knowing that soon the dawn would break and help me to make faster progress. I continued looking out for some wild berries, but the general vegetation in the area gave me little hope of finding any.

Because there were no "war-noises" I still had no clue what was going on. Ever since my chance encounters with the Russian forces I had seen nobody and, if it had not been for a small amount of wildlife, I could have been all alone on earth. Wildlife had indeed been scarce enough. On my journey I had seen some squirrels and rabbits; there were also crows, woodpeckers and the odd buzzard but that was all. The solitude was beginning to get to me.

The day wore on and I could not progress as fast as I would have liked. Tiredness and lack of food had blunted the sharpness of my brain, but it was still functioning in a sort of automatic way; evaluating the terrain and any potential dangers that might lie ahead. I had no eyes for the attraction of the scenery around me, my only thought was of getting back to some German unit, no matter where.

When settling down for the next night I took stock of my condition. I was physically weaker than I had expected to be; maybe the mental strain of being alone for so long was beginning to tell. The real danger would come when my sense of judgement began to be affected by my hunger and tiredness and I started to make mistakes. How well would I function even on the coming day?

When I awoke, the dawn was breaking and, for the first time, I had overslept. This was a bad sign, but the sharpness of the morning air revived me and I began to feel better when I was again walking along at a good pace. An hour later I reached the end of the wood and assessed the territory ahead of me. Glancing to my right I saw a dilapidated small cottage, part of which had collapsed. A barely recognisable path led to it and I was convinced that the cottage was deserted. The prospect of finding food seemed remote, but I could safely approach the building from the rear under cover of the wood. With my rifle at the ready and the safety catch released, I crept up to the cottage. All was quiet as I looked through one of the broken windows into what had been a bedroom. Only the frame of a bed was left, everything else had gone. Moving along the back of the house I looked through the window of the only other room left intact. This had been the kitchen and also gave the impression that the cottage had been abandoned a long time ago. The kitchen had an outside door to the back which opened readily to my push. I made a quick search for food, but found only some mouldy grains of oats.

A door led to the tumbledown part of the cottage and, after some trouble, I managed to wrench it open. I found myself looking into a store-room which was empty apart from a small barrel in one corner. When I lifted the lid of the barrel my breath was almost taken away by acid fumes rising from the contents. Steeling myself for a closer look I discovered that the barrel was full of green, pickled tomatoes. The vinegar had kept them fresh, so I quickly tried one after first wiping the surface dry on my uniform. To me, they were delicious! Despite my resolve to be prudent and go easy on them, I found myself wolfing them down regardlessly. However, I soon came to my senses and stopped to check the reaction from my stomach. It seemed to be quite happy with the unexpected windfall, so I slowly ate a few more. I then selected a handful of the smallest and hardest tomatoes which I dried and carefully put into my pockets.

Emerging from the cottage I heard the sound of an exchange of gun-fire which, in this case, was a good omen because it sounded as if the German lines were now within reach. It seemed they were about five miles away and in a north-westerly direction. By crossing a short open space I would be able to reach the next wood and continue westwards. If I moved fast enough I might be able to get past the conflict area and behind the German units before they retreated any further.

Freshly fortified with my doubtful green diet I got across the open area without incident. After that my luck again evaporated. The wood became almost impenetrable, forcing me to make detour after detour so that I lost much time and was no longer sure that I was going in the right direction. It was now midday, two hours since I had heard the last gun-fire and I began to despair of making the contact which had been so tantalisingly near.

Suddenly I came across a logging path which cut diagonally across my route. This was a godsend and I quickly followed it keeping well to one side. It soon ended at an open clearing and there, to my delight, stood a German truck with my divisional markings. Was this salvation or another disappointment with the truck already in Russian hands? I made a wide circuit of the clearing until I got to the far side and there, to my incredible relief, I saw a small group of soldiers belonging to my division. I had arrived in the nick of time because they were about to climb onto the back of the truck. There was now just the usual tricky bit of being recognised before getting accidentally shot.

It was well-known that Russian soldiers practised the trick of putting on a German uniform and, approaching a man on guard-duty, would call out, "Nicht schiessen, ein Kamerad" (don't shoot, a comrade). If the German soldier trustingly lowered his rifle, the Russian would shoot him. This had happened so often that one could not blame any German soldier for being trigger-happy.

With this in mind I hit on a ruse which, I hoped, would save me from danger. My sudden inspiration was to hail the soldiers with a Hamburg idiom, "Hummel, Hummel," (a greeting with no translatable meaning) recognised all over Germany; it was unthinkable that a Russian would happen to use it. The idea worked and I was quickly accepted by my new mates. They told me they had been separated from their unit and were on their way to an assembly point. When they learned that I had been walking for five days they immediately offered me food, and real, "genuine" ersatz coffee. We drove off to the assembly point and I made a report covering the time from when I had started my vigil in the fox-hole to my meeting with the German soldiers. I was given no information on the fate of my unit and did not know if anybody else knew any more about it. It always struck me as odd that on this, and other occasions when I got separated from my unit, I never again heard anything about its fate.

Not knowing whether my mates had survived the last days, I felt ashamed when I remembered my anger at having been left so long in my fox-hole without any communication. Whatever my suffering, I was alive and probably lucky to have been in my fox-hole when the assault on my battery took place. Had I returned even minutes earlier, the outcome for me could have been very different.

I was given replacements for all army issue that I had lost and was told that next day I would be assigned to a new unit. No suggestion was made of rejoining my old unit and somehow it did not seem to be my place to ask. Once again, I had come up against a situation where normal human concern or curiosity did not seem to figure. It was as if nothing mattered that was not of practical immediacy. I found that I also was being drawn into this web and asked no questions which I did not expect others to ask.

That night I slept as if I would never wake up again. In the morning I awoke refreshed, even my insides had slept well and made no complaint about the abuse they had received the day before. I now heard about my new unit. It would again be a group of 20-millimetre self-propelled guns and its commander was Lieutenant Trapp.

Having just weathered two very tight spots, I felt a sense of confidence and looked forward to the next assignment. I was not to know that my service would be soured by a personality clash and culminate in my most dangerous mission on the Russian Front.

8

BRIDGEHEAD ON THE RIVER PILICA

The next morning a van brought me to my new battery operating in the Warka area, again west of the river Vistula. The Vistula had attained a particular significance at that stage of the war and its defence became the theme of many classical books on war-strategy. One section covering a Front-length of about 95 miles was defended by Army-Group Middle, to which my Division Göring was assigned.

My boss, Lt Trapp, was about 37 years of age and five-foot seven-inches tall; a lean and wiry man with a ruddy complexion. He displayed a somewhat indifferent attitude to me when I reported for duty, but he was not unfriendly and quickly handed me over to my immediate superior.

I served in Lt Trapp's battery for the next eight weeks, throughout September and October, and we first went into action near a town called Glowaczew. We were never in the town itself, but sometimes drove through small villages when moving from one position to another. On these occasions I often saw civilians at work in their farmyards, but they largely ignored us.

I got on well with my new mates, but again it was a sort of neutral relationship. There was only one soldier, called Schmidt, whom I did not like. He was lazy and not as particular about basic hygiene as he should have been. I often wondered how the Division Göring had accepted him as a recruit and then not licked him into better shape during training.

Soon we became involved in plenty of action when the Russians put the German forces under fire all along the lines. This seemed to be aimed at consolidating their positions and discouraging German attacks, rather than setting the scene for further advances.

In the absence of the German Luftwaffe, Russians planes dominated the air-space; their sorties increased and for us there was no respite. How sorely we missed some back-up from the air. However, Allied air-raids on fuel manufacturing plants had been carried out over past months with such devastating effectiveness that the Luftwaffe had become almost totally paralysed. It is interesting to recall that industrial output in Germany reached a peak in 1944, despite the enormous pounding it received from Allied bombers. Of course, the loss of fuel-producing plants had been the most telling.

I had many an occasion to be thankful that I had decided to join the Division Göring. At the time, I had known that I would receive the best possible training and that the division would be given the best equipment available. A further advantage now became apparent to me. With severe fuel shortages continuing, the German elite divisions were the first to be supplied, while many other motorised units had to abandon their trucks, armoured vehicles and even tanks. These sometimes had to be blown up so that they did not fall into Russian hands and the soldiers subsequently became foot-slogging infantry. In the Division Göring we seldom ran critically short of fuel and the fact that I could continue riding on self-propelled guns, while soldiers in other divisions had to walk, must have often saved me from falling into Russian hands.

In my experience, the most common representative of the Russian air-force was the Iljushin Il-2, the "Stormovik" or "Black Death," a fighter-bomber with a crew of two. Although the Russians had many, and quite well-constructed bombers, they did not employ them on any large scale and certainly not to compare with that of the western Allies.

The Il-2 was certainly a formidable warplane. Though rough-sounding and ungainly, it was very difficult to shoot down due to its exceptionally heavy armour plating. It was much slower than the German Messerschmidt-109 or the British Spitfire, but it was highly effective against moving targets such as tanks, transport vehicles and marching troops. Armed with machine-guns and fast-firing cannons, it could also carry rockets or bombs, a veritable flying fortress.

Another outstanding plane, which I saw in action, was the German two-seater Junkers-87, the "Stuka," or dive-bomber. It was also relatively slow and ungainly, but built very strongly to withstand the strain on its fuselage and wings when plunging straight out of the sky. An air-siren operating at a screaming pitch had a highly demoralising effect on troops being targeted. I remember some occasions when I was near Russian tanks that were being dive-bombed and got a mind-shattering taste of what it would be like to be at the receiving end.

During the second half of September 1944, our position became highly critical. Possession of the Vistula had been lost and some German forces had regrouped at the river Pilica, which flowed into the Vistula. My gun-group, together with other units had the task of covering the withdrawal of German forces across the Pilica at a point where a heavy pontoon-bridge had been constructed. The bridge had to be held at all costs until the last German forces had been brought back over the river, only then could we also withdraw.

Our guns were strategically well-placed on a flattish hillock near the bridge. It was comforting to know that we were on the west side of the river which meant there was one less obstacle to overcome when we finally withdrew. We did not dig in our self-propelled guns. There was a certain amount of natural cover from bushes and low saplings and we also wanted to be flexible when dealing with the heavy attacks we were expecting. On this occasion we also did not dig any shelters for ourselves. Instead, we were accommodated in a small abandoned farmhouse next to our position. Beside the house there was a tower, about twenty-five feet high, which we used as a look-out.

The next morning we manned our guns at sunrise when the first German troop columns were expected. I do not know why the withdrawal did not take place at night-time, and this was not explained to us. The area on the other side of the river was heavily wooded and the approach road to the bridge gave excellent cover except for the last half mile. Soon I heard the sound of engines as a long line of army vehicles came in sight.

Movement to, and over the bridge, took place in separate fast bursts with army units awaiting their turn under cover of a group of trees. A pattern began to emerge which was to be repeated over many hours to come. Russian planes attempted to bomb and strafe the pontoon bridge and the approach road as well as the troop movements. They flew in circles until they had unloaded their bombs and fired all their rockets. Sometimes they stayed for a few circuits and then resorted to machine-gun and cannon fire before returning to base to load up with more rockets and bombs.

For their part, groups of German tanks, troop-carriers, trucks and infantry gauged the time to make their crossing with a minimum of interference from Russian planes. I could hear gunfire from German Flak east of the river and, between us, we gave the Russian planes quite a roasting. Every now and then the bridge was damaged when hit by a bomb or a rocket, but men from a sapper unit were ready for this. In no time at all, a temporary repair was carried out and traffic could roll again. Damage was never so bad that infantry could no longer cross the bridge. Many of the retreating units were infantry battalions with their bicycles. Although the German army was very sophisticated in many ways, the bicycle was in common use. Likewise, the horse still had an important role to play transporting artillery and pulling supply carts. A major problem arose in winter when large amounts of fodder had to be carried for the horses.

I cannot say that we gun-crews were continually in danger since the destruction of the bridge was the first priority of the Russian pilots, but sometimes a plane would attack us in suicidal fashion as if making a last desperate attempt to silence us. There were few pauses as my gun spat out its shells and I worked feverishly to keep up a supply of full magazines.

Our policy of retaining mobility paid off. We had no casualties and suffered from no more than the sometimes intemperate language of the gunner trying to get a sight on a plane while our driver reversed or swerved to make us a more difficult target.

During the day the maddening absence of German planes continued. I thought that a few of the fast and highly manoeuvrable Messerschmitt-109s would have quickly dealt with the Russian planes, but none showed up and our Flak had to take responsibility on its shoulders for the whole defence. We certainly gave no thought to saving ammunition and I think my ears soon adopted a permanent ringing as the guns discharged their shells hour after hour.

What does it feel like to be in this sort of a situation? To a certain degree one is an automaton. My actions were purely instinctive, and after surviving some heavy fire from Russian planes I found it difficult to remember details of preceding happenings. Though the mind is numbed and the ears are deafened, a subconscious alertness continues to operate and reaction to real danger is instant.

As usual, the attacking planes had all been Il-2's and were very difficult to bring down. It was not easy to quantify our success rate. Concentrating on one target at a time and continually shifting to another target, as it came within range, meant there was no time to stand back and review the results. In some cases it was obvious that a plane was in trouble, at other times one could not be sure. We were lucky to suffer no deaths or injuries. There were some unnerving moments when shots from machine-guns or cannons ricocheted off our gun-carriers, but no serious damage was done.

I was glad whenever we put a plane out of action, but also experienced satisfaction that no pilots seemed to get killed. No plane was "shot down in flames" and I believed that disabled planes either got back to base or their pilots bailed out in time. My main concern was that attacks should be beaten off and that the lives of German soldiers were protected.

Our task in hand continued for the best part of the day with a number of pauses while waiting for more German units to reach the bridge. I was fairly sure that not a single German tank had been lost. A few trucks were hit while crossing the river and I saw one troop-carrier plunge into the water when a bomb blew a hole in the bridge just in front of it. Some German soldiers had certainly been killed and a number wounded, but I was surprised that, when all was over, there seemed to have been so few casualties or loss of equipment and the pontoon bridge was still serviceable.

Between concentrating on our shooting and watching out for the next attack, I think we had all forgotten about food even though it was now mid-afternoon and we had probably been on our feet for the last ten hours. Once all German units had completed the crossing, the Russians ceased their attacks on the bridge, but I could hear the sound of continuing activity as they harassed the units during their further retreat. I expected the sappers to dismantle the bridge in order to save the components, but, instead, they blew it up and the reason for this became clear to me soon afterwards.

We were given instructions to get ready to pull out and were told that the farmhouse and its tower would be blown up after we left to prevent the Russians making use of them. Having collected my belongings, I made the decision to do something that contravened one of the strictest army rules.

It so happened that food supplies had not been getting through in the last few days; what we got was well below the basic ration and we were all beginning to feel the pinch. I had seen apples stored on racks in the cellar of the farmhouse and I thought it such a waste for them to be destroyed while I went hungry.

So far, I had scrupulously observed army regulations, despite my pangs of hunger, and had not considered taking any of the apples. Now that the building was to be reduced to a heap of rubble I said to myself, "what the hell, anyway does the army not want me to be fit so that I can defend the Fatherland?" Without more ado I dashed down to the cellar, quickly put a few small apples into my pockets and hurried up again.

Just as I stepped out of the house, a BMW motor-cycle and sidecar carrying two military policemen pulled up. It was only a moment before their eagle eyes had noticed the bulges in my pockets and their suspicions were instantly aroused. The man in the sidecar got out and strode up to me. "What have you got in your pockets?" he demanded. I told him that I had apples in them. "Where did you get them?" was the next question fired at me. There was no point in bluffing. He would soon find out that we had received no ration of apples, so I went for a fast and honest answer. "I saw them in the cellar of this house which is about to be demolished. We have gone hungry for days and I have just helped to save the lives of many soldiers crossing the river while we held off the Russians." The policeman was momentarily taken aback by my audacity, but he quickly recovered and snapped, "This is looting, you will have to face a court-martial!" He pulled out a notebook and pencil and demanded to know my name and number.

I made one further attempt and now interrupted him, saying: "If I don't get food, what use will I be ..." This time I was not allowed to get away with any more and was interrupted. "That does not matter a damn, you are guilty of ... "At that moment there was a WHEEEH! and an earth-shattering crash as a heavy shell exploded about fifty yards from us. The sound of a gun told me that the shell had come from a Russian T-34 tank. The brave policeman uttered a startled, "What was that?" Savouring the moment, and speaking with calculated indifference, I replied, "Oh, those will be Russian tanks, we are expecting them any moment now." "What, Russian tanks?" cried the policeman and, before you could say Heil Hitler he was back in the sidecar and the motor-cycle disappeared in a cloud of dust.

This was the only incident on the Russian Front that I thought was really funny, but it also had a serious aspect. On the one hand one might ask, how ridiculous can officiousness become in the enforcement of rules? On the other hand, once discretion is employed, and exceptions are made, this is the thin end of the wedge and how soon is it before standards slip below an acceptable level?

I became guilty of looting for the third time five months later when I was stationed on the outskirts of Breslau in Silesia. During a recent encounter with the Russians I had lost, among other things, my spoon and so had nothing with which to drink my soup. At the time, my unit was accommodated in the basement of an abandoned building. Rooting around I managed to find a spoon that was a close match to my own. As an extra precaution I mutilated it a little to give it the appearance of having "been in the wars" and then kept it. The sum total of my looting during nine months on the front was thus some pickled tomatoes, five small apples and a used soup spoon; three "crimes" of which I am not ashamed.

I do not even think that I was more saintly than any of the others. Although I was never aware of anybody bending the rules, I imagine there must have been times when they acted as I did. About once a week, during assembly, our commanding officer read out a list of men who had been convicted of looting or other misdemeanours. Details were given of each man's name, rank, unit, item stolen and punishment given. The typical sentence for looting small items was one or two days detention. However, the actual punishment was usually deferred until there was a lull in hostilities. The average number of names read out was about three, that is three out of twelve thousand men and in all cases the items were of little monetary value. Some articles I remember were a handkerchief, a penknife, gloves (in winter) and a cigarette-lighter. I do not recall rings, jewellery, or even a watch among the items listed.

I am not suggesting that nobody ever took anything of value, but I well remember how tightly control was exercised. Any significant looting by German armed forces, of which I am aware, was usually officially sanctioned and carried out on specific instructions from a higher authority.

By comparison, I remember seeing destroyed Russian vehicles on German soil which, were piled high with domestic items of every description right down to the veritable chamber pot. Even tanks were crammed with curtains, bedding, lampshades and suits. I remember thinking somewhat bitterly, "it serves them jolly well right, if they had not been hampered with all this loot they might have avoided getting knocked out."

The Russians were not the only Allied troops guilty of looting in Germany. I remember when I was employed by the British Control Commission in post-war Germany that the main topic of conversation was how much everybody had been able to get his hands on. One officer boasted openly that he was sending home an average of twenty-five pounds worth of goods every week, possibly worth fifty times that amount in to-day's money. I was not aware that this officer or any of the other men were put on trial, let alone punished.

Germany has come in for much justified criticism regarding acts of barbarity carried out by the GESTAPO and some SS units against civilians, apart from the unspeakable concentration camps. I also accept that there were instances when units of the regular army carried out illegal acts under official orders. Likewise, it has been proved that there were cases of heavy reprisals being carried out, especially concerning guerrilla activities.

However, I must say in all honesty that I never experienced any lack of discipline in any German unit or any individual soldier during all my time on the Russian Front. No prisoners were shot, there were no reprisals and I never heard of anybody who had been raped. The aforementioned cases of looting, or pilfering, were the only breaches of discipline that I ever encountered. I certainly remember distinctly how different was the tone of instructions given to army units compared to the invariably belligerent and inflammatory Nazi propaganda, which was internationally so well known.

It is interesting to consider an extract from an edict issued by Field-Marshal von Mannstein to German forces invading Russia. "Do not look down on Russians, either individually or as a race. Do not give the Russians the impression that Germans are a superior race. Respect Russian women and girls as you would respect German women and girls and avoid any coarse or indecent behaviour. Do not take it upon yourselves to requisition any food or articles, this is strictly forbidden. Russians must not be beaten. Maintain discipline without pompous behaviour, be strict but just. Russians are used to obeying orders. Give them only instructions they can understand and praise them when they work well. Do not discuss religion with Russians, they must be allowed to maintain religious freedom. Treat Russians decently and do not shout at them, they can be reprimanded if they have done something wrong. Remember that many Russians have a small knowledge of German, shouting does not aid communication."

My own memories of pep talks given to us were fully in line with such an ethos. All this was in marked contrast to the Russian army in which soldiers were subjected to widespread and officially-sanctioned propaganda and incited by their commanders and political protagonists to carry out acts of brutality.

Recorded incitements by the Soviet star propagandist, Ilja Ehrenburg, were broadcast over loudspeakers in Russian trenches, exhorting the soldiers to, "Kill, you soldiers of the Red Army, kill any Fascists you find. Kill them and all their brood, none are innocent among them. When you get to Germany, all German women belong to you. Fall upon this proud rabble and rape them till they perish." Russian officers also carried such tracts with them and read them out to their troops.

The happy intervention by Russian tanks, which had saved my skin, also brought my mates rushing out of the farmhouse. Within moments we were aboard the gun-carrier, quickly following the road just taken by the motor-cyclists. I could not tell whether anybody had overheard the exchange between the policeman and me, but I thought that nobody was near enough to do so. Actually, I had not considered what opinion my mates would have had of my taking the apples.

So, once again, fate had smiled on me, albeit not in a matter of life and death. I had been on the front for only eight weeks and the war was far from over. How long could I keep on being lucky; surely the odds must already be shortening?

9

ANOTHER LUCKY ESCAPE

On 19 September 1944 my division was suddenly withdrawn from the Glowaczew area and sent north to join in the defence of the east bank of the river Vistula between Warsaw and Modlin. Together with our old comrades-in-arms, the 19th Panzer Division and three top-class SS panzer divisions, we presented a formidable line of motorised armour in a section of the Front-lines which was in danger of collapse. Once again we had to resort to "firebrigade-action." The strategy was to send us to a critical spot, but never for longer than was necessary to stop a Russian advance or to push back Russian forces. Less strong units then took over from us so that we could move on to the next hot-spot. Since a division consists of only a relatively small number of men, in the overall context of the Front, it was usually necessary to use the combined strength of two to three top-class divisions to make a significant impact on overwhelming forces. Being catastrophically short of armies on the East Front, this was the only practical way to counteract the advance of the Russians. Apart from the 19th Panzer Division we were later to go frequently into action with the elite Divisions Brandenburg and the Panzer Corps Grossdeutschland. With such a strong combination of troops we usually came off best, but once we left an area the Russians again often advanced.

It is not generally known that of the thirty-nine SS divisions in the German army, only eight were purely German divisions. Eight were a mixture of German and ethnic Germans, while no less than seventeen were foreign divisions. The well-known and very successful SS Division Wiking had the highest number of volunteers from different European countries. They came from Denmark, Norway and the Netherlands and there were also Flemings, Finns, Swedes and some Swiss.

When my division arrived on the scene, we took up our position with the river Narew on our left flank and the SS Panzer Corps on our right. Wave upon wave of attacks were launched on our lines and once again the days were dominated by the crescendo of guns in action. Over and above, the ear-splitting crash of shells intermingled with the noise of Iljushin-2 planes swooping down, bombing, strafing and discharging their rockets.

On this occasion I saw many German tanks in action, mainly the Panther with its distinctive long barrel, and the heavier Tiger. Although I was never one to wax enthusiastically over military matters, I was constantly thrilled by these enormously powerful, steel monsters as they rumbled along majestically with unhurried ease. The presence of these German tanks, more than anything else, made me feel safe and protected. Whenever I came across one that had been destroyed, I felt a deep sense of sadness as if I had lost a dear friend. To me, the tanks became almost like living beings. Of course, though our light Flak guns could cope with dive-bombers and light armoured vehicles, we would have had little chance had we been attacked by heavy tanks unless we managed to disable them with a good shot in their propulsion system. This explains why I was able to view Russian tanks with relative equanimity once German tanks were around and why I developed such a sense of profound gratitude for their presence.

During those days I found myself faced with an unexpected dilemma. The attitude of my commanding officer, Lieutenant Trapp, was highly puzzling. Any time the battery was in action there was no problem, but once things quietened down in the evening and we began to put our equipment in order, I became increasingly aware that something was wrong.

On regular occasions the Lieutenant would walk from gun to gun, taking in the condition of the equipment and observing us at work. Whenever he stopped near me I could sense a growing irritation in him, but then he would abruptly turn on his heel and walk away without having said anything. During my training in Holland, and ever since, I had never had a problem with dexterity and I could match the fastest among us when it came to chores around the equipment. So what was wrong?

What made the matter more puzzling was that neither Schlemm nor my present chief gunner, who more than anybody else depended on my efficiency, ever criticized me and seemed perfectly satisfied with my performance. I suppose that nowadays a soldier would request an interview, or get on to his immediate superior in a situation like this, but in my army days that would have been almost unthinkable.

It would have been good to be able to consult my parents about all this, but what a forlorn hope that was. I had often thought of my family over the past months and, above all, longed to be back home again, but I was never actually homesick. Anything not associated with my immediate activities assumed a sense of unreality and I avoided prolonged thinking about it to avoid getting morbid. The German army provided a very efficient mail service and I exchanged letters regularly with Erika, my Aunt Helen and the Soukals, but, although I loved getting these letters, I never brooded over them.

All in all we remained in our present position for two weeks and continued to rebuff every Russian attack. I saw no sign of the Polish population in our vicinity; intensive warfare had become the daily norm and local residents must have fled the scene. It was only in the past months that I had sometimes seen adults and children at their farms, or working in the fields.

I thought there was something depressing about the farms. Even allowing for the fact that Poland had been overrun five years ago, and was still under military occupation, I thought the general standard was very low. Everything looked untidy; equipment was rusted and usually in bad condition and there was mud everywhere. It would be wrong to compare Polish conditions with the exceptional tidiness of the Dutch, but I must confess that I had never seen farms which were as dreary and neglected as those that I saw in Poland and I was familiar with small farms both in Germany and in Ireland.

Considering that up to two thirds of Poland's pre-war population had been engaged in agriculture and 54 per cent of the whole country was under tillage, it was disappointing that the areas I saw left such a bad impression on me. A likely explanation for these conditions could be found in the high percentage of absentee landlords, as well as the fact that farms are often less tightly run in systems where labour intensiveness is high.

Towards the end of September 1944 the expansion of the Division Göring to a full panzer-corps, consisting of Division 1 and Division 2, began. This was a considerable undertaking, especially in the final stages of the war, and it was not fully completed until Christmas 1944. Units from training establishments were taken over to make up the numbers and they naturally lacked Front-line experience. This in turn led to a temporary weakness of the divisions. I became a member of the Göring Division 1 and remained with it until the end of the war.

The training facilities in Holland were retained, with a large number of troops held there in readiness. It is remarkable that as late as January 1945, there were also 8,000 troops held in readiness in the Panzer Corps' Reserve and Training Brigade in West-Prussia. Retraining schools for officer-candidates and NCOs were also still being set up.

By the first days of October, a degree of stability had been achieved north of Warsaw. Suddenly we got orders to pull out of our positions and move by rail to a new trouble-spot about sixty miles south of Warsaw and near Radom. Together with another group of self-propelled guns we were given a train to ourselves. The train was made up of flat-loaders to take the self-propelled guns with their attached trailers and the supplies trucks associated with the gun-groups. There were also about twelve enclosed railway-wagons each of which had already been loaded to a height of one metre with boxes containing heavy shells and various other ammunition.

This was my first experience of transporting guns by rail and I was amazed to hear that the total embarkation time would be only fifteen minutes. The exercise turned out to be much simpler than I had expected and Lt Trapp barked out his orders in quick succession so that everything ran smoothly. The twelve enclosed wagons were all together at one end of the train and removable bridging plates had been provided between adjacent flat-loaders. The end of the train which had the flat-loaders was driven onto a siding which ended in a loading-ramp. It was now just a matter of each self-propelled gun and its trailer, as well as the trucks, driving up the ramp and along the train using the bridging-plates to get from one flat-loader to the next one. As soon as each vehicle arrived at its destination, the bridging-plates were removed and clamps were attached to the flat-loaders to act as chocks so that all vehicles would be firmly held during the course of the train's journey.

We soldiers were accommodated in four of the wagons and a layer of straw had been put on top of the ammunition boxes to give us some creature comforts. The wagons were marked in the usual manner, "40 MEN OR 8 HORSES". By the time the last vehicle had been made fast, all soldiers were aboard and the train moved off promptly. Army units in transit are always very vulnerable to attack by enemy aircraft and it was essential that not a minute was wasted.

It was a pleasantly warm autumn day when we set off. The soldiers in my wagon pulled open the sliding-doors to the fullest extent and we crowded around the opening to get the maximum benefit of fresh air. In typical fashion, some of us sat at the edge with our feet dangling in space, while others crouched or stood behind.

Our trip through the countryside allowed us to unwind after the preceding hectic days. The area we passed through was fairly flat and interrupted only by short ranges of low hills, but it was nicely-wooded. At that time of the year, wild flowers were no longer in bloom, but field grasses and low bushes abounding on the railway embankment looked attractive in the bright sunshine.

Half an hour passed and I decided to lay out my groundsheet in anticipation of later enjoying the luxury of a midday nap. A golden opportunity like this was unlikely to arise again and I remembered the tension of the past days and weeks when I could never be sure what the next hour would bring. Having got my bed in apple-pie order, I rejoined my mates for some more relaxed conversation.

The train progressed steadily and the gradually increasing warmth of the sun made me feel drowsy. This was a good time to enjoy the nap I had been looking forward to, but, as I moved into the interior of the wagon, I was in for an unpleasant surprise. Stretched out on what had formerly been my tidy "bed" was Otto Schmidt. He was fast asleep and my bed was in complete disarray. Schmidt was lazy by nature, but this was too much and my first impulse was to land a well-placed kick in his midriff with a few appropriate suggestions as to what he should do next. Then I decided that I would not let him spoil my day. I had now been put off my nap anyway, so I decided to ignore the incident for the moment and go back to my other mates.

A further twenty minutes went by and then the train came to a stop on an embankment. This was a great chance to stretch our legs and some of my mates immediately jumped off the train. I had been waiting for just such an opportunity and I quickly joined the others. By walking alongside the train in the direction of the locomotive, we could guard against being left behind if the train suddenly began to move off again. Jumping back onto it would be no problem for us.

A few minutes later I suddenly began to feel uneasy, but, looking around, I could see no reason for this. Everything was peaceful, the only sound to be heard was the contented wheezing of our locomotive. Looking up, I first saw nothing, but then there was a sudden glint in the sky beyond the end of the train. A split second later a sound could be heard and two shapes became visible. There was no mistake, Russian aircraft were attacking our train with the sun behind them and, from their outline and their method, they were obviously IL-2 fighter-bombers. By a stroke of good fortune there was an underpass below the railway line quite close to us and it was just a matter of seconds before the soldiers and I had dived down the embankment and reached what was an almost perfect air-raid shelter. Within moments the train was struck.

There was no question of getting back on board. The train was a sitting target in open country and, with all the ammunition on board, constituted a bomb ready to explode at any moment. All we could do was to stay alive and then try to salvage whatever was left of the train after the attack. By strafing the train with bombs, cannons and machine-guns, the Il-2s set fire to some of the wagons containing shells and other ammunition. A chain-reaction then set in with ammunition exploding in an almost unbroken sequence.

As the fire spread along the train, explosions reverberated again and again. It was as if I was hearing a giant display of fireworks and the air became filled with flying lead and shrapnel. Several times we ventured forth from the safety of our shelter in the hope that we could separate parts of the train and so stop the fire from spreading to the end of it. However, each time we suffered casualties or were driven back by the shrapnel buzzing past our ears like a swarm of angry hornets. The prospect of achieving anything practical was non-existent and we were compelled to give up the heroics and wait until there was an easing off.

I think we were all fairly frightened on that occasion - I certainly was. Although I was perfectly safe in the underpass I felt a great compulsion that it was my duty to get to the wagons even though further attempts would be suicidal. Common sense told me that I should stay where I was, but the fact that I had no control over an incalculable danger made me afraid.

When we finally emerged about an hour after the attack started, I saw a scene of utter devastation. The train had been reduced to a smouldering wreck and all ammunition wagons had been destroyed. When we approached the train, we were relieved to see Lt Trapp already there with three of our mates, while another group was making its way towards us from further down the line. On first inspection, three of our guns seemed to have survived the attack, apart from suffering some surface damage. The fourth gun, which was nearest to the ammunition wagons, and had acted as a shield for the other guns, had taken the brunt of the explosions, but looked repairable.

On the positive side, we were extremely lucky not to have been caught by the Il-2 planes while the train was travelling at speed, otherwise personnel losses could have been very heavy. As it was, a number of soldiers had minor injuries caused by small shrapnel fragments. Some of the wounds did not look too bad, but metal fragments could still be lodged quite deep in the fleshy parts of the men's bodies and be difficult to remove. Although shrapnel wounds can be horrific, in this case the fragments had just raised uneven lumps on the surface of arms and legs below which they were lodged. Some wounds bled a lot, others hardly at all with marks only barely visible where the metal had sliced into the flesh.

Only one man on the whole train had been killed. He had the bad luck to be right in the line of machine-gun fire, just where he lay sleeping peacefully on my groundsheet! It seemed, as I learned later, that the men who had stayed back in my wagon were caught by surprise by the suddenness of the attack. They had jumped off the train at the last moment and were very lucky not to have been hit during the strafing before they were able to reach a safe spot. It was only poor Schmidt whose luck had run out.

Strangely enough, few events on the Russian Front affected me as much as Schmidt's death, even though I had never liked the man and also could not hold myself responsible for his death. The most likely explanation may have been the memory that my ill-will possibly constituted the last thoughts anybody had about him before he was killed; it was as if he had died while being cursed by my lips. Thinking about this episode in later years, I was intrigued by the quirk of fate that had caused Schmidt to stop the bullets that were meant for me and resulted in my life being spared yet again. How lucky I was to have resisted the natural impulse to boot him off my tarpaulin and to lie down in his place.

When the damage to our equipment had been assessed, Lt Trapp called us together to give us our orders. A sergeant, together with our drivers and co-drivers were to stay with the guns while the rest of us marched off to a town about ten miles to the south. When we arrived there we heard that arrangements had been made to clear the railway line and to bring all surviving rolling stock after us. It was now early afternoon and events were beginning to move smartly. Our injured had their wounds dressed. Fortunately, nobody was seriously hurt and all our mates were able to rejoin us that same afternoon. It was also lucky that no major damage had been done to the railway line. After the debris had been cleared away, the train got moving and soon our guns and the body of Schmidt arrived at a nearby station.

Since we had lost most of our personal belongings when the wagons carrying the ammunition went on fire, we were refitted and also given fresh food rations. That night we had a roof over our heads, but we expected to stay only until sometime on the following day when our self-propelled guns would have been inspected and repaired in an army workshop.

Lying in bed that night in an army camp, I thought of my close shave; not so much with a sense of horror, but rather with a wry detachment. The thought struck me that fate was playing little games with me, but, in the end, was allowing my run of good luck continue.

10

A BUBBLE BURSTS

After a refreshing night's sleep, unbroken by guard duty, I woke up wondering what surprises were awaiting us next. All that could be gleaned at the army camp was that the general situation on the East Front was very serious. Rumour had it that we were only waiting for our guns to become serviceable before being sent to the northern section of the front.

In those early October days the situation on the Eastern Front had indeed reached new crisis proportions. In mid-September, Germany was desperately fighting on two Fronts. Hitler and the Supreme Army Command were in a Catch-22 situation, arguing over which Front should be given priority. General-Oberst Guderian feared that any weakening of the Eastern Front would prompt a further Russian offensive. He was also afraid that, with winter approaching, the frozen terrain would be to the advantage of the Russians. Hitler insisted on a strong Western Front and finally got his way. An already weak German Eastern Front was to suffer further depletion, when vital troops were withdrawn and sent to the west.

At the end of September, the German Front-lines had still been ten miles east of the East-Prussian border. After a massive build-up of troops the Russians attacked on the 5 October. Opening a fifty-mile breach, they then had a clear path to the Baltic Sea and on 9 October their first tanks rolled onto German home ground. On the same day my division was transferred from the 9th Army at Warsaw to the 4th Army in East-Prussia. It was here that the brunt of the next Russian offensive was expected.

East-Prussia was the first German province to witness the tragedy of its people becoming refugees. When the war went through its final stages, the fate of millions of East-German civilians was very much in the hands of National-Socialist Gauleiters. A Gauleiter was a high-ranking Party functionary with sweeping administrative powers over an extensive area, usually the size of a province. These officials exercised their control not only in Germany, but also in occupied territories. They had the right to decide whether a German army should defend a city and they could allow the civilian population to flee, or order it to remain.

The National-Socialist Gauleiter of East-Prussia, Erich Koch, had given permission for the civilian population of the town of Memel to be evacuated in early August, but rejected all urging after the end of August that evacuation of the whole district of Memel should also be permitted. It was not until 7 October that he finally gave his approval, but by then it was too late. As it was, many of the refugees could still have escaped had it not been for bureaucratic rules which stipulated that personal possessions had to be checked before people were allowed to take them with them. While party officials carried out the farcical exercise of checking out the waiting refugee columns, Russian troops were advancing all the time.

However, the fate of the refugees was truly terrible with Russian armoured vehicles shooting up columns of civilians on the roads. Many people still in their homes were raped, others were shot. The town of Memel itself was declared a "Fortress." That means it did not surrender, but became part of the war-zone with strict orders that the town must be defended to the last. No troops were allowed to break out and so five German divisions remained encircled there as well as some 30,000 civilians. Bitter fighting for the town was to go on for months.

French prisoners of war deserve special mention. A large number of these were employed as farm workers in East-Prussia. When the German civilians fled, the French soldiers remained loyal to them, helping them during their flight and often sharing death with them at the hands of advancing Russian troops. This speaks well of the good relationship that had developed between these prisoners of war and the civilian population.

At about this time a desperate measure was taken in Germany by mobilising the "Volkssturm," a type of Home Guard Militia. A total of six million men were called up. The Volkssturm was composed of males as young as 16 and up to 60 years of age. Badly equipped and often without a uniform, just wearing an identification arm-band, these mainly old men and boys failed to be of much practical use, especially as they were under the control of Party functionaries, who had very little military experience. Hitler officially approved its formation on 25 September, 1944, but forbade direct attachment of its units to any regular armed forces. Instead, they came under control of Heinrich Himmler and his local Party functionaries. The Volkssturm was usually employed in the defence of German towns. Sometimes they were successful with their bazookas against enemy tanks, but in the last months of the war they seldom had enough rifles to go around and then, maybe, had only 5 rounds of ammunition available for each rifle. They made their final sacrifice when they were taken prisoner, for then it was often their terrible fate to be shot as partisans.

A further source of extra troops was tapped at that time by sending half a million industrial workers to the front under the heading "Totaler Kriegseinsatz," (Total War Effort). The loss to industry was made up by drafting women into factories and workshops and this helped to keep industrial output virtually unaffected. However, the writing on the wall was now clearer than ever. Defeat and the end of the war were not far off.

On the morning after our disastrous train journey we were given time to go over our equipment. As usual, we started with our boots, softening the leather and replacing steel studs, as well as going over our rifles and other equipment. While attending to these chores my mind drifted to the odd behaviour of Lt Trapp. I found it hard to believe that a seasoned campaigner, who had six years of army service behind him, could become prey to such feelings of insecurity, which was what I felt his problem must be. For some time now I had been waiting for the bubble to burst, and suddenly it did.

My musings were interrupted by an NCO who instructed us to fall in for weapon drill. Apparently, one of our self-propelled guns had survived the attack on the train fairly well and had been returned to us after being checked out and pronounced fully operational. As soon as the gun had arrived at our army camp, Lt Trapp decided that we should do a bit of weapon-drill.

In this exercise we had to perform specific tasks such as carrying out safety checks and preparing the gun for action, dealing with simulated mechanical failures and replacing parts of the firing mechanism. It was a case of perfecting precision at maximum speed. During previous lulls in front line activities, I had been trained in these operations and the exercise had become a forte of mine. It was here that the manual dexterity, which I had acquired as a boy, pursuing a multitude of hobbies, proved to be of great advantage to me. I may have been one of the smallest men in my unit, but I made up for it in skill and fitness.

The procedure was that we would line up at the gun and each of us was then called up in turn to go through the same programme which took about seven to eight minutes. The first five men to be called went through their exercise competently and there was a good, relaxed atmosphere. When my turn came, I streaked through the actions without a hitch. After completion, I stood back from the gun awaiting the order to "fall back" and that the next man would then be called forward. I did not expect any acknowledgment for my fast performance, but to my utter amazement I saw Lt Trapp staring at me red-faced with the veins standing out on his neck and temples.

However, a moment later he gave me the order to "fall back" and then called the next man forward. This was Klaus Wagner, a big hulk of a man, who was as strong as an ox. Wagner was one of the most mild-mannered and likeable men I have ever come across, always cheerful and ready to give a helping hand to anybody, no matter how unpleasant the job was. I have never forgotten the picture of Wagner standing there with a big grin on his good-natured face; his hands, the size of dinner-plates, hanging down his sides itching to go into action. The only problem with Wagner was that he was all thumbs and, whereas he could almost lift up one side of a truck by himself, he was at a disadvantage when a large element of skill was involved.

However, nothing could daunt him and, as soon as he had received his order, he flung himself upon the gun as if to wrestle with some monstrous brute. He heaved and pushed and tugged, attacking the gun from different directions so that soon he was panting and perspiring heavily. Unfortunately, in his eagerness, he sustained a nasty gash to his right lower arm from a sharp corner of the gun mechanism. I do not think he was even aware of his injury. He bravely battled on to the end when he stepped back, grinning triumphantly, while his injured arm was now bleeding quite heavily.

It was at this stage that Lt Trapp appeared to lose his senses. He stared at Wagner for one moment, as if mesmerised, and the sight of Wagner's blood seemed to drive him berserk. Whirling round he strode towards me, his face and neck had by now assumed a deep purple colour and I thought he was close to having an apoplectic fit. Screaming at the top of his voice, he began to rave at me, "THERE YOU ARE, STIEBER, DID YOU SEE THAT? THAT IS THE WAY TO DO THE EXERCISE. WAGNER DOES NOT GIVE A DAMN, EVEN IF

HE LOSES AN ARM, AS LONG AS HE GETS THE EXERCISE DONE QUICKLY!"

My immediate reaction was one of outrage. I would have dearly liked to retort that, in the first case, I would be a fat lot of good in the army if I was running around with only one arm. Secondly, I had done the exercise in less than half the time that Wagner had taken. Of course, it would have been the height of folly to talk back to my commanding officer and, anyway, nothing would have forced me to say anything that would have hurt Wagner's feelings. So I remained silent and just looked back at the Lieutenant, who was now fighting to regain his self-control. The expression on his face showed that he was not succeeding very well and after a few tension-laden moments he abruptly cancelled the rest of the exercises and ordered us all to dismiss. I was now really in trouble; Lt Trapp would be unforgiving and any hope of an understanding between us was well and truly dashed. Over the next hours he did not show up and I was still shocked by his complete loss of self-control and the intensity of his outburst.

I was a bit surprised that none of my mates made any remark to me about the incident, even though I was on excellent terms with every one of them. They just behaved as if nothing had happened and went back to their chores. Maybe they were scared of drawing Lt Trapp's wrath on themselves if he got wind of their discussing the matter with me. For my own part, I decided to say nothing to them. I would not have put it past the lieutenant to report me on a trumped-up charge of inciting others to insubordination if he had found out about it. It was a bitter pill to swallow, but I was determined to keep a clear head and to act prudently. Since I had full confidence in myself and did not want to have any blemish on my official army record, I decided to let the matter go, but from now on to be doubly on the alert.

It was not until a few years later that I developed a greater understanding of Lt Trapp's behaviour and how my calm manner must have increased his feelings of insecurity. Maybe he felt insulted by the apparent ease with which I mastered his beloved guns instead of showing more respect for their "awesome technology?" I can also understand how social background could have been a factor and that Lt Trapp would have had a much greater kinship with Wagner than with me. If I had had the maturity of more years I might have thought of purposely making mistakes and introducing some blunders into my activities so that Lt Trapp could have cursed me to the heights and got rid of his tension. Instead, I was innocently doing the very opposite by trying to be perfect.

What was left of the morning passed quickly and soon we were tucking into our lunch and savouring the unusual experience of sitting down at table to do so. One of our drivers told us that good progress was being made in the workshop on our three self-propelled guns and we should have them back by late in the evening. There were no tasks laid on for the afternoon, so I decided to go for a short stroll outside our barracks. I was unconcerned about setting off on my own because I had not heard of any case where German soldiers had been attacked by the Polish civilian population. I saw many men, women and children about and got the impression that nobody had yet fled the area.

Turning a corner I was amazed to see what looked like a group of attractive women with apparently rouged, prominent cheekbones and wearing Asiatic-type army uniforms. They were armed with rifles and long curved swords and a number of them were sitting on strong, wiry ponies while others were standing beside them. I did not want to stare, but was nevertheless highly intrigued by this unusual sight. Hearing their voices and taking a second look I realised that these were men. They were, in fact, Kalmucks, a tribe of Mongol people who lived in central Asia. This was, of course, the explanation. Kalmucks often fought in Cossack regiments and were known as extremely brave warriors and daring horsemen. Being of short build, usually under 5 feet 6 inches in height, and having almost doll-like, flat, round faces with very soft features, it was small wonder that I had first taken them to be women. This impression was strengthened by their pink, seemingly hairless faces. I thought their uniforms were very smart. They wore long silver-grey coats with shining leather-ware and on their heads they had grey fur hats with a flat red top which was emblazoned with a cross-shaped decoration. All the soldiers were of perfect build and bore an air of proud self-confidence.

Soon after the start of the campaign against Russia, large numbers of Russian prisoners of war volunteered to fight with Germany. They came mostly from areas which were opposed to the Bolshevik doctrine on political, religious or historic grounds.

Despite German party-political opposition, the use of active Russian volunteer-units spread and they repeatedly got honourable mention in military reports over the German national radio. They were particularly successful because of their knowledge of land and language, and also in deployment against partisans. Some of the most fanatical units were Cossacks from the rivers Don and Kuban who had an old score to settle with Bolshevism. The Kalmucks I saw were quite possibly members of one of these famous Cossack cavalry regiments.

By the middle of 1944 there were a total of 300,000 Russian volunteers in the German army. All volunteers fought bravely right up to the end of the war. Although it became obvious to them that Germany would be defeated, there were no desertions. After all, where could they go? It was a tragically sad end for so many brave men who were at heart Russian patriots who loved their country and hoped to see it freed from a ruthless regime.

It was late afternoon when our other three guns were returned to us from the workshop. However, our destination was now altered; and with the situation in East-Prussia deteriorating daily, we were being sent back to the northern section of the Front. We would again travel by train, but this time it would be at night and we were unlikely to suffer the same fate as on our last journey.

Lt Trapp appeared on the scene that evening, but he did not look my way and acted quite normally. Once again, embarkation proceeded smoothly and soon we were on our way.

What was different about our new assignment was that, so far, we had been fighting the Russians on Polish ground; now we would be defending our own country against the mighty Russian steam-roller and against a ten to one superiority.

11

I JOIN A SUICIDE SQUAD

As I settled down for a night's sleep and began to relax to the gentle rocking of the train, my thoughts drifted back to the happenings of the last day. Could so much have really taken place in little more than twenty-four hours? Our departure from Modlin to Warka seemed like an eternity ago. Since then our train had been destroyed, another fluke had saved my life and I was now in deeper trouble than ever with my commanding-officer. A bright spot in the day's events was, of course, my interesting encounter with the Kalmucks.

I had never been to East-Prussia before, so I was looking forward to seeing a new part of Germany. Like the whole of northern Germany, East-Prussia had a very flat landscape, most of which was not much above sea-level. There was a widespread system of lakes in the northern part and there were only two hilly areas, both small, in the south-west. East-Prussia was one of the main corn-growing areas in Germany, where many wealthy farmers had lived and worked for generations. Although I prefer hilly, wooded countryside, I was very impressed by the lush and well-cared for farmlands that I saw everywhere.

Our journey to the northern part of East-Prussia was about 300 miles, so dawn had already broken by the time we got there. When our train reached the East-Prussian town of Tilsit we quickly disembarked. My division was stationed in the Russ/Kuckernese area of the Memelland province, quite close to the Baltic Sea.

Since it was now broad daylight we dug in our guns with all haste and soon we were ready for action. By this time I had mentally absorbed details and landmarks of the local terrain.

This quick familiarisation with the surroundings was an essential on-going exercise which was carried out automatically at all times. The ability to immediately relate Russian troop movements to all aspects of the terrain depended on having stored such information sub-consciously. Such knowledge was also invaluable if one had to find one's way at night-time.

The morning passed with nothing to disturb the tranquillity apart from the distant noise of battle. With just over two months of service behind me I had, so far, acquired quite a degree of self-confidence. Nevertheless, my new environment in quite a different section of the Front made me feel a bit like a "new boy."

Early in the afternoon the order was given for us to "fall in" for a briefing by our CO. (Commanding Officer). Under the circumstances there was nothing unusual about this. Although I had no reason for any apprehension, my sixth sense told me that this was something ominous and that it was to concern me personally.

After we had lined-up, Lt Trapp told us that a new major offensive by the Russian forces was expected. However, there was a snag. German intelligence sources had failed to get reliable information on when and where the attack was to be launched and what was the strength of the Russian units involved. In order to impede the Russians in their advance, it had become necessary to have special task forces set up. In that moment I knew what my fate was to be and that this was where my good luck had finally run out.

It was the practice in the German army that where details of an impending attack by the Russian army were not known, or where details were known, but the German lines were weak, special units were established. Their job was to hold up the attack long enough to give the German units maximum time to re-group for optimum effectiveness. These task-forces were almost invariably deployed in "no man's land," that is they were placed well ahead of the German lines of defence, but still some distance from the Russian lines. This was somewhat on the principle which the Greeks had applied in the Pass of Thermopylae. The positions occupied by the task-forces were selected so that, as resistance pockets, they were difficult to wipe out while, at the same time, they could effectively hinder the attackers in the speed of their advance. Members of these task forces had no hope of staying alive, because there was no way back to their own lines. The Russians took no prisoners when they had to keep advancing and it was a case of just firing to the end and keeping the last bullet for oneself.

Having given some more details on the general situation, Lt Trapp went on to say, "Each unit-commander in this section of the front has been instructed to contribute two men towards setting up these task-forces and I will now give the names of the men I have selected." At this point I experienced a feeling of indifference since, to me, it was blatantly obvious what was to come and I just wanted him to get on with it. It may seem hard to believe that I could have felt indifferent about being "sentenced to death," but that was exactly how I reacted.

"The first man I have selected" went on Lt Trapp, "is Gefreiter Offenheim. My second selection is .... " and here there was a pause in which I thought I could sense him savouring the satisfaction his announcement must be giving him ".... Kanonier Stieber." Then a most peculiar thing happened. Although there was no obligation on the lieutenant to add anything; he was quite within his rights to select anybody he chose, he turned to me and addressed me for the first time in two days. Speaking in a calm and, incredibly, almost friendly voice he said, "This is a very important assignment, Stieber. We need good men on it."

One could have knocked me down with a feather. What was this latest inexplicable trait in Lt Trapp's behaviour? It was a well-known fact that commanding officers invariably selected their least accomplished men, or troublemakers, to go on these task-forces. No skill, much beyond the ability to pull a trigger, was required and men of good proficiency would be wasted there. Actually, it was quite valid to pick the youngest, and thus most inexperienced, man and so I would have been a legitimate choice. But where was the rationale in this sudden, and unexpected, praise? I thought this was pure hypocrisy, but I was puzzled as to why the lieutenant had made the statement at all.

Was he pricked by his conscience into making some obscure apology for his decision, or was he telling me that if I thought that I was all that good a soldier, here was my chance to prove it? Those were the thoughts that crossed my mind at the time, but I still felt baffled by a personality which I could not understand. Having made his pronouncement, Lt Trapp said that Offenheim and I would be picked up by truck that night and brought to our new position. Well, the dice had been cast and I was now up against what must have been the toughest test of my mental fortitude that I had ever experienced. How was I going to cope in a situation where I knew that nothing could save me?

After the order was given to "fall out," Offenheim and I packed our kit and spent the next few hours having a last chat with our mates. When the truck arrived that evening, Offenheim and I reported to Lt Trapp who wished us good luck and hurriedly dismissed us. I was quite happy to have Offenheim as my fellow-sufferer in adversity. He had a pleasant personality and seemed to be well-balanced, the sort of person who would not be a problem in a desperate situation. Since it was known that nobody ever returned from a suicide-mission, the psychological pressures on us all would be very great and I knew nothing at all about the other soldiers in my new unit.

The drive to our position took about half an hour and we arrived as night was falling. The many advantages of this new position, for what that was worth, became quickly apparent. First of all, it was ready for occupation and so we would not have to spend the night, and maybe further nights, digging trenches and providing protection from enemy-fire. Secondly, although our unit was comprised of only thirty men, the position had been designed for three to four times that number and it consisted of an extensive labyrinth of interconnecting trenches and of generous underground accommodation, a veritable Hotel Ritz. Some well-protected machine-gun stations were also provided, so it wanted for nothing. To the west of the position there was a small wood, about six acres in size, quite close to us. Other conscripts to our task-force arrived much later that evening, so it was not till the morning that we got our first formal briefing by our new commander, Lt Breding.

The third advantage of the position became evident the next morning when I saw that a number of trenches connected with the wood, thus providing access to a place where we could safely stretch our legs. Our little wood immediately proved its usefulness and the briefing took place in a clearing, well hidden from any observation by the Russians. Lt Breding informed us of the strategic options for attack that the Russians had, and he explained the situation and weaponry of the other German task-forces in the area. We had been supplied with machine-guns, bazookas, hand-grenades and, of course, we had our own army rifles, so our targets would be ground-troops, troop-carriers and any light tanks or armoured vehicles that came within our range. Our machine-guns, of the type MG-42, were much superior to all others used in the Second World War. They were absolutely trouble-free and fired at the then incredible rate of 25 rounds per second. Despite the good quality of these weapons and of the hand-held bazookas, I did not see us making much of an impact on a determined Russian attack and I thought that even neighbouring task-forces with their heavier equipment would have been brushed aside like flies when the Russians advanced.

My new companions seemed to be an average group of soldiers. Against my expectations, none struck me as being in any way of a lesser standard than my previous mates. They all went about their work without hazarding any opinion as to what they thought of our mission or why they had been singled out for it. I thought that Lt Breding handled the situation extremely well. He struck a shrewd balance between not giving us too much free time to brood and, on the other hand, not making us engage in purposeless activities just for the sake of killing time. Good disciplinary control was exercised and I thought we had quite a lot of free time without it ever hanging heavily on our hands.

Our little wood proved to be a tremendous boon and saved us from the claustrophobic environment that members of the other task-forces had to endure. Although our situation was hopeless, it would have been very much worse if one had to wait for death like a rat in a trap. In the case of my unit all formal activities took place in our wood and, during our free time, we were at liberty to ramble in it as long as we kept well out of sight of any Russian observers. Since the wood was fairly dense, this was not a problem. Admittedly, Lt Breding was taking a small chance in allowing us this freedom, but we were never far away and a Russian offensive was highly improbable during the daytime.

Dieter Offenheim was a nature lover, just as I was, so he and I would go for walks together, chatting about our homes and families. Offenheim was twenty-four years of age and came from a town in the Hannover area. He had worked with his father in the family painting business which he had hoped to extend when he came back from the war. He found it hard to believe how I had ended up on the Russian front when my home was in Ireland. Although he knew that conscription was enforceable by law, he was convinced that I could have avoided it somehow. It seems strange to look back on the two of us, walking and chatting together in the peaceful wood, while just the occasional chirp of a bird intruded on our conversation. Was the war really so close by, with death waiting to claim us? Offenheim was actually one of the only two soldiers with whom I ever had a more personal conversation during my year in the army. The particular situation we found ourselves in was probably the reason why we overcame the barrier of reticence and spoke to each other of our homes and our hopes.

Since it had been late the previous evening when we arrived, I had immediately gone to sleep after spending two hours on sentry duty, but on this evening I was able to further appreciate the luxury of our new accommodation. The internal height of the bunker was about six feet and we had strong paraffin lights so one could read in comfort. I still had my slim volume of Lord Emsworth and Others, which I had held onto through thick and thin. Somehow I had repeatedly managed to salvage it, even though I had not always carried it on my person.

If I had had to choose between Wodehouse and a few extra slices of bread, I think I would have discarded the bread and kept the Wodehouse. A link with normality, even if this was represented by the antics of some absurd characters in a book, was an essential need of mine and I was still able to chuckle over stories I had read so many times. My mates were interested in the source of my laughter, but how could I explain Wodehouse to them? I did not even attempt it and just said that these were funny stories written by a very popular English writer. I was afterwards surprised that nobody had taken exception to my reading a book by an English author, even though Germany was at war with England.

So far, I still felt no anxiety about my short life-expectancy. Ever since I had been posted to the Russian Front I had carried the conviction in me that I would know in advance if my end was nigh. My sixth sense had sent me no signals, as yet, so I retained an optimistic "wait and see" confidence.

The second day progressed much in the same way as the first day, but then there was a development. During the afternoon briefing, Lt Breding told us that a colonel would be inspecting our position in the following morning and that we should go all-out to make a good impression on him. This announcement filled me with excitement and gave me a sudden feeling of hope for which there could have been no imaginable reason. Visits by "top brass" were made as morale boosters and had no further significance, yet I felt that there was a message behind this interruption to our routine.

Next morning we assembled in our wood in good time for the inspection. A Mercedes staff-car arrived punctually and out stepped a colonel, his adjutant and a captain. As they came nearer, I could not believe my eyes when I saw that the captain was the same officer who had chatted to me when I was in my fox-hole on manoeuvres at Alkmaar in Holland so many months ago. Now I was sure that there was a meaning behind this development. Maybe it was a signal that I was to live?

After delivering the usual pep-talk, the colonel turned to Lt Breding and said that he would like to see us carry out some machine-gun drill. I felt like bursting! All the signs were pointing directly my way. In that instant I resolved to go all-out and to follow the path that providence seemed to be showing me. My last gun-drill had sentenced me to death, maybe this gun-drill would return me to life?

Up to this point I had been inconspicuous near the end of the second of three rows of a faceless blur of blue/grey uniformed soldiers. Now I had the opportunity to stand out and be noticed, maybe even recognised by the captain. In anticipation of the order to be given, I poised myself ready to push through between two soldiers in front of me so that I would be the first to go forward and immediately draw attention to myself.

Lt Breding asked for three volunteers and the moment the order was given I catapulted forward and stood to attention. Everybody seemed stunned by this sudden eruption and nobody else moved. However, Lt Breding quickly reacted and irritably shouted, "I said three men! I want two more men, and on the double!" Two men quickly stepped forward and we picked up three machine-guns for our drill. The exercise was simple. Each man was to set up his machine-gun ready for action, then to replace the barrel by a spare and then to replace the firing-mechanism. All this suited me perfectly and I now had the opportunity to distinguish myself from the group of three men. Maybe the captain would recognise me and wonder what I was doing on this suicide mission?

I went through the drill as if my life depended on it, which it did. My fingers flew as they had never flown before and then I was up on my feet, standing to attention. When the last man had completed his drill, the colonel thanked Lt Breding and then came the magic words, "I would like to speak to the Kanonier on the left."

I got my order to step up to the colonel who proceeded to congratulate me and to say that I had given an exceptional demonstration in the handling of a machine-gun. Although I had to keep my eyes on the colonel while he was speaking, I was strenuously trying to send a telepathic message to the captain at the same time. When the colonel had finished speaking, my role would have been to give a simple "Danke, Herr Oberst" (Thank you, colonel) and wait for the order to return to the ranks. But this would not be enough. I still had to get through to the captain, but how could he remember a face in a fox-hole, partially obscured by a steel helmet, and this over five months ago?

The answer was my voice. People can forget faces, but they do not forget a voice. I had to take the liberty of going beyond the formal three-worded reply and to start waffling at the colonel. So, what came out was, "Thank you, colonel, I have always taken a particular interest in all forms of drill on machine-guns and light anti-aircraft weaponry." There, that was as much as I could risk, but I was already conscious of the captain's interest.

The captain came up to scratch and, before I could be dismissed, he said that he would also like to speak to me. Things were now running smoothly and, at last, I was at liberty to look straight at him. There was a puzzled expression on his face and he said to me, "Tell me, have we met somewhere before?" I replied, "Ja, Herr Hauptmann" and went on to remind him of our meeting in Holland. The captain admitted that he now remembered, but he continued to look puzzled and I imagined he was wondering how I had got into this situation.

Time was getting short and I could hardly burst out with a detailed explanation. Then I had a flash of inspiration, the best I probably had in all my life. Suddenly I knew how I could convey all in a camouflaged manner. I went on to say, quite innocently, "After completing my training in Holland, I was sent to the Eastern Front at the end of July and last served with the Anti-Aircraft Gun-Group Nr.... commanded by Lt Trapp." When giving the number of my unit and the name of its commander, I tried to speak very distinctly without making it too obvious what I was up to. I had now managed to give him a lead and it was up to him if he wanted to find out more about Lt Trapp. There was nothing else that I could do. With that I was given the order to "fall-back," and we three volunteers rejoined the soldiers lined up behind us. The inspection came to its formal close and the "brass" drove off.

After the colonel and his party had left, I felt a sense of subdued exultation. Surely all this could not have been without purpose? It was a miracle that the captain had arrived at this very spot and this was compounded by the miracle that the colonel had asked for machine-gun drill. He could have asked for many other things or he could have just left after five minutes.

But the odds against me were astronomical. The captain had to understand the hint, he had to remember the details I gave him and he had to want to do something about it. Then he needed to have time to follow it up, he had to obtain permission for my transfer back to Lt Trapp's gun-group and my return had to be effected. All this had to happen in turn and there was no time to lose since the Russians could stage their offensive at any moment. My spirits remained elevated, but I tried not to be too optimistic. It looked like an impossible race against time, if there was a race at all, and maybe I was just deluding myself?

Many hours later I still felt dazed by the events. I knew that no great developments were possible the same day, nor even likely during the next day. None of my mates referred to my conversation with the captain and I did not think they were even aware of any of its undertones.

The day drew to a close and that night I got off to a good sleep. Unfortunately, I was picked for sentry-duty from one to three o'clock in the morning and as the minutes dragged on, one by one, I had to constantly fight against my thoughts dwelling on my chances of a reprieve.

Things became easier the next day when my mind was occupied with various activities. Again, I was able to walk in the woods with Offenheim, but I avoided any reference to the happenings of the previous day.

After breakfast on the following morning, I was getting out my equipment for the morning-drill when a soldier came dashing along one of the trenches and shouted, "Stieber, you are to report to the CO in a hurry!" Surely this had to be it! The urgency of the call and the way I was singled out could mean only one thing, but I had to keep calm and not let my hopes rise too much.

Like a shot, I bolted through the trenches and stood before Lt Breding who said to me, "Stieber, I have just received a communication that you are to report back to Lt Trapp immediately." He then went on to say, "There is a supply-van here at the moment, but it has to leave in ten minutes and I cannot let it wait. If you are ready by then, you can leave on it, otherwise you will have to wait till tomorrow." I rushed back to my bunker, calling out to Offenheim that I was being sent back to base. Grand fellow that he was, an instant look of delight crossed his face and he scrambled to help me get my things together. There was no sign of envy, only joy at my good fortune and I suddenly felt a pang of remorse at leaving this fine person behind to die. I had a fleeting urge to go slow and miss my van, but Offenheim was already pumping my hand and wishing me good luck, so I shook off all thoughts of staying. Anyway, I would have been foolish to risk my life just to delay the departure for one day until the next van was due to arrive. I wished Offenheim good luck and, after hurried farewells to my other mates, went to report to Lt Breding.

Jolting along in the van, my mood was not so much one of celebration, but rather a feeling of being at peace. I was still going back to the Front lines, to a situation where I could be killed, but an immediate danger had been averted. It was difficult to comprehend the miracle that had saved me, but my faith in my future was now stronger than ever. I felt no animosity towards Lt Trapp, only compassion, and so I resolved to make our meeting as easy as possible for him. There must be no suggestion of triumph and I would have to guard against appearing condescending. I knew exactly what I had to do, but would I get it right?

I arrived at my destination and made my way to Lt Trapp's underground bunker. It was a brilliantly sunny day and, as I walked down the steps with the sun at my back, I could see him writing at a table facing the open door. After walking up to him I stood to attention and saluted, giving him my formal "Kanonier Stieber reporting for duty." I felt I had achieved a natural expression on my face and waited for his reaction.

Lt Trapp had obviously known that I was coming, but he still stared at me for some moments as if mesmerised. All he had to do was to say, "All right, Stieber, fall out," but that was not what happened. Instead, he began to rise in slow motion, his knuckles showing white as he clutched the edge of his table. He did not seem to be able to achieve a standing position, but remained crouched behind the table staring up at me. Then his face slowly went into a hideous contortion and his clenched teeth parted to give me what, I realised to my horror, was meant to be a smile. Words came, pushed slowly and painfully through his rigid jaws; "Yes, …Stieber, …glad to have…you…back with us." Having said that, he remained crouched before me with the same expression on his face; it was as if his whole body had suddenly been cast in stone and he was unable to stand up or sit down. I saw only one way out; the spell had to be broken. I saluted and left the bunker.

I do not think Lt Trapp ever spoke to me again and, thanks to the Russians, there was no shortage of action to hold our attention. I was occupied on my gun-carrier and he dealt directly with his NCOs. It was also not long before the Russians brought about the final parting of the ways between Lt Trapp and me.

I never came across "my captain" again, so I do not know what role, if any, he might have played in my transfer. It seems inconceivable that he could have got me out of the suicide squad, especially so quickly, or that he would have even decided to try. Whatever happened, I did return to my unit, I am still alive and so the episode will always remain a mystery to me. The significant date of the morning when I reported back to my unit was 15 October 1944. During the next night there was a major alert and all hell broke loose. The Russians had completed the build-up of their forces and at four o'clock in the morning on the 16 October they launched their awaited offensive.

It was just eighteen hours earlier that I had boarded the van to leave the suicide-squad; if another day had elapsed, my luck would finally have run out.

12

CAUGHT IN A RUSSIAN PINCER MOVEMENT

The 16th of October heralded the start of a two-week period of bitter fighting with no respite for either side. My division, as part of the 3rd Panzer Army, faced a seemingly impossible task as Russian forces fanned southwards to attack us in the Russ-Kuckernese area. This constituted part of a pincer movement designed to capture 2,500 square miles of German territory. If this move had succeeded, not only would one German army have been encircled, but all civilian inhabitants and refugees in that area would have been trapped with no hope of escape.

On being roused by the general alert at 04.00 hours that morning, it soon became obvious that something very big was in the air. The Russians kept up a continuous barrage of heavy shelling for several hours and supplemented it with air strikes against our lines. This military action was clearly on a more massive scale than I had hitherto experienced and there was a new dimension to the way the ground now trembled beneath my feet.

The Russian action had begun about two hours before sunrise and I had to operate in almost total darkness. My ears were numbed by gunfire and shells exploding and I had to rely almost totally on my ears for trying to sort out what was happening around me. During previous action in daytime, experience had taught me how to keep my bearings, but circumstances had now changed. On top of this the noise of flying shells and of echoes was different during night compared with daytime.

I have sometimes been asked whether I was very frightened when I was on the front and my answer was always, "No, I was not really afraid." Although it is often said that only a fool or a liar would claim that he was not afraid, many soldiers will give a similar answer. I agree with what I have read that soldiers in infantry units are the most likely to experience fear. The more prolonged exposure to enemy fire, from both long and short range, the claustrophobic influence and horrors of trench war-fare and the heavy casualty rate must have a highly demoralising effect on soldiers. The situations confronting other branches of the services can seldom be as bad. This would also seem to be confirmed by a British study of sample cases which showed that casualty rates and desertion in infantry companies ran at four to five times the army average.

My situation was different, even though death never seemed to be far away. Luckily, I was never involved in hand-to-hand fighting or attacked by soldiers at short range. This would have been a frightening experience and one that I was grateful to have been spared. My main danger usually came from shells and I could predict their point of impact fairly accurately from the characteristics of their whistle. If I expected a shell to land close to me I could only duck low behind whatever protection might be near me and hope for the best.

I think the fact that we were never short of ammunition and had fuel to give us high manoeuvrability, was the main source of reassurance for me. Being on the move almost daily gave me an impression of "freedom" and of not being stuck in a spot waiting to be killed. The reason why I felt no fear in the "suicide-squad" must have been based on my sixth sense which had not given me any message of impending death. Somehow I never thought about becoming afraid. Since I do not consider myself to be a brave person, the explanation must have been my preoccupation with the present. To me, the future was as unreal as the past.

The idea of deserting never entered my head even though there must have been occasions when I experienced extreme anxiety. I certainly never considered crossing over to the Russians and could not have run away from my responsibilities. More than ever I saw it as my duty to help prevent a total collapse of the Front and to stop the Russian armies from storming into Germany. According to various reports I have read, desertion was never considered a problem in the German army.

It is curious how at times of great danger, the mind often latches onto some trivial happenings around one and relegates the noises of warfare to the subconscious. Lying on the ground while taking cover from shell-fire, I remember becoming absorbed in a beetle's attempts to climb onto a stone. Movements of other insects, flowers and blades of grass also attracted my attention. Emerging unscathed after intense shelling I have found myself worrying about whether a bit of butter I saved for my evening meal had survived. I recall many such trivia to this day, whereas I probably could not remember details of some of the military action as soon as it was over. Such are the vagaries of the human mind, but similar instances have been well documented and what I experienced was quite usual.

I have sometimes wondered what my attitude to serving in the German army would have been had I known the truth about the concentration camps. That the population at large could have been ignorant of the facts is generally met with absolute disbelief outside Germany, but that is exactly the way it was. People just did not know about these things and I have since had nothing but confirmation that this was so.

Had I known what I know today, I do not think that I would have behaved differently because the war was in its final stages and the days of the Nazi regime were numbered. Among other priorities, the saving of the lives of refugees and German soldiers would have been at the forefront of my thoughts. Of course, it would have been different and I would have had a problem had I been called up at the start of the war.

There is one other point that has intrigued me. The Nazi fixation about purity of an Aryan nation was well known in Germany, but I never heard of the expression Master Race until after the war. Undoubtedly it was used somewhere by extremists in word and print, but I would certainly not have forgotten a word like "Herrenrasse" once I heard it.

After my battery had survived the shelling during the early hours of 16 October, Russian Il-2 planes stepped up their attacks, but we were able to effectively beat them all back. The following night we moved to a new position, as we did on the next night again, but each time we dug our guns into good and well-camouflaged positions which we managed to hold without suffering any casualties. These nightly moves reduced our time for sleeping, but the longer autumn nights gave us more time for rest than we had got previously.

While operating in the Russ-Kuckernese area our main task, apart from holding back the Russian armies, was to keep a channel open through which fleeing refugees could safely travel. Every day I saw refugees on the road and their situation was hopeless. At their rate of progress, how many of them would be lucky enough to escape being overtaken by advancing troops? Already we heard reports that straggling columns had been fired on by Russian planes.

I noticed very few men among the refugees, nearly all of whom were women and children. Any of their men-folk who were still able-bodied, despite their age, would have been kept back on the orders of a Gauleiter for trench-digging or other futile tasks in the defence of the Fatherland. The condition of many of the refugees' horse-drawn carts and their wagonettes, loaded high with people and possessions, was very poor. Shot at by strafing Russian planes and with make-shift repairs, or just plainly overloaded, their prospects of reaching safety were extremely bleak.

Our action over the first two days north of the river Memel was very successful and we brought the Russian advance to a halt. Then, in the night of 18/19 October, we unexpectedly received orders to pull out of the area and move to a new, and far greater, trouble spot.

By attacking the German 4th Army from the east on 16 October, three Russian armies had managed to break through the hopelessly outnumbered German forces. Within three days the Russian troops bypassed the town of Gumbinnen, about sixty miles south-east of my division. Their spearheads reached the river Angerapp near the town of Nemmersdorf by 21 October. As a desperate measure the Göring Divisions 1 and 2 and another panzer division were dispatched to the troubled area to hurl themselves against the Russian units storming westwards.

After only two days in the Russ-Kuckernese area we were now being withdrawn, leaving behind a front weakened even further. I felt as if I had betrayed the pathetic columns of struggling refugees by deserting them, but only a much greater crisis could have warranted removing us at that stage.

It was shortly after darkness on the night of 18/19 October when we began our journey south-eastwards. It was a long drive by road, but we managed to complete it well under cover of darkness. The ride was physically very uncomfortable because the self-propelled gun carriers were virtually unsprung and, sitting on steel plating in a cramped area around the gun, left little room for moving about.

When we arrived at Gumbinnen, the situation there was catastrophic and the Russian attack had now become three-pronged. The main thrust was still westwards, but attacks were simultaneously being launched to the north against Gumbinnen and to the south-west. The two-fold task of our divisions was to stop the Russians taking Gumbinnen and to cut off their main thrust to the west while also blocking their retreat. This was achieved after three days of heavy fighting.

During these days my battery had to provide our fast-operating grenadier and tank units with continuous protection against air attacks. There was no question of digging-in since we were continually on the move as if trying to confuse the Russians about the details of our deployment. During the first two days we steadily gained ground in a southerly direction and there was a lot of short-range action since we were penetrating an area already taken by the Russians, but we did not become involved in any of the ground fighting. Without suffering casualties we were able to put a number of Russian aircraft out of action.

In the afternoon of the third day we suffered our first setback. All through the morning, especially after early ground fog had lifted, there had been increased action around us with our Panther tanks taking a heavy toll of Russian T-34 tanks. Russian planes had also stepped up their sorties and I was glad that it was a cool autumn day since I hardly got a break in the warm job of re-loading the shell-magazines of my gun.

It was at about two o'clock in the afternoon when we took up our position close to a bridge over a large river in order to guard it and the approach roads. We had no problem keeping Russian planes at bay while German tanks and troops crossed over the bridge. Half an hour later we again moved further south. Suddenly we were put under fire by a group of Russian tanks well concealed in a nearby wood. My self-propelled gun was hit by a shell low down at the forward end, causing it to rear up from the explosion and then to keel forward with shattered axle and steering gear.

The sudden stop caused us all to be flung forward but, since I had been kneeling down beside my shell magazines, I was fairly well protected and only suffered a bruised shoulder. We all escaped without anything worse than a few bruises, but our co-driver suffered a gash on his forehead when his head struck the frame of the windscreen. Although more shells had been discharged at us, the other three self-propelled guns had luckily escaped being hit. Exposed as we were to further heavy fire, there was nothing we could do, but immediately abandon our crippled gun. We all jumped up on the surviving gun-carriers which quickly reached cover where we were safe from further Russian fire.

Everything had happened in a flash and we were lucky not to have lost more of our guns. As it was, a heavy explosion and a plume of smoke soon told us that the Russian tanks had continued firing at our crippled gun and caused the fuel tank to explode and set the vehicle ablaze.

It was at this stage that I finally lost my Wodehouse after I had managed to hold on to it for so long. I cannot clearly remember how I came to still have it with me after all the scrapes I had been in. I suppose it must have been in a pocket of my jacket whenever I lost the rest of my kit. On this occasion it obviously was not there and my only priority at that moment was to jump onto one of the gun-carriers already picking up speed and to get away out of danger. Our guns would, of course, have been no match for the well concealed heavy Russian tanks.

My battery was now short one gun but, as the other gun-crews had suffered no casualties, there was no reason to distribute any of the surplus crew among them. My "unemployed" mates and I were now sent to an assembly area nearby to wait for developments, but we did not have to wait long. That same evening we received replacements from our well organised supplies-unit, for the personal equipment we had lost, and on the following morning we were sent to join a new gun group. I could not believe my luck! I was now parting company from Lt Trapp only twelve days after returning from the suicide-squad.

The new gun group also consisted of self-propelled guns, but these were of 37-millimetre calibre and had twin barrels placed one above the other. Compared with the 20-millimetre guns they could fire much higher, while the horizontal range was four miles. The firing rate per barrel was lower, 150 rounds per minute, but the shells were much heavier and therefore of greatly increased effectiveness. We could either use the barrels singly, or both together if we wanted to double the firing rate.

My new Commander, Lt Grossenheim, a man about 24 or 25 years of age, seemed to be a very straightforward sort of a person. Maybe I could now settle down to a more natural relationship with my superior officer.

Since my job, once again, was filling magazines with new shells, I needed no instruction, but the work was a lot tougher than it had been previously. The heavier weight of the 37-millimetre shells was no problem, but the magazine springs past which the shells had to be pushed were much stiffer. This made the job a lot more tiring and my right hand became quite sore until the skin had toughened up.

There were many grim reminders of the presence of Russian troops in the wrecks of refugee carts littering the sides of the roads. The area south of Gumbinnen was particularly hard hit by the lightning advance of Russian armoured units who had simply shot up refugee columns, or driven over them with their tanks if they got in their way on the clogged roads. It is estimated that 1,000 refugees had been killed there during the Russian progress. The tragedy of the refugees was a new element in the suffering of the German civilian population which was already being subjected to terrible ordeals in air-raids on cities.

I was now nearing completion of three months' service on the Russian Front. How was I generally adjusting to that way of life? First of all, I did not spend any time thinking about my situation, but instead, took every day, every hour and every minute just as they came along. My mind concentrated on each job in hand as if it were all a routine day's work.

At this stage my senses and brain were becoming ever more like what would nowadays be called a computer. I found my ability to take in and process a huge amount of detail through my eyes and ears to be quite phenomenal. It seemed to become effortless and basic that I was able to differentiate between the sounds of different guns, planes, tanks and trucks and make good estimates of numbers involved and their distance away from me. I also discovered that sounds enabled me to gauge the speed and direction of tanks, trucks and other vehicles and the direction in which guns were being fired. At the same time I automatically took into account the strength and direction of any prevailing winds which could affect the sounds.

While all this was going on, my "computer-mind" was processing visual impressions of movement, topographical details of the terrain, light and shade effects, the position of the sun and many other factors. Although much of this information is not needed all of the time, every detail is stored in a sub-conscious way. I found that if anything became important, it would immediately surface in my brain and prompt an instant reaction from me.

I discovered that the situations where this had the greatest importance were when I was on my own behind the Russian lines or in "no-man's land." Whenever I was on foot in such a situation, and heavily dependent on my "computer," I had the feeling I was being guided by remote control. I was able to move swiftly and safely across the terrain, every now and then automatically adjusting my rate of progress and direction of movement. I saw myself like an animal in the jungle that makes its way stealthily, with all senses tuned to receive the faintest signals. Although I clearly remember the unusual sensation I experienced, it is something I find difficult to describe adequately in words.

I got on well with my new comrades on the 37-millimetre guns even though we had, once again, the usual neutral sort of a relationship but there was good all-round co-operation, which was the main thing. In fact, throughout my service in the army I never knew anybody to shirk his duty. There may have been grumbles, but if a job had to be done everybody co-operated fully.

Towards the end of October, temperatures dropped noticeably. I began to wonder what it would be like living in the open in the depths of winter. Since the catastrophic loss of life in Stalingrad, when thousands of German troops had frozen to death, supplies of winter clothing had been well-organised and I therefore did not expect any undue hardship over the coming months.

I had an unpleasant scare when on guard duty in the early hours of one morning, as it was just getting light. There was a fairly heavy fog around, so I had kept within twenty yards of the gun nearest to me. Suddenly a light breeze sprang up and enveloped the whole area in a blanket of impenetrable fog. Being caught unawares, I lost my sense of direction and no longer had the remotest idea where the battery was, even though I knew it must be right beside me.

Since I was in a field with no salient features, there was nothing I could use as a guide. I could hardly shout to my mates or stand there for hours like a fool waiting for the fog to lift. I took the logical action of walking twenty-five yards in one direction and retracing my steps when I had not found the battery. After repeating the exercise at right angles in three other directions I had still drawn a blank and started to get worried. In the dense fog I could not even see the mark I had scratched into the ground with my boots before I initially started my search. Hoping that I had not veered off too far from my original starting point I set off again choosing different angles. At the third attempt I breathed a sigh of relief when I made a familiar contact. I was saved extreme embarrassment, and probably a rebuke, if I had had to be rescued. My experience gave me a warning about fog and orientation that I never forgot.

By 31 October Russian forces virtually abandoned their attempts to gain a greater foothold along our Front. Ten weakened German divisions, two of which were Göring divisions, had defeated forty fully-equipped Russian divisions and many armoured units. Over the preceding twelve days Russian forces had lost 1,225 tanks, 330 heavy guns and 312 planes and suffered a major defeat, and were therefore forced to abandon any plans for a further incursion into East-Prussia. Along the northern front the 3rd Panzer Army had managed to stabilise the lines of defence after conceding some small territorial losses. For the time being, the front in East-Prussia was secure.

Near the end of October, I managed to knock out a Russian tank single-handed. Early one morning the Russians had unsuccessfully launched an attack and tried to break through our lines to give assistance to groups of their own troops who had been cut off. Our guns were in a well-camouflaged position to the south-east of a small wood in a terrain providing plenty of cover in the form of trees and bushes. I could hear Russian tanks and soon made out the silhouettes of five T-34 tanks passing us in an easterly direction on the far side of the wood. Suddenly they stopped when they were about a few hundred meters away. Lt Grossenheim decided that our self-propelled guns should stay in their position and that a very good opportunity had presented itself for an attack on the tanks by bazookas, the hand-held rocket-launchers.

A Gefreiter and I were instructed to pick up a bazooka each and to attempt to creep up near enough to get in a shot. Slinging our rifles over our shoulders, and carrying our bazookas, we set off making fast progress thanks to the generous ground cover. The rumble of the stationary tanks gave us a clear sign of the direction we had to take. As we got closer, we stayed together since it was essential that we got in our shots simultaneously rather than have one of us giving the Russians an early warning.

Moving through the wood we got within 100 yards of the nearest tank. Having primed our bazookas and erected the sights we moved on, keeping behind a small mound ahead of us. We skirted it on one side, but found ourselves out of luck. The nearest Russian tank was still too far away and the tank commander was standing up in the turret; he would have seen us if we tried to get any closer. To dodge round the other side of the mound was a much better idea, so we made our way there hurriedly in case the tanks started to move on again. This time we were able to get much closer.

Between taking crouching steps and crawling, we got within forty yards of the nearest two tanks. They presented a side-on view giving us a large target area and we now also had the advantage that they were blocking a direct line of sight between the other tanks and us. Dropping down on one knee and pressing the bazooka hard into my side I took aim. My mate counted to three after which we each pressed our release button. There was a huge explosion as the tank my mate had selected burst into flames while my own shot hit the other tank lower down. As we jumped up to run for safety in the wood, I heard the tank engines rev up. I saw the tank I had hit begin to move forward and then slew round as its right propulsion track burst where my exploding rocket had damaged it.

It was some moments before the surviving tanks were able to drive past the two tanks that we had knocked out and spray the wood with machine-gun fire, but by that time we were well away and safe from their bullets. Soon we arrived at our battery and made our report. Lt Grossenheim was obviously delighted by our successful venture and gave us his congratulations. Meanwhile the surviving T-34s had moved off and I could hear the rumble of their engines as they receded into the distance. Nobody in the burning tank was likely to have survived and the crew of the other tank had probably been taken on board the surviving tanks.

I must say I felt happy that my shot had been the one with less spectacular results. Despite knowing what Russian soldiers had done to German refugees, I thought that the tank crew could have been just as unwilling conscripts in the war as I was and I felt glad to have put the tank out of action without killing or maiming its occupants.

13

WINTER ON THE RUSSIAN FRONT

Over the next eleven weeks, from 1 November, 1944, to 20 January, 1945, there was only a small change in the territory held by German and Russian armies in the central and northern sections of the Eastern Front.

Weeks of gruelling action had left German and Russian troops physically exhausted. Abandoning further attempts to attack the German lines, the Russians began a massive operation bringing forward supplies of armaments, equipment and food to bolster up their forces prior to their next major thrust forward.

All units of my division became engaged in developing and improving the lines of defence, while constructing sound shelters against the coming winter. The infantry dug an elaborate system of trenches, which were manned on a continuous basis and in some places were separated by a distance of only forty-five to fifty yards from the Russian trenches.

A standing order was issued that, in principle, vehicles of all descriptions should be well dug in so that they would be protected against direct hits and shrapnel. This made for an extremely tiring, but worthwhile, chore. The staff of regimental and battalion headquarters were housed in cellars of abandoned farms; sometimes ruined outbuildings provided excellent camouflage for vehicles temporarily parked there.

We now dug small communal shelters, one for each of our gun-crews, instead of each soldier digging his own. Although these were still only glorified "holes in the ground," they provided a place where one could sit and have a bit of room for moving around. The air was less fresh, but it was warmer from the presence of many men than it had been in our individual shelters. Despite the "pong," I was glad to be able to face the cold nights in warmer accommodation since I had no idea what it might be like sleeping in one-man shelters when the icy blast of winter hit us.

I do not remember topics of conversation, but there was quite a cosy atmosphere and we had a paraffin lamp by which we could read or play cards fairly comfortably. I cannot say that I missed a more personal contact with my mates. By nature I have always been a self-sufficient person and, if being reserved about oneself was the norm in the army, that was alright with me.

Our position was in undulating terrain with small hillocks, which gave us some good look-out positions, but in other places it favoured the Russians, so each side was able to keep a good watch on the others' lines. Our guns were located on a hillock named "Height 102", which gave us a good view over a distance of about a mile. Life was not so easy for our infantry in the forward trenches close to the Russians and they even had problems getting supplied with food. The Russians fired at men carrying food to the trenches and went as far as to use flares at night-time to continue their shooting when the ferrying of food was switched to the cover of darkness.

Il-2 planes still kept up their sorties, but I do not recall being in any action specially worth recording during that period. Russian snipers remained active and other Russian fire seemed to be intended more for its nuisance value than to have any specific military objective.

Another bit of psychological warfare that the Russians engaged in was their practice of sending an Il-2 fighter-bomber over our lines every night. The plane would circle monotonously, keeping soldiers awake. Some nights it dropped a few bombs and on other nights it did not. Instead, the next morning we would see the area littered with thousands of propaganda leaflets. All of them carried incitements in German to desert. Many had a cajoling text offering all sorts of good times to anybody who surrendered; others threatened that soldiers who fought on would be sentenced to twenty years of hard labour when they were taken prisoner.

Sometimes the Russians spread their propaganda by way of loudspeakers turned up to maximum volume. At other times they broadcast music which was suddenly interrupted by an announcement that we would now hear the "Stalin Organ;" only seconds later we would hear it. "Stalin Organ" was the nick-name for the "Katjuscha," a multi-barrelled shell launcher which could despatch forty-eight projectiles within seconds. Although very inaccurate, the sheer number of shells and the frightful, howling noise of the launcher could have a considerable psychological effect on troops.

Fully aware that it would be only a matter of time before the Russians began a massive offensive, the German Army made a special effort to look after the creature comforts of the soldiers. Warm winter clothing was distributed in good time and I remember remarking on the excellence of the winter boots with their thick felt shafts. Not only were they wonderfully warm, but they were softer and extremely comfortable; quite different from the standard jack-boots we had been wearing.

Special efforts were also made to improve the quality of our food; the cooks of the field kitchens were sent on courses at corps headquarters to learn new methods of preparing meals and giving us more variety. Staff-officers were detailed to accompany food carriers to the trenches so that they could have contact with ordinary soldiers and get first-hand impressions of any deficiencies.

Ever since the Eastern Front had stabilised, a steady trickle of refugees began to return to their homes. Although there had been an almost hundred per cent exodus, most of those who survived the Russian advance did not flee further than the western parts of East-Prussia. Anxious about the state of their homes and the livestock they had left behind, they began to arrive on bicycles or on army trucks which had given them a lift. Although their presence could hamper the activities of our units, and they often lacked food and other bare essentials, every effort was made by army personnel to help them in their need.

Up to the end of November the weather had been very cold, but over the weeks temperatures dropped well below freezing point. A blanket of snow settled on the countryside and made the landscape look beautiful in sunshine, but bleak and depressing when the light was gone. How lucky I was to be in my communal shelter where the cold was nothing compared to the conditions the poor devils in the trenches now had to contend with.

During daytime I was able to keep my circulation going by pacing around in the open and out of sight of any Russians. The only problem was keeping my nose from freezing up, but the smarting of my eyes from cutting winds often became quite painful. I was issued with a "head protector", a sort of woollen muff which was pulled over the head to cover ears and the lower half of the face. However, it got damp on the inside from my condensing breath and every now and then I used to pull it down over my chin to get a few unrestricted lungfuls of air. Of course, in time the outside of the protector began to freeze over and the whole arrangement got to be irritatingly uncomfortable, so I always tried to keep going as long as possible without covering my face.

The worst conditions of cold I ever suffered were on the self-propelled gun itself. Even sleeping out in deepest winter, which I often had to, was nothing compared to this. Looking through military records I discovered that the lowest temperatures with which I would have had to cope reached minus twenty-five to thirty degrees centigrade in January 1945. I had to take my position on the gun with hardly any room for moving about. There was no effective way to keep my circulation going and I suffered sheer agony. As if this was not bad enough, the steel studs in my boots took up the arctic temperature from the steel plating on the gun-carrier. The nail part of the studs acted as perfect transmitters of cold to within millimetres of the inside surface of the boots. In no time my feet felt like two lumps of ice.

Sometimes I tried to stand on one foot to get a bit of relief, but that only made conditions worse for the other foot by increasing the pressure on its boot. Another thing I tried was curling my toes under my feet in order to raise the soles of my feet off the inside of the boots. That was quite effective, but it made things worse for the toes, especially the big toe, which had to be pressed down hard only to quickly feel an answering icy jab from below. There was no solution to the problem, so I just kept on doing different things with my feet, and constantly moving my toes, while fighting off feelings of despair and angry frustration.

On 7 December, the Division 1 of the Army-Corps Göring, to which my battery was attached, was withdrawn from its forward position. Together with other elite divisions it was held in reserve between the towns of Gumbinnen and Insterburg. In the knowledge that the Russians would soon launch a major offensive with an overwhelming superiority in manpower and firepower, it was essential to have well-equipped, fast strike forces in readiness to be flung into action at trouble spots at the shortest notice. Our Division 2 was kept at its position in the forward lines.

I now found myself in even better accommodation, as gun crews were now housed in the outbuildings of a deserted farm. The guns still had to be dug in and this was a difficult task since the frozen layer of soil extended to well below ground level. Before any digging could be started, this layer had first to be broken up with pickaxes; a job which sent sparks flying up whenever a pick struck a stone frozen into the ground.

Over the next weeks the only action of the Russians that affected us was frequent, if not very intensive, air-raids on the town of Gumbinnen, an important junction point of main roads and railway lines. Our position lay too far south-east of the town for us to become regularly involved, but we still had to be ready for any Russian planes coming our way. Sometimes we had to remain on our guns and at other times we were allowed to jump off and stay beside them. This hanging around, while the cold made its inexorable passage through my boots and invaded my feet, remains one of my worst memories of the war.

A lesser, but nevertheless unpleasant, ordeal I had to suffer was when I had to wake somebody to relieve me for guard duty at night-time. As long as we had been in our one-man shelters it was just a case of my kneeling down and tugging a man's foot till he sat up and I knew he was fully awake. It was different in the communal shelters, where I had to use a torch to step across the sleeping bodies and look at their faces to make sure I woke the right man. Even the quickest, most cursory, glance at a man's face was enough to give me the creeps. The men invariably looked as if they were heavily drugged and would never wake up, but often their faces wore an expression of frightening grotesqueness that literally sent shivers down my spine. I suppose that past physical tolls and lack of rest gave them a sleep of exhaustion, but whether the contorted faces reflected nightmares or suppressed tension, I can only guess at. However, I can still picture some of their expressions and well remember my feelings of queasiness whenever the boredom of guard-duty ended with this eerie task.

As Christmas approached, much was done to provide us with small treats. There were special rations of cigarettes, alcohol and sweets. Working night and day the division's bakery produced 45,000 large "Christmas Stollen," a German-type Christmas cake, so that everybody was well provided for. Since East-Prussia was a county well covered with beautiful forests, we had no difficulty finding a small fir-tree which we set up in our quarters on Christmas Eve and decorated with candles. During the day we also put up some greenery and decorations which we had made ourselves and by evening the place began to look quite festive. The army mail service must also have made a special effort since everybody seemed to have Christmas post.

I had letters from Erika, the Soukals and my Aunt Hella. Erika wrote that my parents were well, but her words were couched in very general terms and nothing she said gave any clue that they did not live in Germany. It may not have mattered to be more frank, but she was wise not to take any unnecessary risk.

As we settled down to enjoy the evening, I was struck by another contrasting image. Our quarters looked cheerful and festive in the flickering light of the candles and, though our uniforms were by no means drab, it was the sameness of us all that spoilt the picture and lent it a forbidding aspect. However, everybody was in good cheer; our CO made a short speech and we enjoyed several helpings of a punch that our field-kitchen had brewed up for the occasion. The occasional sound of Russian planes in the night failed to disturb us as we sang popular evergreen songs and played cards. Nobody was tipsy and everyone was in good humour. For a few hours we had been able to banish all thoughts of war from the forefront of our consciousness.

On 29 December, General-Oberst Guderian was still imploring Hitler to allow troops to be transferred back to the Russian Front, but his entreaties fell on deaf ears. Hitler's over-simplified solution to the problem was that soldiers in the German armies should dig in where they stood and not give any ground.

The serious depletion of German armies in the east can be gauged from the following figures: On 1 June, 1944, these armies still had 2,62 million men, but on 1 November they were down to 1,84 million men. 112,800 soldiers were dead, 524.400 were missing and 538.800 were wounded. A net figure of about 700,000, including 12 per cent of the wounded, were considered to be irrecallable.

In his book, <u>Panzerleader,</u> Guderian estimated Russian superiority to be 11 to 1 in infantry, 7 to 1 in tanks and 20 to 1 in guns. As an overall evaluation, he put Russian superiority on the ground to be 15 to 1 and 20 to 1 in the air. Another important factor was that Russian armies were far better off for fuel and in their ability to replace soldiers and armour lost in battle. With 78 per cent of conscripts from Germany's last desperate attempt at recruitment going to the Western Front, only an inconsequential trickle was available to the Russian Front.

On New Year's Eve we had no celebrations. I thought that for the first time my mates, though not despondent, were more quiet than usual. Everybody must have been thinking that the coming year would bring the defeat of Germany; perhaps some of us were recalling the saying that "terrible as the war was, peace would be even worse." Maybe some of my comrades thought they would be killed in the crushing advance of the Russians or be taken prisoner and spend the rest of their lives in a Siberian death camp.

I did not expect the war to last another year. Ever since I had seen large numbers of refugees on the road and realised how they often had to make their way unprotected, I was sure that the German army could not hold out for long. The possibility that I would be killed or taken prisoner had become greater, but my confidence remained strong and I rejected any such thoughts.

And so 1945 started. The New Year was ushered in with heavy falls of snow which made the plight of refugees even worse than it had been. None of us knew anything of what was going on in the outside world. We also did not have the slightest concept of the enormously superior strength of Russian forces soon to be unleashed upon the depleted German lines, and maybe it was just as well.

Though the New Year had started, there was still no sign of the Russians launching their offensive. It is thought by military historians that they overestimated the strength of the German army and wanted to conserve their forces and not have to negotiate with the Western Allies from a position of military weakness when the war was over.

As one day followed the next in the New Year, I felt as if time seemed to have suddenly slowed down. On 10 January, 1945, a major alert was declared, but it so happened that it was not in East-Prussia where the first blow fell. Two days later word went around that the Russians had attacked south of Warsaw, but we heard no further details. Everything remained quiet in my section of the Front, but on 13 January I was left in no doubt that war had also woken here from its winter sleep. At six o'clock in the morning we were put on first degree alert even as we could hear the distant thunder of guns.

My division, being held in reserve, was about fifteen miles behind the Front-lines, but I knew that our Division 2 must be suffering the full effects of the bombardment. After two hours of shelling and air strikes, the Russians attacked along the line Gumbinnen-Goldap, but the Göring Division 2, together with two extra infantry divisions placed under its command, rebuffed all attacks.

On 14 January we were given the surprising information that our division was to be loaded onto a train. This could only mean another long journey. For the second time we were being withdrawn from a critical battle area in East- Prussia and I wondered what our destination would be this time. On the evening of 16 January we drove our self-propelled guns to the town of Insterburg where we boarded a long train.

By morning we had still not arrived at our destination and I wondered how we would fare against Russian fighter-bombers in the daytime. It was our good fortune not to be attacked and by the afternoon we arrived at the city of Lodz, about 75 miles south-west of Warsaw, after travelling some 400 miles. In no time we were driving through the suburbs and then on country roads towards the town of Lancellenstätt, about twelve miles further south. That night we did not dig in, a fact for which I was grateful because it would have been a murderous job breaking up the deeply-frozen ground. Instead, we drove our guns in among some outbuildings of a farm and were able to get a comfortable night's rest in a small barn.

The following morning, the 18 January, started quietly enough, but when daylight came I saw groups of exhausted soldiers passing through the town in a westerly direction; their uniforms torn and dirty. Every now and then lines of trucks or armoured vehicles, obviously on the retreat, passed along the road. Many of the soldiers I saw wore bandages and some walked with difficulty as their comrades supported them. The sight of such bedraggled soldiers affected me deeply and the picture of these beaten groups of men gave me a sinking feeling, which the sight of wounded men had not given me before. What must have increased my foreboding further on this occasion was that I missed a sense of purpose in our presence at Lancellenstätt. So what had gone wrong with the German defence of the Eastern Front?

The opening Russian onslaught on 12 January had been launched 120 miles south of Warsaw. A merciless bombardment by artillery spaced at an average of one heavy gun for every fifteen feet of the whole Front length was kept up against the German lines for five hours. Then the Russians advanced. A handful of already weakened German divisions faced a tenfold majority of well-equipped Russian divisions and suffered dead and wounded of up to 25% in some units.

Coming on top of expected defeats in East-Prussia, all hope was lost of holding the eastern Front between the Baltic Sea and Czechoslovakia.

The catastrophic developments exceeded all fears and Russian armies swept forward along a width of 375 miles advancing as much as 190 miles in only six days. In East-Prussia the Göring Division 2 was trapped and facing extinction. Not far from my own position 100,000 German inhabitants of the town of Lodz had already taken to the roads, grabbing only a handful of possessions.

As the hours passed on 18 January, we waited in readiness on full alert. Although I could hear plenty of action east of the town, no Russian planes came our way and my battery remained inactive while I just felt myself getting colder and colder. Lancellenstätt remained in German hands on that day, but in the afternoon shells began to hit the town and, as night fell, the noise of artillery and tank fire increased. Many buildings in the town were burning and the sight of the night spectacularly lit up by the flash from discharging gun-barrels could have been thrilling if it had not all been so deadly.

There was no sleep for us that night. Pacing around my gun and trying to keep warm as temperatures plummeted, I finally heard the order to mount up. The relief that some positive decision had been taken was tempered by the dread of maybe spending the next hours trapped on my travelling ice-box. We slowly drove out of Lancellennstätt in a north-westerly direction and then stopped in a field for the night.

We had no shelter and it was pointless to start trying to dig our holes in the frozen ground, so we prepared to sleep in the open. Four of my mates and I cleared a small area of hard snow and spread out two of our ground-sheets on it. Then we simply lay down close together, covered ourselves with our rugs and then manoeuvred our remaining three ground-sheets over the top. It was amazingly warm, cocooned as we were, and I quickly fell into a deep sleep.

The next morning presented us with a problem. Snow had fallen onto our covering ground-sheets during the night, it had melted due to the heat from our bodies and then re-frozen, forming a nicely-contoured sheet of ice that was itself frozen to the ground around us. Hardly able to move, we tried in vain to push upward. After a while I found that I was able to wriggle painfully through a narrow gap we had opened up and ran to fetch a pick-axe. Unfortunately, it was necessary to hack all around our sleeping spot, because using force to separate the ground-sheets could have split them. The other men in my battery had fared similarly and I had to smile at the bizarre sight of strangely-shaped sheets of ice being stacked on our truck because only the warmth of a fire could thaw them out again.

For breakfast we managed to get some hot coffee from a nearby field-kitchen to go with our bread. Soon we were on our way again. We drove slowly along farm tracks just north of the road to the town of Pabianice, stopping only occasionally. Our task was to guard the right flank of marching columns of soldiers and strings of motorised traffic, all on the retreat.

Suddenly, heavy fire erupted from our right as a group of well-camouflaged Russian tanks began to fire from afar with their heavy cannons and machine-guns. The immediate effect was disastrous. Shells slammed into vehicles, causing some of them to burst into flames, while raking machine-gun fire hit marching soldiers. Our guns were already loaded with anti-tank shells and within seconds we were firing back at an enemy we could barely see. By this time German tanks accompanying the columns had swung off the road and opened fire on the Russians tanks. My battery emerged unscathed from the conflict, but we had to wait some time while the dead and wounded in other units were attended to and supplies and equipment had been transferred from damaged vehicles to those which were still operational.

Later that day we arrived at Pabianice, one of the many towns in the west of Poland with a sizeable population of Germans or people of German extraction. Gangs of Poles had been on the rampage murdering German civilians, looting houses and setting them on fire. We stayed the night in houses on the outskirts of the abandoned town and were able to light stoves to warm ourselves and thaw out our frozen ground sheets.

The following day our first destination was the town of Lask, about fifteen miles west of Pabianice. We soon had to leave the road, because it was cut off by Russian tank formations and we had to conserve our ammunition as far as possible. We had begun to run low and, for the first time, were not sure when fresh supplies would reach us. Keeping mainly to snowed-over farm tracks we travelled north-west, but had to change direction a few times when despatch riders told us of heavy Russian armour ahead.

We were now a much smaller group. Probably the order had been given not to present the Russians with such a large attractive target and the forces had been split up to make their way separately to Lask. Due to our criss-cross driving we must have still been some ten miles north of Lask. Over the last hour we had had no contact with any Russian units and our group moved into the cover of a wood to give the marching units a short rest.

My NCO instructed me to go to the driver of our supplies truck to help him on a short mission. As soon as I got into the cab beside the driver, Gerhard Wilkens, he drove off quickly and told me that we were headed for village a few miles further north. A motor-cycle despatch rider had brought the information that we could pick up a dozen jerrycans of fuel from a small depot that was being cleared out. The whole job should not take much more than twenty minutes, but we would need to hurry before more Russians turned up.

We had no trouble getting there and we got our fuel alright. It was when we were racing back in the gathering dusk that disaster overtook us. A sudden skid sent the truck sliding sideways along the road and despite Wilkens' valiant attempts to correct the skid we ended up bruised and shaken with the truck lying on its side in a field. There was absolutely nothing we could do about the truck so, cursing our bad luck, we picked up our rifles and a road map in the cab and started off on a race against time.

After less than half an hour's hurried walking our hopes were dashed when we saw a line of Russian armoured troop-carriers crossing our path ahead of us and coming to a stop. In an instant we were off the track and lying flat on the freezing ground as we waited to see what would happen next. It was unlikely that we would be seen unless the Russians had powerful night-glasses, but there was no point in taking any chances. Our best bet was to wait till it got darker and do a detour if the Russians were still there. However, this was not our lucky day. As I lay there with the cold beginning to bite into my body, I heard Russian T-34 and Stalin tanks approach from our left side and head toward the group of armoured carriers. Again we had to await developments, before deciding on our next move.

A short while later the whole group drove off in a westerly direction. After waiting a few moments, Wilkens and I jumped up and set off at a jog-trot. It was some time before we arrived breathless at the wood where we had left our mates, but now there was no trace of them. Looking at our watches we were horrified to realise that almost two hours had passed since we had set off in the truck. It was too long for our group to have waited and they could not have scoured the countryside in search of us. They had no option but to move on and leave us behind.

It was now pitch dark and beginning to snow; we were on our own without food and only our rifles to protect us. Already we could consider ourselves to be behind the Russian lines. Unless we managed to get to Lask by the early hours of the next morning our chances of staying alive were going to be very slim indeed.

14

A BRUSH WITH PARTISANS

We now had to think clearly. We were in trouble and would be foolish to make an impulsive decision. Fortunately, Wilkens had the map and so we struck a few matches and began to study it. Luck had not deserted us because we discovered that there was a country road nearby leading to Lask which was about 10 miles away and almost exactly due south. Even if the night remained overcast and no stars were visible, we would still have the road to guide us.

Another stroke of luck was that a main railway line ran in an east-west direction north of Lask. If we had to leave the road during the night for any reason, and lost our bearings, we could still hope to see the railway once daylight broke, and use it to find our way to Lask. But was it a good idea to go there at all, since the Russians could already be in possession of the town? Alternatively, we could head due west on the basis of trying to get as far away as possible from the advancing Russian troops. But they might be carrying out a pincer movement around Lask on the north side, in which case we would be keeping inside Russian-held territory.

We had to think of something better than that. In the end we agreed that we would head straight for Lask, but we would not approach the town. As soon as we got to the railway line, we would head west and away from the town. After that we would make our way to Lask in a wide, circuitous movement. With luck we might run into some German units and find out whether Lask was still in German hands and whether parts of the Division Göring had already passed that way. There was, of course, one hazard we could come across and that was partisans. We knew that they frequently made use of abandoned homesteads as hideouts from which they attacked German soldiers on the retreat, especially if they were in small splinter-groups rather than in fully-armed combat units.

Having decided on our course of action, we set off while we were still warm from our recent exertions. Unfortunately, I had a slight niggling worry about Wilkens. He would not have been my choice of a companion if I thought that a sticky situation might arise. Wilkens was about five years older than I and was a good all-round soldier. He was extremely fit and strong, but what bothered me about him was his slight tendency to grumble. It may sound pettish to have been critical of such a normal human failing, but if we landed in a tight corner the outcome could well hinge on a small point like this.

It was six o'clock in the evening when we started on our march. On the basis of an estimated total distance of some twenty miles, including detours, it would be practical to allow about eight hours for walking plus time taken for rests, but not allowing for major problems. Finding the road to Lask was easy enough, but then it began to snow quite heavily. Our plan had been to walk near the road, but now there was the danger of losing sight of it as a thick layer of snow began to cover the landscape. We had to risk walking on the road, but decided to keep well to one side to lessen the risk of being seen.

Soon the snowfall became lighter and the sky was less overcast, allowing the moon to throw a dim light over the landscape. I found there was something refreshing in our movement along the road and across the Polish countryside. The events of the day had had a draining effect on me, so I now relished the freedom of walking in the cool night air and hearing the soft crunch of fresh snow under my feet. The fact that I had been sitting and standing around a lot in the cold over the last few days meant that my muscles needed some vigorous activity. Most of the exercise I had been getting in the past was on guard duty which meant doing just enough pacing to and fro to keep reasonably warm.

Occasionally we came across small farms beside the road, so we had to take to the fields on the opposite side of the road to avoid being seen. There was no real danger of injury walking through fields in the near darkness because previous falls of snow had turned into a frozen crust on the ground and covered small holes that could have given us a twisted ankle. Occasionally, there were stretches when it was safe for us to raise our voices to comfortably talk with each other for short spells at a time.

After walking for an hour we were startled by suddenly hearing what sounded like voices ahead of us. The sound of our steps had been muffled by the snow, so it was unlikely that we had been detected. Stopping instantly, we strained our ears to try to catch further sounds in the hope of discovering whether we had come across fellow Germans. We found it impossible to tell because the sounds became more indistinct without moving further from us and then petered out altogether. Perhaps it had just been some nocturnal animal we had heard, the sound of which had been exaggerated or distorted by our stretched senses in the spooky lighting. After waiting for about ten minutes we decided to move on, but we made a wide detour on the down-wind side of the road. All went well and we soon recovered from our shock without knowing how real the suspected danger had been.

Following this delay we kept going for another two hours and continued to make good progress. Seeing that Wilkens was moving prudently, I had begun to feel more confident in him and my uneasiness slowly receded. Frankly, I was also relieved that he had not set a pace that I might have found hard to match. We had been walking for over three hours, quite apart from the dash from our overturned truck to the wood, so we both felt like having a rest. We stopped for ten minutes, but we had no food with us and decided to keep the last bit of coffee in our flasks for later. Instead, we made do with melting snow in our mouths and swallowing it.

We agreed to walk for another two hours and then try to get some sleep for about three hours since we had to be rested for whatever we might be up against on the next day. A short while later I came in for a shock when Wilkens began muttering about being hungry. This was an ominous opening, so I quickly said that I was hungry too and was it not a good job that we had only a few hours to go before we could get something to eat. My transparent ploy failed to work and Wilkens countered by saying, "I think we should look for some food at the next farmhouse." Being as persuasive as I could, I said that it was sheer folly to go anywhere near a farm and I went on to say, "I think you are daft; we are not starving and we are not weak from lack of food. We may feel a bit of discomfort, but at least we are alive." The intensity of my little speech seemed to have its effect and, crankily, Wilkens said, "Oh well, I suppose that you are right." I was able to breathe a sigh of relief, but it was with some trepidation that I continued on my way.

Things went well for a while, but I noticed that Wilkens was getting very quiet and not reacting to anything I said beyond giving a short grunt. Suddenly he stopped dead, saying, "look, I am not going on like this. I intend to go into the next farmhouse and see can I find something to eat." Although I knew it would be to no avail, I said that we were now only a few hours' march away from the railway-line. Why risk everything when the end of our trail was in sight? However, I got no reply. Wilkens' mind was obviously made up and we walked on in moody silence. It could not have been more than ten minutes later when we came upon a farmhouse which was on a slight rise to our right. It was at the end of a straight tree-lined avenue about one hundred and fifty yards long leading to it from our road.

As expected, Wilkens stopped and said, "look here, I am going into that place. I know you don't agree with this and I don't expect you to come with me, but I want to ask you to do one thing for me. Will you wait till I get back?" As far as I was concerned, it was sheer recklessness to delay unnecessarily in partisan country. Our progress had been good so far, but there was always the chance of a major problem and we had to be west of Lask by dawn. At the same time, I did not want to desert Wilkens, so I said, "I think you are crazy to risk spoiling everything when we have almost reached safety, but, OK, I am prepared to wait for you." I then went on to say, "But I will only wait for exactly ten minutes. If you are not back by then or if I hear any shooting before then, I will go on and leave you. There is no point in my joining you in getting shot in the darkness if you run into trouble."

Wilkens seemed quite grateful for my proposal and thanked me before going on to say, quite unnecessarily, as I thought, "if I do find food, I will share it with you." This struck me as being so much like a bribe that I found myself reacting rather sharply. I replied, "I have already said that I will wait for you. If you take the risk, you can enjoy whatever food you find. I don't want any of it." I had not been able to keep the sharpness out of my voice, but Wilkens did not appear to resent it and off he went, moving swiftly from tree to tree. As soon as he had gone, I looked at the luminous dial of my watch and took up a waiting position hidden by bushes some fifty yards further along the road. From there I had a good view of the avenue and for a while there was no sound to be heard apart from the rustling of leaves in the breeze. A short time later, I suddenly became aware of hurried movement on the avenue. A short glance at my watch told me that seven minutes had elapsed since Wilkens had gone off on his quest. I could see a lone figure speeding towards the intersection with the road, and from the outline it was obviously Wilkens. As soon as he came near to me, I stepped forward from my hiding place so that he would recognise me. I then needed to make quite a spurt to keep up with Wilkens, who had not slowed down as he passed me. All I heard from him was a gasped, "run like hell, the place is swarming with partisans."

A new danger had now emerged, but I was less worried about the partisans than our headlong flight which, despite the muffling effect of the snow, sounded terribly loud to me. Wilkens just had to be slowed down, but this was where his superior physique put me at a disadvantage. Somehow I managed to pull abreast of him and panted, "For God's sake, slow down, we're crashing along like a couple of mad elephants."

To my great relief he reacted immediately and slowed down. Though normally a good soldier, in this instance he had allowed his complaint to preoccupy his mind to the extent that he had made two serious errors of judgment. This episode proved that even the smallest human failing can assume a critical significance in a situation of life and death.

A few minutes later we had both got our breath back and I heard what had happened. Apparently, when Wilkens got to the farm, he felt sure that it was deserted, but had not been able to get into the building. While trying to open a window at the side of the house, he suddenly sensed danger. Then he heard the soft sound of voices and saw a group of men come spilling out of a barn at the back of the house. As they emerged, they were adjusting their clothing and releasing the safety-catches on their rifles - they were obviously partisans. It was probable that they had not mounted a look-out and that a light sleeper had raised the alarm. Their lack of organisation had given Wilkens a good head start and he was lucky to have got down the avenue without being shot at. Since we had heard no sound of a vehicle starting up, we could consider ourselves to be fairly safe and lucky to have escaped what might have become a very sticky situation.

After our unpleasant fright all went well, we made good progress and then stopped for our planned longer break. It was doubtful whether we would be able to rest very well. An earlier fall of snow had been accompanied by a rise in temperature, but since then the night sky had become clearer and it was again bitterly cold, certainly at least minus twenty degrees centigrade. For a resting place we picked a spot under some trees and broke off branches of bushes to lie on and to insulate us from the freezing snow. As a matter of prudence, we decided to take turns keeping awake and I volunteered to take the first stint. I was surprised that, huddled up in my army coat with the collar pulled in front of my face, I did not feel as cold as I had expected. After all my practice on guard duty, I had no trouble keeping alert until it was time to wake Wilkens and get him to take over from me.

I did not manage to sleep. Maybe it was because I had, after all, got quite cold or I was not sufficiently relaxed. However, I did feel a lot more rested when Wilkens nudged me and I stood up to get the circulation in my body going again. This time we allowed ourselves some tepid coffee from our flasks and moments later we were off again.

Finding the railway-line turned out to be no trouble at all, though it did take longer to get there than we had expected. After crossing it we walked west for one hour and then turned south again until we reckoned that we were about two miles west of Lask. It did not take us long to find a wooded area where we stopped for a rest. As soon as the light improved and we could see the terrain better, we would decide on our next move.

After a while we took a walk around the wood, keeping just inside the perimeter. We could hardly have been more lucky; within minutes we came across a German unit of reconnaissance vehicles parked in the wood. Once again I used my "Hummel, Hummel" as a hailing call which had worked so well the last time I had to overcome the suspicion of a German soldier on guard duty. Again it was a success and we were accepted. Before long we were sipping hot coffee that the men of the reconnaissance unit shared with us. In answer to our anxious questions they told us that units of the Division

Göring had driven into Lask late in the previous night and could be expected to move out any time now.

Wilkens and I immediately set off and as soon as we got to Lask we were thrilled to come upon vehicles with the distinctive markings of our unit. Our mates had not given up hope of seeing us again and congratulated us on managing to rejoin them so quickly. We were saddened to hear that in a skirmish with Russian armour during the previous evening they had suffered a number of dead and wounded.

It was now 21 January and our next destination was the town of Sieradz on the west side of the river Warthe. I was made to think of Napoleon's retreat from Moscow as I watched the columns of German troops, sometimes interspersed with refugees, flooding westwards. Late that evening we crossed the Warthe and arrived south-west of Sieradz, where we joined up with the Panzer-Corps Grossdeutschland. I felt heartened by the presence of this trusted Panzer-Corps and even more so the next day when the elite Division Brandenburg also joined us. We were now a formidable force and were all part of a significant unit in the final stages of the Russian Campaign. In German, we were known as "Der wandernde Kessel," loosely translated this could be called a wandering pocket of troops.

Our "pocket" was made up of many fragmented divisions and splinter-groups which joined under the command of General Walther K. Nehring, commander of the 24th Panzer-Corps. It gradually swelled to a force of almost 100,000 men. Short of ammunition and first-aid supplies, and critically short of fuel, it nevertheless presented an impressive army which the Russians were reluctant to attack.

Although we suffered mainly harassment at the hands of Russian forces, there were many occasions when German units found themselves cut off, or encircled, and had to fight their way out again. We ourselves became encircled at the towns of Kalisch and Ostrowo and had to break out through the Russian lines, partly under the cover of darkness.

In contrast to Pabianice, where Polish mobs had wreaked vengeance on German civilians, it was very different in Kalisch, where the Polish population watched us depart with dread in their eyes, knowing what could befall them when the Russians moved in. Sadly, the fears of the Poles in situations like these were only too often well-founded. It has also been recorded that there were countless incidents when Polish civilians gladly helped German soldiers by giving them information about the Russians. They also gave them food and sometimes hid them without being coerced to do so. By doing this they put themselves in great danger when they could just as well have refused to give any assistance.

On 31 January we approached the German border and, once again, Russian forces blocked our path to the west, but this time they seemed to be less strong. By breaking through the Russian lines at night, we finally escaped through the main ring around the "pocket" and the road to the river Oder, some twenty-five miles away, was clear.

My battery had suffered no further casualties, but day by day I saw a steadily mounting number of wounded soldiers, who marched heavily bandaged or rode on vehicles. It was not that the daily skirmishes took such a great toll on the troops, but, as there were no field-hospitals to take the wounded, they had to be brought along and every day there were more.

Riding on my self-propelled gun I was one of the lucky ones, but enormous physical endurance was required from those on foot who were exhausted from long days of marching, often across very rough terrain. Weak from lack of food and sleep, on top of their wounds, they struggled on gamely and, as if that was not enough, they still had to fight off the Russians when the need arose. As trucks and armoured vehicles were disabled by Russian fire, broke down, or just ran out of fuel and had to be abandoned, more and more troops swelled the number of marchers on the road.

By successfully leading such a large conglomerate of troops from diverse divisions over 200 miles and under appalling conditions of cold and deprivation, General Nehring achieved an extraordinary feat. Much has been written about this retreat from Lodz via Sieradz and Kalisch to the river Oder and it has become a classic of military history.

At last the semblance of a more stable front had been reached where the army General Nehring had saved would be able to help stem the headlong surge of the Russians. This was going to be all the more important since, once again, German refugees were suffering the consequences of the blind stubbornness of Party functionaries who had refused to accept the possibility of a German defeat and had delayed evacuation. Handicapped by their late start, any breathing space that could be achieved was of vital help to refugees in giving them time to get away.

Gauleiter Greiser of the Wartheland had forbidden the preparation of evacuation plans until the Russians arrived; burning, murdering and raping. Houses were going up in flames everywhere and on 20 January, Greiser finally gave his consent for evacuation. For most civilians the order had come much too late, but, true to form, the Gauleiter was the first to flee. For the refugees there was only panic and chaos with cold, hunger and death accompanying them everywhere on the roads. Children who had frozen to death were taken along wrapped in sheets. Over a three-day period in late January 20,000 - 24,000 farm wagons were estimated to have crossed the river Oder.

After witnessing many distressing sights of refugees and retreating army units, I came across another scene that affected me deeply. It was that of dead tank crews whose tank had been on fire. The first time that I experienced this was when I saw what looked like large, black dolls scattered on top of burnt out Russian tanks. It was only a moment later that I realised to my horror that these were the charred remains of men who had been incinerated when their tanks went on fire. Although death must have come very quickly, their last seconds, when they realised that they were faced with a horrible death and scrambled desperately to get their burning bodies out through the turret, must have been terrible beyond description.

It is thought by many people that being a member of a tank crew must be one of the most fascinating activities in an army. Tank men are certainly a special breed and very proud of their job. In reality, theirs is one of the most uncomfortable and stressful jobs in the army. Cooped up in a space in which they have hardly any room to move, they are tossed around violently when their tank negotiates a difficult terrain. The temperature inside the tank becomes stiflingly hot, especially if the turret has to be kept closed, and the deafening noise from its engine makes all communication impossible except by way of microphones and headsets. To this must be added the crashing noise of the gun when it is fired.

Tanks usually required a lot of maintenance and this had to be carried out by their crew during the evening. It took about three hours, most of which came off time for sleeping. Sometimes the crew had to sleep for weeks in their tank and this became a nightmare with men wedged into impossible contortions as they tried to accommodate themselves in the irregular spaces available.

After retreating across the river Oder on 4 February, we had only the barest respite before we were to face the Russians again. True, we were now back to hot meals and normal rations, and were no longer retreating, but a massive Russian build-up was taking place and so our break would be a short one.

When the Russians attacked, the ferocity of their onslaught forced us to move back from our positions and by 9 February my division had retreated six miles. We were lucky that our vehicles had been refuelled and our stock of shells replenished, because we were using far more ammunition than previously.

Our targets were now not so much aeroplanes as tanks and other armoured vehicles. In such a fluid situation, digging in did not arise and our usual action was to fire at stationery or moving targets for a while and then to make a dash to a new vantage point from which we again used our rapid-fire guns to destroy or incapacitate Russian armour. My battery remained lucky and we had no casualties, but it was distressing to see other units carrying their dead and wounded with them as they retreated. I think I was very lucky with my humble job of re-filling shell magazines as it meant keeping my head down while I worked and so missed seeing much of the carnage around me.

There was no sleep for any of us in the night from 9/10 February. Russian forces had already by-passed us on our north and south flanks and we were in danger of being cut off, so we retreated further west. Once again we found ourselves part of a huge trek, marching and driving along a road already partly blocked with units from other divisions, either on the move or waiting for their next orders.

By dawn our progress had deteriorated to a painful crawl and the road was now really jammed solid. Because of varying rates of progress, members of different divisions had begun to intermingle and this resulted in utter chaos. As divisions lost their cohesion, officers tried in vain to retain contact between units separated from each other. On a road already blocked, motor cycle dispatch riders were just about able to worm their way through as they brought information and orders back and forward. I saw many high-ranking officers fuming impotently in their marooned staff cars at a situation which had got out of control. This was the only time I witnessed a breakdown of military organisation and, knowing that Russian tanks could not be far away, it was frightening.

We were not able to progress more than a couple of miles over the next few hours. When we had started off in the morning, my gun group, together with some of our Panther tanks, had brought up the rear of our division in order to give it cover from pursuing Russian forces. But now, due to our snail's pace, units of other divisions had caught up with us and we became sandwiched in between. The inevitable was bound to happen.

All of a sudden, Russian artillery opened fire from somewhere ahead of us on our left side, scoring hits on the trapped convoys of trucks and armoured vehicles. Although we could not actually see the guns, we had a clear view across the intervening fields and were able to rake their likely position from where we stood.

Suddenly, I noticed a long row of heavy Russian Stalin tanks spread out about half a mile away and heading straight for us from a north-easterly direction. Glancing back to the left, everything looked unchanged to me when, out of the blue, the landscape took on a life of its own. As if appearing out of the ground, huge numbers of Russian tanks and armoured vehicles came to view in the distance and bore down on us from a westerly direction. Moments later we were under fire from both sides and the drivers of my battery had to use all their skill to get our self-propelled guns off the road in order to have more room for manoeuvring.

I do not know how anybody in overall command could have decided in this chaotic situation which units should take on the tanks to the north-east and which would go for the huge assault force to the west. However, my unit was among the self-propelled guns and tanks which took on the larger force. Within moments we had driven onto the field on our left and were racing for a good vantage point from which to protect the almost defenceless columns of troops.

We fired as fast as we could at the semi-circle of Russian armour heading towards us, but, whatever success we had made little or no impression on the unstoppable forces. Our Panther tanks had moved on ahead and were successfully picking off Russian tanks one by one, but every now and then one of the Panthers was itself put out of action.

I saw that two of our four self-propelled guns had stopped firing, but in the crescendo of bursting shells and gun discharges, I had not noticed what happened to them. I never did find out and the last thing I remembered was the violent bouncing of my own self-propelled gun as we raced across the field to take up a new position, when suddenly the whole sky caved in on me.

15

GIANT "DODGEMS" GONE MAD

When I regained consciousness, I found myself lying on my back on the ground. I was deafened by the noise of vehicles travelling at high speed and the tortured sounds of engines being over-revved, all intermingling with the cacophony of guns firing and a myriad of explosions. Galvanized into action by the danger all around, I quickly checked whether my limbs were intact while trying to decide what to do next.

Apart from a spell of unconsciousness, I seemed to have come to no harm, but when I looked about me an incredible sight met my eyes. As far as my eyes could see, vehicles of every description, tanks, armoured cars, troop-carriers and many others, were hurtling around as if in a frenzy. There seemed to be no pattern to what was happening. German and Russian motorised armour, all mixed up higgledy-piggledy, were dashing around firing at each other for all they were worth.

It was as if I was lying in a huge field of giant dodgems which had all gone completely mad, but this field was about a square mile in area and skirmishes were going on everywhere. The din was incredible and, dazed as I still was, it took all my will-power to force my brain to start functioning again. Already I was in danger of being crushed by the next set of wheels and tracks bearing down on me, but where could I go?

If only I could float up over the battle area or instantly burrow deep into the ground, but whatever I did I had to get moving quickly. Rolling over, I jumped up into a crouching position and started to run even as I looked around desperately searching for inspiration. It was obvious that I could not keep on running through the line of fire and it seemed that the only place of relative safety lay in the actual shelter of the vehicles that were a danger to me. As I ducked and dodged I caught sight of my self-propelled gun about fifty yards away with a big hole in its side, but no sign of the crew; just a stationery Russian armoured car drawn up beside it.

I also saw that there was more action going on in the half mile between me and the road still packed with German units than there was to the west of me. It would have been suicidal to try to get back to the road on my right and I did not even have my rifle, as if that would have been any help. There was no time to lose, I had to get out of this mêlée superfast if I wanted to stay alive.

What happened next was one of the most bizarre episodes in my army career. Seeing a nearby Russian tank driving in a northerly direction I raced to it, bending low, and managed to take cover on its west side which I thought was not exposed to German fire at that moment. Running alongside the tank I had to watch out for fire coming from my side while looking out for "traffic" going west that I could latch onto. Since the road that I had been on ran in a northerly direction and could be clearly seen by the concentration of vehicles, I could easily tell in which direction I was going. Soon I became quite proficient at "changing horses" and began to feel more confident. Sometimes it was Russian vehicles that I tagged onto and sometimes they were German and there were also times when I had to accept going in the wrong direction, because it was safer to do so. Unfortunately, the German vehicles I used were invariably tanks which could not have taken me on board because of shortage of space and the danger of stopping, so I was left to fend for myself.

The ear-shattering noise I had to endure all the while was almost unbearable. Worst of all was the firing of tank guns near me which sounded like huge timber boxes being smashed to pieces right beside my head. Several times I was quite close to the muzzle of a tank gun when it fired. Since it was almost at the level of my head, I always felt as if I myself had been blown up in the explosion and each time it became harder to shake off the numbness of my senses. Then again, if I ran around a tank I had to duck very low because the machine-guns were located far down and I did not want to get my head shot off.

The ground I was running on was terribly treacherous. One moment I could be on patches of deep snow and the next moment on smooth, slippery bits of ice and then again bounding over deeply churned up ground, trying to keep my balance. Tanks can swerve sharply and as I ran beside them I had to watch the turret for signs of danger on my side while trying not to fall flat on my face or be crushed under their tracks.

Once again, as on previous occasions, I experienced the feeling that tanks were like living creatures. There was the anguished squeal from over-stressed tracks, the sight of a tank backing away and spitting venomously like a cat at another tank bearing down on it, and then the "dead" tank with its gun askew and its life blood pouring out in huge clouds of black smoke.

As I strove to keep going, there seemed to be a pneumatic drill in my head getting louder and louder and I began to feel dizzy and see everything around me as if through a haze. At the same time I felt fully in control of the situation and I think this must again have been an occasion where my "computer mind" guided me. I always seemed to know what to do next and my actions were confident and deliberate.

I do not know how often I swapped vehicles or for how long I zig-zagged back and forth. It must have taken over a dozen swaps and a quarter of an hour before I was finally near enough to the edge of the battle-field to make a dash for safety. Diving into some bushes where I could safely recover my breath, as well as keep an eye on the fighting, I sat down to steady my nerves while contemplating my predicament.

Once again I was on my own, but this time there were far more Russians around and God knows how far their advance units had already progressed. What were my options? I could sit tight for a while and see how the battle went. With luck I might be able to latch onto a unit of my division that managed to survive the chaos. The alternative was to strike out in a westerly direction and try to get through one arm of the Russian pincer-movement in which I was caught. I would then have to keep going until I made contact with some German unit. My mind was made up by the appearance of Russian infantry who approached from my right keeping to a line between me and the scene of battle, now moving slowly away from me. It had become far too dangerous to stay, so I went for my second option and headed west, keeping to the limited natural cover available.

After walking for about ten minutes I was amazed to see Gerhard Wilkens ahead of me. He was sitting down talking with a soldier I did not know. They had not seen me and, as if guided by instinct, in a flash I had taken cover behind some bushes. In that moment I automatically made a decision that meant violating one of the cardinal rules that had been drummed into us recruits in Holland. If fragmented units have to break up into small groups in enemy territory, then the smallest viable number of men is three unless the circumstances are exceptional, in which case the number becomes two men. Nobody must be on his own if he can team up with at least a second man. I made up my mind to break the rule as the memory returned to me of how Wilkens had previously been prepared to jeopardise our lives for no good reason. Of course, I also knew nothing at all about the man with him and to what extent I could rely on him.

I could expect to be up against some very tricky situations and, if I teamed up with the other soldiers, Wilkens could always pull rank on me if I refused to support him in some decision of his. I was just not prepared to waste my life if I thought I had a better chance of rejoining my division on my own. Thinking back on the dangers I knew I would have to face, and remembering my decision in the light of it all, scares me now, but I recollect being quite calm at the time and absolutely resolved to go it alone. Seeing that Wilkens had a companion with him removed any feelings of guilt I had about not accompanying him.

I was not surprised that Wilkens had escaped the ambush. When the first tanks had appeared on the scene, a number of trucks and other vehicles managed to escape the line of fire by breaking out into the fields on our left and Wilkens had quite possibly been on one of them. There could have been any number of reasons why he subsequently abandoned his vehicle. I did actually feel awkward about not making myself known to the men, but then I would have had to give up my plan. So, being determined not to weaken, I just sat it out until they moved on a few minutes later.

I gave them a good start and then carefully set off in a direction a bit more southerly than the one Wilkens had taken. Natural cover became better and I was able to walk faster especially when I reached a thinly-planted wood. Now that the initial danger was behind me and I was moving freely, I experienced a lessening of tension. Suddenly I remembered, to my chagrin, that I had saved an especially large pat of butter for my tea and this had been with my kit when we were attacked. If only I had eaten it for my breakfast or put it in my belt-bag, it would not have been wasted! Ludicrous as these thoughts were, considering how lucky I was to be alive, they preyed on my mind for quite a while as I made my way.

After walking for about twenty minutes I was overjoyed to see a German open truck among the trees ahead of me. About a dozen soldiers were sitting on the back of it and a few more were climbing on. Just as I broke into a run, the driver started the engine and I waved frantically because I knew nobody could hear me if I shouted. I was still some distance away when the truck began to move and all I could do was to curse it as it disappeared from view. It was incredible that nobody had seen me and I was quite shattered that I had missed the truck by seconds. If only I had given Wilkens a few moments less of a head-start I would not have suffered this terribly bad luck, but now there was nothing for it but to continue my lonely walk.

Half an hour later I thought I was seeing a mirage. There was the same truck parked in a clearing ahead of me quite close to the edge of the wood; I easily recognised it by its identification symbols. But why was there not a soul in sight? Gingerly I stepped nearer; I did not want to call out and I initially thought that the engine had broken down and the men had to continue on foot. Suddenly I knew there was something terribly wrong and felt the hair rise on the back of my neck. Glancing around quickly, I noticed a grassy embankment just outside the wood. By making a small detour I was able to see round the other side of it.

A feeling of nausea immediately swept over me as my suspicions were confirmed. Over a dozen German soldiers lay dead. They had all fallen over on their faces and, clearly visible on the back of their necks was a neat bullet hole, a standard way Russian soldiers executed men they did not want to take prisoner. My horror at this discovery was mixed with another feeling that gave me an eerie sensation.

Schmidt had died in my place on the ammunition train, my observation duty in the fox-hole at Magnuszew had saved me when Russians attacked my battery, I alone had been transferred out of the suicide squad in which all the men must have perished, I had been on the fuel run when my other mates suffered casualties and now all soldiers on the truck that did not wait for me were dead. It was staggering to think that none of my mates had been hurt when I was around; it was only when some fluke had taken me away from them that they were harmed. Although all this had to be put down to pure chance, I clearly remember feeling devastated at the time and responsible for what had happened to the other soldiers, as if my absence had sentenced them to death. It is a fact that such guilt feelings among survivors of military action, or civil disasters for that matter, are perfectly normal even when they are not associated with strange flukes as in my case.

Before leaving the site I did a quick check on the truck and was lucky to find a couple of army rifles in the cab, but there was nothing else of use to me, not even a map. Grateful for small mercies, I took one of the rifles and started on my way.

As a result of my gruesome discovery, I decided to alter my plans slightly. More vigilance was now called for and, since dusk was not much more than an hour away, I decided to look for a spot that gave me a good view into the distance and to lie low until it got dark. After that I would walk on again and make plans as I went along. Since the terrain was not hilly I soon found what I wanted and settled down in good cover where I was able to rest and keep a look out. The sound of gun-fire in the distance had now decreased considerably, but I could see plenty of Russian troop movements to the east of me, and heading in a north-westerly direction. I would just concentrate on heading westwards.

The first pangs of hunger began. I had only one slice of bread in my food-bag and a small amount of coffee in my flask, but I wanted to save these until I really needed them. All I allowed myself was some snow that I melted in my mouth, but it did nothing to alleviate my hunger, even though I felt somewhat refreshed.

When it got dark I set off, but I really had only a very vague target in mind and began to think that the chance of meeting German units before the Russians got me looked very slim indeed. Fortunately, the night was not cloudy, and stars were visible most of the time, so I was able to check my direction. I thought I was making good progress when I ran into trouble trying to cross some fields. A flash of light from powerful searchlights suddenly lit up the landscape and I had to drop to the ground to avoid being caught by one of the beams as it swept across the open spaces. Since it was obvious that it was not Germans who were operating the searchlights, I had to beat a hasty retreat during the dark spells and do a very unwelcome detour of my projected route.

My progress was generally quite good, aided by the flat Polish landscape. In Poland I seldom came across ditches or hedges between fields. Occasionally there were just a few strands of wire supported by stakes and it was no problem to step over these. There were also no ditches beside the roads which were often tree-lined and at the same level as the adjoining fields. Strangely enough, I have no recollection of ever having had a problem crossing rivers or streams. It must have been a matter of pure luck that I always found a bridge across, or that I did not happen to run into such obstacles.

It was approaching midnight when I decided to take a break. I had been walking for over four hours since seeing the dead soldiers, but unless I knew exactly what I was doing, I thought it would be better to wait until daylight and then look out for signs of German units. It was going to be a long night, so I set about getting myself some shelter from the cold by constructing a sort of mini-igloo as was recommended in such situations. First, I selected a bit of a hollow in the ground and broke off some small fir-tree branches which I stuck into the snow. I then wedged others across them to produce a box-shaped framework with an opening on the down-wind side. Finally, I threw loose snow onto this and, by patting it from the inside and the outside and throwing on more snow, I was able to form a shell looking a bit like a lop-sided sphere that was open on one side. I now had a small, but quite, snug shelter for the night that was surprisingly warm and proved that Eskimos have the right idea.

As I settled in and began to relax, it suddenly struck me that I had not removed the identity discs of the dead men I had found. It was pure shock that had made me forget this guideline. Since the men were obviously dead, I had had a natural aversion to going any nearer, which in turn would have probably jogged my memory. However, I have always felt remorse for my lapse and that I left behind confirmation of the death of men on whose return family members must have pinned their hopes for many years to come.

The next seven hours to daybreak passed comfortably enough for me and I managed to get a restful sleep before I awoke as dawn was breaking. After my breakfast of melted snow, I cautiously started off again, keeping well inside the edge of a wood. A short while later I saw a small group of soldiers crossing my path ahead of me. To my great relief they were German. Almost as soon as I noticed them they had seen me and identified me as a compatriot of theirs. It was an undramatic ending to what had started with a very dramatic beginning less than twenty-four hours ago.

My new mates were Panzer-Grenadiers in the Panzer-Corps Grossdeutschland and were well-equipped with rifles, two machine-guns, a map and a compass. They were heading for an assembly point and invited me to join them because it was most likely that there I would meet up with other soldiers of my division. After a fast march of several hours we came across more stragglers, some of whom joined us and it was not long before I saw the familiar blue-grey uniforms of the Division Göring. Although the colour did not stand out from a distance, it was easily distinguishable at shorter range from the dull grey of other army uniforms. I might also mention here that the Division Göring had an excellent identification system for its vehicles, whereby they had a clearly recognisable symbol representing each main- and sub-unit prominently painted on the front and the rear. A colour code was used and the symbol sometimes incorporated a pointer like the hour hand of a clock to denote numbers, all of which was a big help towards instant identification.

When we got to the assembly point, the time had come for me to part from the grenadiers and to approach an officer of my division for further instructions. This I duly did and now found myself to be part of a mini "wandering pocket," only this time I was no longer privileged and had to walk. The cross-country marching was tiring, but at least it gave me warm feet and I was not frozen stiff as I would have been on a self-propelled gun. The route took us in a southerly direction and our destination was the town of Lauban about two marching days away.

I was now in a column of some 200 soldiers and we were accompanied by a few armoured cars. Sometimes the sound of gunfire came nearer and other times it receded, but we did not become involved in any fighting with the Russians. Frequently altering our direction, we marched with hardly a break till well after dark when, to my great relief, we were housed for the night in a group of abandoned buildings. In next to no time stoves were lit and an official search party was set up to look for food, which was then distributed among us. The thick stew of potatoes, meat and vegetables that we cooked for ourselves was one of the most delicious meals I remember having in my life. Since we were such a large group of men, lots were drawn for guard duty. Only six men were needed per stint and I turned out to be one of the lucky ones to get an unbroken night's sleep.

While I was asleep, and dead to the world, one of the greatest tragedies of the Second World War was taking place less than eighty miles away, the bombing of Dresden. The war had almost reached its end and it was thought that Dresden had been spared because its art treasures were of international importance and it was not an industrial city. During the night of 13/14 February, 1945, Dresden was to become the German city to suffer most under the "fire-storm" bombing technique. Seas of flames created hurricane force winds that made fires spread faster than people could run. Those who were not burnt alive suffocated from lack of oxygen. In less than fourteen hours the city was almost wiped off the face of the earth. 202,040 corpses were collected after the raid and it was estimated that the actual total of dead was nearer to a quarter of a million. Contrary to popular belief, Air Marshal Harris was not the inventor of the "fire-storm" technique, just the executor. When Churchill received Royal Sanction to appoint the civilian Arthur T. Harris as Air-Marshal in 1942, the basic design of the new bombing warfare had already been completed, but not yet put into practice.

The following morning I was roused from a deep sleep at five o'clock. I felt refreshed, but my joints were still a bit stiff after the previous day's long march and I could expect another equally long day of foot-slogging ahead of me. Before we started off, I purposely manoeuvred my way to a position near the head of the marching column because of what I had experienced on previous occasions. What had happened was that when the soldiers got to be extremely tired the columns became more and more strung out and gaps opened up. Although these closed again, it spoiled the rhythm of marching and I found it especially tiring having to close up repeatedly. Knowing that men who dropped out on forced marches often had to be left behind to fend for themselves, I was determined that I would not march under avoidably adverse conditions if I could do anything to prevent it.

The countryside we passed through was fairly flat, but it was densely wooded and very attractive in its covering of crisp snow. One drawback of the snow was the lack of contrast and the never-ending whiteness that spread as far as the eye could see. As I became more tired, the landscape lost its attractiveness and began to have a psychologically negative effect on me, in the same way as when I was walking through woods for days on end. There were times when my eyes became strained from the reflection of the sun on the snow, but I never actually suffered snow-blindness or saw snow turning red before my eyes as happened to men walking through snow for weeks on end. Marching in a column with my eyes fixed on the back of the soldier in front of me cut out a lot of the glare, but I still found myself closing my eyes for periods at a time, especially after I became very tired. As I became more exhausted during the day, I felt myself walking almost like a zombie with my legs moving automatically and my mind a blank.

I suppose that in a situation like this, a person will economise on any unnecessary physical or mental drain on his energy. Often, while I walked with my eyes closed, I had quite lengthy naps before being rudely awakened by my boots knocking against those of the man in front of me, or being kicked by the feet of the man behind me who was probably having a nap just like I was.

When our day's march finally came to an end and I was able to let myself drop down exhausted, I wondered whether my weary limbs would ever obey my commands again. At the same time I knew that I had overcome the threshold of pain and had been able to continue marching for hours afterwards, so I supposed that the same thing would happen the next day and I would just go on and on for as long as was required.

That night we were again accommodated in abandoned buildings and after we had finished our evening meal an NCO came around to instruct us about new units to which we had been assigned. When my turn came I heard that I was to join an ammunition transport unit the next day; a few of the soldiers in my accommodation would join artillery units, while the bulk of the men were destined for the infantry.

Well, the Division Hermann Göring was obviously not going to produce new self-propelled guns by magic for my benefit, but how lucky that I was not to become a foot-slogging infantrist. Ammunition transport sounded like heavy work and I was surprised that they had picked a light-weight like me for it, but then I was probably just a number on a list when they made their selection.

At that point in time I knew nothing about the dangers I would be exposed to when going on cross-country supply runs, effectively unprotected on the back of a truck. All I could think of was that the new job suggested to me wheels and re-acquired mobility. Surely this was a sign that luck was still faithfully remaining on my side?

16

BEHIND THE RUSSIAN LINES

The following morning I got a lift from a truck that brought me to my new destination where I reported to the Oberfeldwebel (staff-sergeant) in charge of my new unit. He explained that we were part of a larger supplies system and that our unit consisted of eighteen men, including drivers and co-drivers. We had three trucks and our main job was the transport of heavy shells for flak-artillery, but it could also be medium and light shells, medical supplies or food.

Our trucks were all of Italian make, pride of place going to a huge, immensely powerful, open 7-ton Alfa Romeo which also pulled a large trailer. Then there was a 5-ton Lancia, again open-deck which was a great "mud-plugger," that is it could keep going through terrible conditions of mud and slush. Finally, there was a 3-ton Fiat with a tarpaulin-covered loading area. The Fiat was our only truck with a petrol engine. In general appearance it was like a Volkswagen van with a rounded front end and no protruding engine bonnet, but it was much larger. The blunt front end made it tremendously manoeuvrable in woods and on narrow tracks and it could accelerate extremely quickly.

The purpose of our unit was threefold. Firstly, it was to collect loads from main supply depots and bring them to the ammunition dumps of batteries in action. Secondly, to shift shells from front line dumps to new action spots. Thirdly, to bring ammunition, food and medical supplies to German units cut off by the Russians. The 105-millimetre shells we carried were packed two at a time in timber cases which weighed just over one cwt (approx.. 51Kg) each, while the 88-millimetre shells were packed three at a time in wicker cases of similar weight.

On my first run we used the Lancia to bring shells to the front lines. Six of us, apart from the driver and the co-driver, travelled with the truck and I soon learned what a hard job I now had to do. During loading, two of my mates stood on the truck and two others stood at the stacked shell cases in the depot, while another man and I did the carrying.

The procedure was that a shell case was placed high up on my shoulders and I gripped the end above my head with both hands to steady it. The distance of some twenty-five yards to the truck was covered at a fast walk, almost a jog-trot, and when I got there, I had to turn around so that the bottom end of the case rested on the loading edge of the truck. The two men there took over my case and commenced stacking on the truck. Tough as the loading job was, the unloading turned out to be much more strenuous. First of all, the dump to which we delivered the cases was at least fifty yards from the approach road and, secondly, we had to carry the cases through undergrowth, over tree roots and rocks; and all this at a jog-trot.

On subsequent runs we used to switch around our tasks, but I found that handling the boxes on the truck itself was often even more strenuous since I had to do a lot of lifting while bending down. I also had to slide the cases along the truck floor and push or pull them into place where they were stacked, all of which was harder on the spine than the ordinary carrying.

How grateful I was for my logging training in the Labour Service, which had taught me to lift and carry with minimum strain to my back, because it was no mean task for a slim eighteen-year-old to handle one hundredweight loads under such difficult conditions and over prolonged periods. I did not mind so much carrying the wicker cases. Being flexible, they distributed the load evenly across my shoulders, but the timber cases were an absolute curse even though they were no heavier. Their sharp edges dug into my flesh, as if to the bone. Then, being so smooth, they tended to slide down my back, forcing me to uncomfortably bend lower and grip them harder during my already torturous journey. As if all this was not enough, it was normal to keep the truck's diesel engine running during loading and unloading, so the atmosphere became heavily polluted. In conditions of winter fog I found myself choking on air saturated with exhaust fumes when I needed all the fresh oxygen I could get into my lungs. Sometimes the driver and co-driver would join in, but they were not obliged to and usually did odd chores on the vehicle while waiting for us to finish our job.

None of us, apart from drivers and co-drivers, were associated with any particular truck, so we took it in turns going on runs and if more than one truck was used we all worked together to the finish. The average time taken to load or unload a truck was about twenty minutes, so there was a total of forty minutes of concentrated labour involved in each run with a spell of rest while we were travelling. Our work load varied from day to day. If there were many changes in the Front-lines we could be on the go all day, whereas on other occasions we might have three to four runs taking up about half of the day. We varied the number of men on each run to suit the load to be carried.

One of the main advantages of being with the transport unit, apart from being driven everywhere, was that we were almost invariably accommodated in deserted buildings and did not have to sleep in the open. We were still in the depths of winter and it was extremely cold, but we now had warm and dry shelter at night-time; the food was good and the supply was reliable. Occasionally, we came in for a special treat. Because of the fast retreat of the German army and the panic exodus of civilians, large central food depots had sometimes been left behind still stocked with tinned foods of all description. There were preserves of meat, vegetables, fruit, dripping, soups and jams and many other things. We were occasionally allowed to pick up certain items to supplement our rations and I remember often feeling it was like Christmas as I walked among shelves loaded with a variety of goodies from which we selected our allowance.

Of all the men in the transport unit, there were only four whom I remember well. The driver of the Alfa Romeo was Ober-Gefreiter Hensel, a very thin, fair-haired man. I never saw such wizardry in truck driving as he demonstrated over and over again when flicking his huge vehicle across an impossible terrain. At night he had the eyes of a cat. Aided only by the useless pin-pricks of light from his blacked-out headlamps, he often kept his engine at full throttle as we thundered along narrow roads. I forever marvelled at his skill and would have been absolutely terrified out of my wits if I had not had such utter faith in the man.

His co-driver, Gefreiter Detlev Hansen, was an amiable slim man from Hamburg who used to wear an informal black seaman's cap, a type that was very popular in his home town. Of course, he put on the standard steel helmet whenever we drove into a battle area. Though we were a well-disciplined unit, there was a more easygoing atmosphere than had been the case in my previous units.

Ober-Gefreiter Heisig was another man I remember well. At about thirty years of age, he was the eldest. Heisig came from the eastern part of Germany and spoke with a heavy Slav accent. He was of very stocky build, quite a rough diamond and given to a constant use of Polish swear words. I can still hear his "psiakrew pieronie" or "pieronie, pieronie" ("blood of a dog" and "dog, dog") spoken in his gravelly voice at every opportunity, but he was good-natured and always managed to enliven a situation with his witty comments.

The last man I remember was Gefreiter Willy Gerkens, who came from a small farm south of Bremen. Willy was a bit of a dreamer by nature and full of plans for what he was going to do when the war was over.

My transport unit, which I joined in the middle of February 1945, was based north-west of the town of Lauban, which itself was about eighty miles west of the city of Breslau. Russian forces in the county of Lauban were massing for a drive aimed at Saxony and, once again, it was the Panzer-Corps Grossdeutschland and Göring and the Division Brandenburg, which were involved in attempting to stop the breakthrough. Despite the usual numerical superiority of the Russians, their aim was successfully thwarted by the German forces over weeks of bitter fighting.

During this time our runs went off fairly trouble-free, but not without danger when we came under fire from planes or artillery. In these situations it was the skill of Hensel and the other drivers that saved our lives many times when they managed to get the trucks into the shelter of a wood in the nick of time. Another hazard they avoided was getting stuck in slush, or bogged down in the rough ground we often had to cover.

There was one particular instance when Hensel clearly saved the lives of all of us on his Alfa Romeo. We were driving along a snow-covered road at high speed late one evening in an area supposedly free of Russians when we suddenly ran smack into heavy fire from ahead of us and it seemed as if it would only be seconds before we were all dead. However, undeterred by the fact that we were lumbered with a heavy trailer, and that the fields on either side of us were several feet lower than the road itself, Hensel swerved off the road sending truck and trailer flying through the air.

Even as we landed in the field with a sickening crunch that knocked all the breath out of my body, Hensel had engaged a lower gear and we were churning through the snow in a wide arc gathering speed all the time. Fate was on our side when Hensel managed to find a spot that he could charge and get us back onto the road in a manoeuvre that all but overturned us. It was also our good luck that from the moment we left the road the Russians had stopped firing at us. Maybe they could not believe their eyes or they were spellbound by the incredible sight of our splendid Alfa Romeo truck and trailer sailing through the air. The way the Alfa Romeo responded to the demands made on it and never broke down, is a testimony to the great engineering product that it was.

The speed with which we did our loading and unloading in a battle area played a significant part in our ability to get out of danger quickly. We enjoyed a great team spirit and there was never an occasion when anybody tried to get out of doing his share of work. A lot of our runs took place during daytime, but there were many times when we had to bring ammunition and supplies to batteries which had been cut off by Russian units. In those cases we travelled by night, but frequently ended up running the gauntlet when the Russians saw us and opened fire.

We always used the most suitable trucks depending on the weight of a load and conditions we could expect to encounter. On night runs we set off well after dark and drove on a mixture of roads and tracks, across fields or through woods and usually criss-crossed along a pre-determined route. Sometimes we got through the Russian lines undetected. Other times we had to change plans repeatedly and try different routes. Other times again we had to give up and go back to base when it was either getting too near to dawn or too dangerous to try again. Riding on the back of a truck I was always unprotected. If any shooting started, I could only lie down flat and hold on for dear life if I did not want to be thrown off as the driver began swerving or accelerating to escape the Russian fire. We always had our rifles with us, but it never became practical to use them.

Unloading at our destination was usually done at a gallop so that we could quickly start on our return trip, but sometimes, when it got late, we had to wait for the next night to go back to base. Whenever that happened we gave our beleaguered mates whatever help we could by joining them in the defence of their position and doing guard duty for them. They had invariably gone through a rougher time than we had; they were exhausted and undermanned, so it was natural that we should help out, however briefly.

At the time I joined my transport unit, the western Allies had reached several points on the river Rhine, but we knew nothing of this. On the northern part of the eastern Front the Russians had reached East-Pommerania, while Berlin was being subjected to round-the-clock air-raids. We could see for ourselves that things were not good on the Russian Front, but all that mattered to us was keeping our troops supplied. There was no alternative anyway; we could not all go home and let the Russians sweep over Germany; I certainly did not want to be taken prisoner and I looked on each day on which we held off the Russians and maintained an intact Front-line as a positive achievement.

As a result of German resistance, the Russian forces were making no headway. In the section defended by the 4th Panzer Army, to which my division belonged, stability was achieved in the early days of March. Other divisions from Army-Group Middle successfully defended the Front-lines right down to the Tatra Mountains in Slovakia. As a result of this concerted stand, streams of refugees managed to make good progress on their trek to the west. The tenacity with which German soldiers were defending home soil against enormous odds was something the Russians had not expected. Between the Baltic Sea and the Slovakian border there was nothing more than three worn out and ravaged German armies opposing twenty-eight fully equipped Russian armies and fourteen army-corps.

It was at this time that I got my one and only war injury, but I cannot claim to have suffered it in heroic battle. We had made use of a relatively slack period to build up a sizeable dump of assorted ammunition at our base, by ferrying several loads from a main depot. Our dump was inside the edge of a wood bordering on a small village and we maintained a continuous guard on it.

One beautiful, sunny day I was standing guard at the dump. It was close to mid-day and all the world seemed at peace, there was even a touch of spring in the air. Suddenly, I was startled to see white smoke rising up between the cases at one end of the dump. My immediate guess was that a piece of glass had caught the strong rays of the sun and was igniting dry grass and leaves. There was a village pump only a hundred yards away which always had a bucket beside it, so I raced to it and began to fill the bucket while shouting to one of my mates that there was a fire at the dump. When I got back the smoke had become a lot denser and so, without hesitation, I emptied the bucket over a spot that was the obvious source of the fire.

The next instant I felt an agonising pain all over my face as if it had been hit by a wall of flame while simultaneously it seemed that a red hot poker had pierced the top of my left foot. Looking down I saw that the top of the boot and the lacing had dissolved. I instinctively lashed out with my left foot to kick off the boot and shake off the foot cloth even as I started racing to the village.

My eyes were burning and I could hardly see where I was going, but I felt a reassuring grip on my arm from my mate who had seen what happened and knew I was badly hurt. Steering me as if I was a galloping blind-man, my mate brought me to a medical orderly in the town. He immediately told me to get my trousers off in a hurry and only then did I hazily see that the bottom half of my left trouser leg was reduced to shreds. In next to no time the orderly had bathed my eyes and smeared ointment all over my face, my left foot and parts of my leg and he then swathed all affected areas in bandages. That was all that could be done for me at the moment, but I experienced no relief and felt as if my whole face and left foot were on fire. The orderly told me to report to the Oberfeldwebel and then to lie down and rest; he would come and visit me shortly. So off I went. My head was a mass of bandages with only slits left for me to see through and my injured foot and leg were likewise bandaged up. The poor Oberfeldwebel got a terrible shock when he saw me with my huge, white, pumpkin-like head. I quickly gave him my report and he ordered me to rest immediately and not to worry about anything.

When the orderly visited me a short while later he told me what had happened. The explanation turned out to be quite simple. For once I had suffered an extraordinary bit of bad luck. For some unknown reason, one of the wicker cases contained canisters of a smoke-generating solution. This solution only remained in its liquid state as long as it was in a sealed container, but once it made contact with air it turned into dense smoke.

It seemed that one of the containers must have been faulty and suddenly developed a heavy leak of fluid which formed a pool in the grass and began to give off smoke. Throwing water on the pool had a similar effect to throwing water on a pan of boiling fat, it immediately vaporised and shot explosively in all directions. It was mostly light vapour that had hit my face, whereas the larger and heavier droplets had bespattered my left boot and trouser leg. Since the solution was highly acidic, the corrosive effect of it hitting parts of my body or my clothing was devastating.

In the midst of my bad luck I had still been extremely fortunate. One droplet had burned a deep hole above my left eyebrow and others produced a few minor craters in my face, but none had hit my eyes otherwise I would have been instantly blind. Some light vapour must have struck my eyes because of the searing pain I felt, but the natural eye fluids had given me enough protection, since I did not suffer any long term effects. I still have some of the burn marks on my face, but they are almost invisible. My face healed up reasonably well in a week and was then no longer painful, but my foot troubled me for many weeks to come. The acid had burned right through to the bone at one spot near my big toe and this obstinately refused to heal over.

It was two weeks before I could do any heavy work, so I was put adjusting cases on the stockpiles where very little walking was required. A week later, though not fully recovered, I was back on full work, but paid the price of having to endure a much longer healing period than I would otherwise have had. Strangely enough, despite the severity of the foot injury, no scar has remained to tell the tale. Painful as my single war wound was, I still think I was amazingly lucky that the outcome was not more serious.

The front-line situation continued to improve and by 6 April further stability was achieved. Though German forces were retreating all along the line, at least the fighting Front remained intact and there was no break-through by Russian forces. After a short while, a phased pull-back over forty-five miles to the west was carried out by my division. The troops were to get a badly needed rest and casualties were to be replaced by soldiers from reserve units. Since depletion of soldiers in some units had gone beyond a critical stage, the units had to be dissolved and new units created from the survivors.

While my Division 1 had been defending Silesia and suffering heavy casualties, our sister division in East-Prussia fared much worse. Short of food and with guns rationed to a ludicrous eight rounds per day their casualties mounted. Losses in some units reached sixty-three per cent between January and the end of March; a terrible toll of human life mixed with suffering. At this stage, what was left of the Göring Division 2 was withdrawn by sea and sent to join the Division 1 in Silesia.

One of the most dastardly orders given to army commanders was that large or important towns be designated a "fortress", i.e. given a military status. Even as late as 12 April 1945, the Supreme Command of the Armed Forces, made up of Hitler's henchmen Keitel, Himmler and Bormann, directed that any town commander of a "fortress" who surrendered or retreated without express permission would be sentenced to death. Declaring a town a "fortress" invariably spelt death and rape to many civilians, apart from the pointless sacrifice of troops and equipment. Many such orders were given when the war was almost over, which just goes to show the stupidity, blindness and irresponsibility of which human minds are capable.

Some statistics relating to east-German refugees forcibly demonstrate their tragic fate; In East-Prussia, 1,09 million people were evacuated by the German navy and a further 350,000 left by road, leaving behind 614,000 dead civilians. In East-Pommerania the number of civilian deaths was 375,000.

I received my last letters at the front in early April 1945. Between bombing raids in Germany and the catastrophic situation on the eastern Front, it was surprising that army mail had still continued to reach me.

In mid-April, we received an addition to our unit in the form of a heavy 5-ton German Henschel truck and a further six soldiers. The truck was diesel-engined, but unusual inasmuch as it had a small 3-speed gear box bolted onto the front end, used only for cranking the engine before starting it. What happened was that two of us, standing face to face, operated a huge four-handed cranking-handle. A stubby gear lever was first pushed into the low gear position and we would crank away till the engine was spinning freely. Then we paused an instant, pushed the lever into middle gear and brought the engine up to a higher speed. Repeating the operation in top gear, we waited for a signal from the driver. When he was satisfied he nodded, we immediately stopped cranking and he engaged the starting clutch. If the engine did not fire there was no question of continuing cranking in top gear, or even middle gear. We had to start all over again in low gear, straining to get the heavy engine moving once more. The army must have been terribly short of transport to have provided us with such unsuitable equipment in a war zone.

During the last three weeks of the war, we were kept busier than ever. It was not that there was an abundance of ammunition available for us to fetch, but rather that we had to continually re-ferry dumps so that they were not lost to the Russians over the retreat in the last fifty-five miles. Though sometimes short of fuel for our trucks, we never actually ran out of it. I suppose the obvious reason was that, important as tanks and other armoured vehicles are, they are useless if they cannot use their guns; and so my little transport unit probably took priority over them.

One day Willi Gerkens approached me with a proposal. He said the war would soon be over and we should then stick together for our mutual benefit. His proposition was that if I, with my knowledge of languages, helped him to get back to his parents' farm near Bremen, without being taken prisoner, he would put me up until I was able to return to Ireland. He added that if I managed to locate my sister, she would also be welcome to stay at his home. We could expect the western half of Germany to be occupied by British, American and French troops and so, since Gerkens spoke no foreign language, this was quite a shrewd suggestion. The idea also appealed to me, since it would mean having accommodation that was a long distance west of Russian-held territory as well as being also close to the north-west German coast.

Soon afterwards I got one of my worst scares in the transport unit. We had gone to retrieve a stock of ammunition from a dump in an area from which most units had been withdrawn. Having arrived shortly before dawn, we worked at break-neck speed to complete loading up because we knew the Russians could arrive at any moment. I do not know why on this of all times we used the Henschel truck. Also, the engine was shut down while we were loading, probably because the driver was afraid the Russians would hear us. However, the upshot of it all was that the engine failed to start when we had flung the last cases onto the truck and we had gone through the tedious cranking procedure.

Twice already the driver had released the clutch and each time there was just a cough from the engine before it spluttered into silence. Our driver frantically waved for a fresh pair of men to take over from the first team who, in spite of the cold weather, were covered in perspiration. Another mate and I jumped forward and took over the job of man-handling the engine through its three starting gears.

Just as we were about to engage second gear three Russian armoured troop-carriers appeared about half a mile away and began to head towards us. Rather than desert the truck and head into the safety of the woods, we nodded our immediate agreement to continue with another try. By the time we got to third gear, desperately trying to get up more speed on the engine, the Russians were much too close for comfort. Our driver now held the balance of our lives in his hands. If he tried the ignition too soon, the chances were that the engine would again fail to fire. But if he waited longer for us to get up more speed then, even if the engine fired, the Russians could be upon us. Outnumbered, and with only rifles to defend ourselves, we could be wiped out in minutes.

Seconds dragged on like an eternity and still the driver held back, I could almost sense the fingers of the Russian soldiers hovering over the release of their guns as they waited to get nearer to us. I was beginning to feel that I could not keep up the cranking any longer and would myself become a drag on the spinning engine when, at last, the driver gave his signal. As my mate and I stepped back, the sweet song of the engine coming to life hit my ears and we were scrambling aboard in an instant. We had not gone many yards before the Russians opened fire, but they were crossing very rough ground that spoilt their aim and within seconds the wood had swallowed us up and we were safe.

On 16 April, the Russians began an all-out offensive with deeply penetrating movements towards the provinces of Brandenburg and Saxony. The Göring Divisions held out until 22 April, but by then Russian advances to the north of us had reached and taken the town of Bautzen, thirty miles north-east of Dresden. Our orders were to retake Bautzen and establish an unbroken Front-line. Together with another panzer division, the Göring Divisions 1 and 2 attacked shortly after midnight of 22/23 April. Within twenty-four hours, Bautzen had been recaptured from Russian and Polish troops. Indescribable scenes of past barbarity were revealed when women and girls were freed from buildings, where they had been held prisoner.

Forcing the Russians out of Bautzen was the last major German success in the East. Russian troops gave up trying to recapture the town and it remained in German hands until the war was almost over. Shortly after we had retaken Bautzen, American and Russian forces met at the town of Torgau on the Elbe. It was 25 April and Germany was now effectively split in two by the invading armies. During the last week of April the Göring Divisions fought a slowly retreating battle toward an area north-east of Dresden, but by this time they were no longer an effective force.

During my research I have come across many names of towns in battle areas that I remember well from my ammunition runs in the last phases of the war. It is so easy to glibly peel off such a list of names, but what of the anguish, the torment and the terrible human suffering associated with each of these places? As for me, not one supply run had been without incident and I treated each day as just another day to be survived. There were periods when I felt that we were spending half our time behind the Russian lines or trying to get our trucks through Russian-held territory. Amazingly enough, we never lost a truck on our runs even though they became badly marked by bullets. Similarly, the rest of the crew and I had luck on our side and suffered no casualties despite all the runs we made past Russian positions.

The news of Hitler's death on 30 April was announced to us, but there was no mention of suicide. Grossadmiral Dönitz, who was appointed by Hitler to take over from him, purposely delayed surrender negotiations so that retreating German armies could give cover to the huge masses of refugees fleeing from the east. It is reckoned that by his action he saved between two and three million refugees being overtaken by the Russians. For me, this is an important concept because I feel that it has vindicated my own attitude and actions as a soldier in contributing in my small way towards saving the lives of civilians and German soldiers.

In the first four days of May 1945, the surviving operational units of the Göring Divisions 1 and 2 fought their last engagements north of Dresden. After that they retreated toward the northern border of Bohemia.

I remember driving through Dresden on what was the last day of war, 7 May 1945. We no longer carried ammunition; there was none left to fetch and nowhere to bring it. Instead, we took refugees on board and hoped that we would be able to get them to safety. I had never been to Dresden before its destruction and what I expected to see was the usual sight of the shattered buildings of a bombed city. What I saw instead was a desert. As we drove along streets cleared of debris I could see for miles across mounds of rubble. Little remained of the buildings to obstruct my view from where I sat on the back of our truck.

I don't know what part of Dresden we drove through, but there was not a soul on the roads and what would they have been doing there anyway? It is not surprising that I got the impression I was travelling through some strange stone formations in the middle of the Sahara Desert. Terrible as the destruction was, I had then no idea of just how horrible a death the citizens had suffered. During my months on the Russian Front I had often come across the sickly, sweet smell of corpses; I do not know if it was my imagination, but I was sure I got the same smell of decay hanging over the city twelve weeks after the air-raid.

After leaving Dresden behind us we heard rumours that the war was over, but they remained rumours and we began driving southwards on a road that became more and more clogged with military trucks and cars as well as fleeing civilians. I knew that the Russians could not be far away to the north and the east and was convinced that the western Allies must also be quite near to us, but I saw no sign of either. In fact, the nearest Western Allies were the 3rd US Army which was then still over seventy-five miles to the west of us, about fifteen miles the other side of Karlsbad and about thirty miles inside Bohemia. At the same time Russian tank forces under Marshal Konjiew were closing fast on us from a northern direction as they headed for Prague.

Despite the rumble of traffic on the road, I was very conscious of the absence of any noise of warfare and it gave me the strange feeling that there was something unnatural and wrong about this day. I did not seem to be glad that the war must now finally be over, nor was I conscious of any feelings of sadness that Germany had lost - there was only an emptiness in me. However, just because the war was over, there was no reason to relax; in the confused situation, into which I was heading, I had to be extra vigilant and my future remained as uncertain as ever.

17

ESCAPING CAPTURE

We were approaching the town of Glashütte, 15 miles west of Dresden, in mid-afternoon on 7 May, when our slow-moving column came to a halt. An officer standing in a jeep at the side of the road used a loud-hailer to announce that Germany had signed capitulation documents early that morning. He said that all soldiers were to stay with their units and these would be surrendering to American forces. No arms or vehicles must be destroyed and everything had to be handed over intact.

When our column moved on again shortly, I noticed that a couple of soldiers on my truck had not returned after ostensibly slipping off to "spend a penny." The reason was obvious and who could blame them? The war was over; fighting had ceased and vows of allegiance no longer had a practical meaning. The biggest danger now was that we might end up as prisoners of the Russians and not the Americans.

So far, Gerkens and I had shied away from making any plans about how we would get to Rotenburg. This may have been because we felt that such discussion was disloyal or impractical at too early a stage, but now it was high time to have a plan of action. Rotenburg was a long way off in the north of Germany, but Karlsbad, where my Aunt Hella lived, was no more than seventy-five miles west. Karlsbad was obviously our first destination. Once there, we would be able to get civilian clothing, food and other useful items for our onward journey. Getting there quickly also meant putting a bigger distance between us and the Russians.

It was lucky for us that the town of Werdau, where Erika had last been living, and Mücheln, the home town of my guardian, were roughly en route between Karlsbad and

Rotenburg. A decision on our immediate action was more tricky. Slipping off our truck now meant a three-day tramp to Karlsbad which was too long for safety. The Russians were probably not far off and there were bound to be Czech partisans in the area. On the other hand, if we waited too long, we might suddenly find ourselves in a prisoner-of-war camp with no opportunity to escape. We finally decided to stay with the truck for the time being, because it was averaging ten to twelve miles an hour and going roughly in the direction of Karlsbad. At the same time we would keep an extra sharp look-out in case of problems so that we could still make a get-away.

Soon after making our decision we saw two young and attractive female cyclists waving to our driver and begging for a lift. We now had more room on the truck, so the driver obligingly stopped and willing hands pulled the girls and their bicycles aboard. I would have thought cycling under prevailing traffic conditions to be quicker, but it may have been too much for the girls who looked more as if they were out for a Sunday jaunt than that they were refugees in flight.

It was not long before the girls found they could do even better for themselves. Once again we had landed in a traffic jam and were crawling along at a snail's pace when an army VW jeep with two young German officers, travelling in the same direction, began to squeeze past us. Our two friends were on their feet in an instant, waving down to the officers and entreating them to give them a lift. It took only one look at the pretty faces for the officers to give a nod before the girls were off the truck and in the jeep, showing amazing agility.

I had been watching these events in an absent-minded sort of a way when I suddenly became aware of Gerkens hissing and whistling at me from another part of the truck. When I turned my head to look at him, I saw a rather funny sight. Gerkens was down on his knees, crouching low, with his arms stretched out on each side, reminding me of an Oriental about to pray. The reason for his urgent hissing was obvious. Each of his hands was clutching one handlebar of a bicycle which the girls had left behind, and he was afraid somebody might claim them. Gerkens had been more quick-witted than I and thanks to him we now had our own transport. Getting to Karlsbad would be much easier and we also had the means to cover the long distance to Rotenburg. How lucky can you get? Yet again good fortune had smiled on me.

Every now and then I noticed another soldier disappear from a truck or from among the marching men, but, as nobody in charge made any attempt to stop them, it seemed unlikely that Gerkens and I would be prevented from leaving. I must pay a sincere tribute to the common sense of the officers and NCOs. To date, strict discipline had been maintained because it mattered, but now that soldiers felt they had a better chance of reaching safety on their own, those in charge turned a blind eye and ignored their orders. I did not have any guilty feelings that I myself would soon be leaving the truck, because my departure could only be of benefit to a soldier or civilian who could then get a ride in my place.

When dusk approached, our column came to a halt near the town of Altenberg, just a few miles short of the Czech border. We did not know if this was in order to stop for the night or whether we were about to be handed over to the Americans, so we decided there and then to make a break. The bicycles were in good condition; barring major difficulties we could easily get to Karlsbad before daybreak. No eyebrows were raised when we nodded good-bye and slipped off the truck with our bicycles. We also kept our rifles, because we might still have to defend our lives. Little more than an hour later we found ourselves on a direct road to Karlsbad. By now it was quite dark, but I saw from a road sign that we had only another 65 miles to go.

I don't know which of us had, what turned out to be a hare-brained idea, but we decided to save time by getting a tow from passing vehicles. There was a lot of westbound traffic in the form of German army trucks and vans and it seemed to be too good an opportunity to miss. We agreed to pick vehicles which were unlikely to drive too fast for us and that any time we lost sight of each other we would let our tow go, so that we would maintain contact with each other.

All this was easier said than done. First of all, it was not easy to see far in the dark and then it took all one's concentration not to come a cropper bouncing along the road at up to thirty miles an hour. Although we were on a main road, the surface had become broken up by military traffic and lack of maintenance. Holding onto a truck with one hand while trying to control my bicycle with the other hand, as the wheels hit stones and potholes, was a hopeless task. We relinquished our tow a few times when the speed became too fast for road conditions, but then we began to have accidents. One time I was sent sprawling on the road and another time I was catapulted into the ditch after hitting potholes. Gerkens had meanwhile fared no better and we decided to give up the madness before we suffered injury or wrecked our precious bicycles.

Looking back on our helter-skelter ride, I think it may have partially been the fear of partisans that made us ignore the other danger. Hanging onto a truck gave us some protection from snipers and ambushes; as lone riders we would have been very vulnerable. Fortunately, our bicycles had survived the crashes without suffering damage or a puncture, so we thanked our lucky stars for our escape and the extra miles we had gained. From now on, there would be no more tows. Near midnight we decided to stop for a break before cycling straight through to our destination.

After our rest we continued on, heading for the river Eger which flowed to Karlsbad. As we cycled beside the river I remembered the scenic beauty of the valley from bygone holidays, but in the darkness only a hint of this was evident. Luckily, our journey passed off without mishap. It was three o'clock in the morning when we arrived at Karlsbad, so I did not feel like bursting in on my aunt at that unearthly hour. Instead, we cycled to her home and settled down at the edge of some woods close by. I knew the area like the back of my hand, so I was confident that I would be able to deal with any problems that might arise. Remembering that Aunt Hella was an early riser, I thought six-thirty was a good time to sneak into the house. Although Dönitz was a German-speaking suburb, there was no point in advertising our presence unnecessarily. I could not ignore the risk that in the post-war atmosphere some Czech neighbours might try to get Aunt Hella into trouble.

My soft knock at the door drew a quick response when somebody looked at me through the spy-glass and then the door was flung open by Aunt Hella, quite beside herself with joy. Gerkens was made equally welcome and I quickly explained where we had come from and what our plans were. Being such a well organised housewife my aunt quickly prepared a hero's breakfast for us while we removed the travel stains from our bodies. While we were eating, my aunt gave me all her latest news. To my delight she was able to confirm that my parents and Erika were all well and that Erika was still living at the same address in Werdau.

Aunt Hella was very disappointed when I told her that we could only stay for one day, at the most. However, she appreciated that it was not safe for us to be in Czechoslovakia and there was also the danger that advancing Russian soldiers might take over this part of the country. She herself had considered the question of leaving, but had decided to stay and I thought she was right under the circumstances. Our most urgent need was for civilian clothing, a map and food for the way. Being recently widowed, my aunt had plenty of men's clothing to spare; Gerkens and I each picked what we needed, but there were no shoes that fitted us so we had to stick with our army boots.

While Gerkens and I lay down for a snooze, Aunt Hella went off to the local shops to chat with people and see if she could glean some useful information on the general situation in East-Bohemia and in Germany. I would never have asked her to do this for us and maybe draw unwelcome attention to herself, but she was just that sort of a helpful and unselfish person. The news she later gave us was that American troops were expected soon in Karlsbad, but nothing was known of the Russians. Gerkens and I decided it would be best not to delay and we should press on for Werdau in the currently confused situation. We would stay for just one night and then leave early in the morning wearing civilian clothes. We also decided to bundle up our military uniforms and take them with us; maybe we might need them again and we could still throw away the bundles if it became dangerous to keep them.

Our biggest problem was what to do with the rifles. The German border was over thirty kilometres north of Karlsbad which meant a two-hour cycle during which we could still come up against partisans. On balance, we decided against taking them, since they would only give us away, while being of little use if we ran into an ambush and were assumed to be ex-soldiers. It was far better to aim for a fast sprint to safety.

We spent the rest of the day chatting with my aunt - there was so much to reminisce about since we had always had such good times together. I was very sorry to be leaving the next day, but it was also important that we should not jeopardise Aunt Hella's safety in any way by our presence. The preparations in the evening did not take long. Aunt Hella's road map told us that it was only sixty-five miles to Werdau, which, barring problems, we would cover inside the day. We would first cycle through the Erz Mountains to the town of Johann-Georgenstadt, just across the German border. After checking out and oiling our bicycles we parcelled up our uniforms, some items of clothing and a small amount of provisions. The last chore was to bury our rifles in the woods after dark before settling down for a night's sleep in the unaccustomed luxury of real beds.

Our leave-taking next morning was helped by Aunt Hella's cheerfulness and optimism that all would go well for us and that she herself would be all right. After a last hug we were on our way at six o'clock. We purposely did not leave earlier to avoid attracting attention to ourselves when roads were still deserted. It was a beautiful morning as we set off and the countryside was resplendent in its spring colours. I would have enjoyed the ride a lot more if I had not been conscious of the hazards we could face before getting over the border.

However, we reached Johann-Georgenstadt without any problems and had now covered a third of the way to Werdau. After that, everything continued to run smoothly for the next hour until we approached a small village. For some time now there had been more traffic on the road consisting of a mixture of German army units, some small groups of soldiers, but very few civilians and we were beginning to stand out from the other people on the road.

Suddenly we noticed the traffic bunching up about half a mile ahead of us and we feared that it might be a check-point. We had seen no sign of the American army, so it was most likely to be the German army monitoring traffic movement. This could be very dangerous for us. The German military police, would have no difficulty recognising us as ex-soldiers and, although they could no longer have us court-martialled, they would certainly detain us and ensure that we ended up in a prisoner-of-war camp. With open fields on either side there was no way to sneak past them undetected. If we went back to try another route we would just waste time and maybe end up no better off.

The argument for keeping our uniforms was now to be put to the test. We decided to hop behind some bushes for a quick change and then to continue on our way like obedient members of an infantry bicycle unit on their way to a surrender point. As expected, there were military police on the road checking out all soldiers and questioning the civilians. When our turn came I said that we were on our way to a POW camp, as instructed, and I made it appear as if we were bound for a specific destination. It must have sounded genuine for we were waved on without any more questions being asked. We then decided to remain in uniform for a while, because the number of German soldiers on the road had increased and we could expect more check points on the way. At this stage it seemed a good time to take a short break. We had covered some steep gradients in the Erz Mountains and after that we had to get through quite an extensive hilly terrain which was tiring on our single-speed lady's bicycles. With only a three-hour ride to Werdau ahead of us, it was as well to be refreshed in case of emergencies.

We came up against two more check points manned by German military police, but on each occasion they no more than glanced at us and we continued on our way. Once again, we were lucky to have made the right decision about what to wear. When we got close to Werdau we decided to change back into civilian clothes in the hope that they would make us look less conspicuous. Werdau was a small industrial town of 25,000 inhabitants and so it was not long before we found our way to Erika's road.

When I rang the bell of an old town house where she lived it was answered by an elderly lady dressed in black. To my query, "Does Erika Stieber live here?" she confirmed that Erika was in at the time. I told her that I was Erika's brother and would she please tell her that I was here. An instant look of suspicion crossed the lady's face, but she went upstairs and I heard her knocking on a door. A moment later Erika came dashing down the stairs shouting, "John, is that you?" In the joy of our reunion I forgot all about Gerkens and it was only after Erika and I had got over our first excitement that I noticed him standing there looking embarrassed. Satisfied about my credentials, the old lady had already withdrawn, so I then introduced Gerkens to Erika and we went up to her flat.

Erika found it difficult to get over her amazement that I should suddenly turn up on her doorstep only two days after the war was over. She went on to tell me that, though her job with the communication centre was over and she did not have the faintest idea where I had last been on the Front, she had intended staying at her address until she got some word from me. Although we had much to tell each other, we first had to plan our next move.

Erika told us that American troops had already passed through Werdau and she was sure that forces of the western Allies occupied all of Germany between Werdau and Bremen. That was good news, but it was still essential that we should be quickly on our way because the troops might move back again and allow the Russians to take over. Even if we became prisoners of the western Allies there was the danger that they would hand us over to the Russians if they vacated the area. I was later to hear that this did happen.

One of us then had the excellent idea that we should forge travel documents to help us get past Allied military checkpoints. Erika's deserted office was in the same building that we were in, so we designed a suitable text and went there to produce our documents on her office typewriter. In my case the wording was:

TO WHOM IT MAY CONCERN

This is to certify that Mr John Stieber is travelling to rejoin his parents at Milford Villa, Mallow, Co Cork, Ireland. All British and American authorities are requested to give him any assistance he may require on the way.

Erika signed the document somewhat illegibly and our unknown benefactor was given the rank of colonel. We thought it was too risky to overdo it and make him a general. Looking around for something to make the document look more official, Erika came up with a German Navy rubber stamp which also depicted the German Eagle and a Swastika. Experimenting with some judicious smudging, we perfected the art of disguising what should not be recognised while allowing the stamp to impress with its suggested authority.

We produced a similar document for Erika, but had to tone down the one for Gerkens. He spoke no English, so we just referred to him as accompanying us to Rotenburg. Actually, we hoped our papers would be necessary only in a fall-back situation; both Erika and I spoke English with a distinctly English accent and we expected that soldiers would be quickly won over by the face of a pretty girl and voices that betrayed no German background. Maybe this would save us from awkward questions and if Gerkens remained suitably mute in the background all might be well.

While Erika was going through her belongings to see what she wanted to take with her, Gerkens and I checked out our bicycles and then tried to construct a more comfortable seat for Erika on one of the steel luggage carriers. Since she had no bicycle, we would have to take her on one of ours. Using an ordinary cushion we folded it over and tied it firmly to the carrier, but there was no easy way to construct foot-rests for Erika. She would just have to let her feet dangle, or try to wedge them over the nuts of the back axle.

When we tried out our transport arrangements on the road we found that, between the luggage of us three on one carrier and my sister on the other one, we were well loaded up. However, the bikes were strongly built and we considered ourselves well-equipped. Erika then settled up with her landlady who was glad to have Erika's belongings that she had to leave behind. By the time we were ready to go, it was well into the afternoon, so we decided to push ahead after having a meal and using up any of Erika's food that we could not take with us. The distance by road to Mücheln was eighty-eight miles and after that it was another 250 miles to Rotenburg. It had been no trouble to us cycling the sixty-five miles from Karlsbad to Werdau in eight hours, but from here on our progress would be much slower.

We had already decided to stick to secondary roads and I took over the bike with its lady-passenger for the first hour. Although Erika was a lightweight, the going was quite tough and I found that even slight uphill gradients took a lot out of me. In a way it was still more tiring for Erika who could not let her legs hang freely and had to keep her feet from hitting the ground. After changing places with Gerkens we cycled for another hour, but then decided to break for the night because we were getting tired. As it was, there had been no snags and we expected to be able to comfortably cover the remainder of the journey after a night's rest.

Although it was a mild night, we decided to ask at a farm whether we could sleep in the hay-barn, it would be more comfortable than sleeping in a field and also keep us safe from detection by the eyes of any busybody. The first farmer we asked agreed immediately to our spending the night in his hayloft and refused to take any money from us. A six o'clock start was planned for the next morning, so we had a light snack, chatted for about an hour and by nine o'clock were ready for sleep. I felt very relaxed and quickly dropped off. Though I slept like a log, my body-clock had me instantly awake at five o'clock in the morning.

Our breakfast was a short affair and afterwards we went over our route on the map and also familiarised ourselves with alternative routes in case we ran into any problems. At six o'clock we were on the road with Erika bravely suppressing the memory of her uncomfortable ride on the previous day. Willi and I swapped bikes after each hour's ride, but every time I had to again get used to the extra strain of the heavier load as I propelled the wobbling bike forwards.

We had been on the road for several hours when we ran into the first American soldiers. We were cycling along a straight stretch of road and could see a barrier in the distance with helmeted soldiers standing behind it. I was on the "luggage" bicycle at the time, so I speeded up to put some distance between our two bikes. Bearing down on the barrier I tried a diversionary tactic by calling out to the soldiers, "Hi, any idea how far it is to Mertendorf?" (a village I knew to be a few kilometres further on). The surprised reaction I got was, "Say, where are you from?" I got off my bike and said, "Oh, I am from Ireland. I'm on my way there now and this... ," here I gestured to the other approaching bike, " ...is my sister and a friend of ours." As the American soldiers crowded around me there were amazed smiles all round and I heard somebody say, "Well, get a load of that, they're from Ireland."

To cut a long story short, Erika and I had a friendly chat with the soldiers and any remarks aimed at Willi evoked from him a sheepish blush which was ideal for our purpose because the soldiers then left him alone. We were then asked whether we had enough food with us. Giving the right answer, "We haven't much, but we will be all right" resulted in soldiers dashing off to come back with delicacies such as peanut butter, tinned coffee, bread and other goodies. Being careful not to overstay our welcome, we thanked the Americans for their kindness and cycled off accompanied by their good wishes.

Before leaving I asked them whether there were any Russian forces between us and Bremen and was assured that they were well to the east of our route, which was very good news indeed. Now that we were inside the part of Germany likely to remain occupied by the Western Allies and we were not likely to meet any more German military police, it seemed opportune to throw away our uniforms. We would be in trouble if they were found by any officious Allied Army personnel and that could put an end to our plans. As soon as I dumped my uniform behind some bushes, I felt as if a huge weight had been lifted from my shoulders. It was final confirmation that my army life was now a thing of the past.

It had been a good idea to start early on the previous evening. Our estimation of the speed we could maintain had been too high and we might be unlucky and have to make some detours. Two hours later we came across another American check point, but again there was no problem;

perhaps the soldiers were bored and glad to have a bit of diversion. As before, we managed to scrounge some food and now felt that we would not be a burden on Aunt Grete when we visited her. Our trip remained uneventful and late in the afternoon the tall chimney of the Mücheln sugar factory came in sight.

When I rang the doorbell of my aunt's house, she was just as amazed to see me as Erika had been on the previous day. She was very well and had recently become a mother, but unfortunately had no news of Uncle Oskar who had since been made a captain in the army. However, we three were made very welcome and there was plenty of room to put us up.

Once again, our decision was that we would not stay long. Aunt Grete could hardly feed four people off her own rations when our supplies ran out and, anyway, our priority was to follow our plan and try to at least get to Willi's farm before being taken prisoner. We agreed to stay for two days and to leave early on 13 May.

As soon as I had a bath and settled in, I went to look at my belongings I had left in the house before being drafted into the army. Of course, my prize possession was the bicycle that I had used during my schooldays and I knew it was in perfect condition. This meant an end to our drudgery on the road and we would now be able to travel faster and in much greater comfort. We could carry more luggage and I would be able to take along some of my old clothes; now I even had my comfortable old shoes. On top of this there was my camera and items of sentimental value including some books that I did not want to leave behind.

It was only after Erika heard about my bicycle that she confessed to the torture she had suffered on the luggage carrier, with agonising cramps in the legs from trying to hold them rigidly in the air. I was very glad that her pluck did not have to be tested further on the much longer trip we had ahead of us.

I relished our stay in Mücheln. It was so relaxing to be totally unstressed for two whole days and to get long nights of refreshing sleep. Aunt Grete enjoyed our company, but she was subdued and obviously worried about her husband. It was nice to be able to share with her the delicacies we had been given by the Americans and so partly repay her for her hospitality during our short stay. I was sad when it was time to leave her behind in her lone vigil, but at least she had baby Christian to take her mind off her worries.

We made our usual early start on a beautifully sunny morning. It was exhilarating to be pedalling along on my trusted bike which revived so many happy memories of past jaunts and my joy was increased by the faster pace that we were now able to set. As before, we slept in a hay-barn during each night and the Americans continued to facilitate us, although we did once have to show our "papers" to emphasise our bona fide. Most of our trip was through American held territory and on the last leg of our journey we were twice stopped at British check-points.

On the first occasion we found ourselves heading towards disaster. Unimpressed by my cheery greeting, which had worked so well up till then, the soldier on duty first refused to let us through and said the road was closed to all civilians. I was about to say that it was no trouble to us and we would go back and take another road when he began to eye me suspiciously and said, "You look like a German soldier to me, I think I should run you in." He did not look like somebody you could argue with, so the only thing was to keep cool and show him our papers. He then began to ask questions which I answered in a friendly voice even if I did not always tell the truth. He must have come to the conclusion that we were not worth all the bother when he finally muttered, "I dunno, I still think I should run you in," and allowed us to beat a hasty retreat.

That was to be our last snag; at the next British barrier it was all smiles and we were able to continue on our way. Our journey from Mücheln to Rotenburg took just under three days. We did 80 miles on the first day and went up to 115 miles on the second day, but found that was too much and slowed down for the last run. On the afternoon of 15 May, 1945, our odyssey came to an end. We had reached a haven that was to be our home for the foreseeable future.

18

PROBLEMS RETURNING TO IRELAND

Rotenburg struck me as a very attractive town with many half-timbered old buildings and pleasantly set on the river Wümme in the Lüneburg Heathlands. Willi's home turned out to be a small farmhouse situated on the outskirts of the town, within a few minutes' walk of the country.

Erika and I were heartily welcomed by Willi's family who were overcome with joy at his safe return from the Front. His parents were both very thin people whose faces reflected a life of toil making a living from their small farm. The only other member of the family was Willi's sister, Ilse, a tall and attractive nineteen-year-old brunette.

Mrs Gerkens brought out her special crockery to celebrate the occasion and we all sat down to home-made cake and the still inevitable Ersatz coffee. During our meal I discovered how cheerful Willi's parents were, and I was delighted by the good humour and laughter that accompanied their conversation. Compared to them both, Willi and Ilse were much quieter. Frau Gerkens very generously offered to put up Erika and me indefinitely even though the family did not have much room for themselves. This presented a bit of a problem because the house had only three bedrooms, a parlour and the kitchen in which the family took their meals. A make-shift arrangement was made whereby Frau Gerkens sacrificed her good parlour to give Erika and me a bedroom. There was already a couch there, so a bed was added and our accommodation was complete. The farm boasted no bathroom, the kitchen sink being used for all ablutions. It was all very simple, but the house was spotlessly clean and Erika and I were grateful to be put up with such heartfelt kindness.

The only compensation we could offer was to pay a good rent for food and accommodation. We thought this might be welcome since Ilse was working at home with her parents and it did not look as if the farm could provide much of an income. I had very little money, having lost most of my army-pay in action, but Erika had saved enough to cover several months' rent.

In characteristic German fashion the farmhouse was situated in the town and separate from the land that belonged to it. There was an enclosed cobblestone yard at the back and side of the house, with access to the road. Behind the yard itself, there was a large barn with room to house the cattle in winter and also a wagon and the one horse which the Gerkens owned. Ducks, hens and a pig were housed in the yard and that was also where the only toilet was located.

During our evening meal we made plans. Our first priority was to get jobs, but we also had to register at the local police-station and we had to apply for ration cards. Willi and I had the extra problem of trying to avoid being sent to a prisoner-of-war camp. Mr Gerkens mentioned that there was a large British military administration department in Rotenburg which might be glad to employ Erika and me with our knowledge of English.

Early next morning Erika and I set off to visit the British Commanding Officer of the town, Major Carver who turned out to be a most gentlemanly person about forty-five years of age. We told him that we had just arrived in Rotenburg and needed a job while waiting to get back to our home in Ireland. I said nothing about having been in the army, and the major tactfully did not ask me although it must have been obvious to him. The major was very sympathetic to our cause and promised to try to get us jobs in the administration department. We were to come back next morning and he would let us know the outcome.

This gave us a trump card for our next important visit. We had to go to the police station for permission to register as new residents in Rotenburg. There was now a danger that some super-officious busybody might start asking me about army discharge papers. When we got there I spoke to the desk sergeant and told him importantly, and tongue-in-cheek, that my sister and I were about to start working at the Administration Department of the British Military Government. Having suitably impressed the sergeant, I went on to tell him that we already had living accommodation and now wished to register.

Whether this build-up was necessary or not I do not know, but it was as well to take the initiative and not leave anything to chance. It was only a matter of minutes before all formalities had been completed and we were on our way to the town hall as fully legitimate residents to claim our ration cards, and these we got without more ado.

During our absence, Willi had cycled to a neighbouring village, where he had worked as a fitter. They did not have enough work to give him his old job back, but agreed to employ him part-time until business improved. Since we had a free afternoon on our hands, we went for a walk in the adjoining heathlands and let Willi show us over his father's land. After a year's living on my wits in almost continuous danger, it was an unbelievable feeling to go for a relaxed ramble and I thought the atmosphere was one of perfect, idyllic peace. Now I could hear the song of birds without listening for the sound of danger, an approaching aircraft was no cause for alarm and distant figures posed no threat to me. I think I must have been on a "high" because I felt a numbing of my senses and it was as if I was viewing everything around me through a screen.

When I saw the land belonging to the Gerkens I was impressed by what good use had been made of it. It was quite tiny, only about six acres, but every square foot had been utilised. Five cows were grazing on a meadow and the rest was intensively cultivated with vegetables and fruit. It was a neat little holding, but it was also obvious that it took a lot of hard work to raise a family on it.

Next morning Erika and I were full of hopeful expectation when we went to see Major Carver. Once again luck was with us and he told us that we had been offered jobs as translators and interpreters. We were to report on the following day to a Major Waring, the officer in charge of the 58th Depot Control Company which was a unit of the British Control Commission of Germany. The offices were located in the administration buildings of a disused military aerodrome, a few miles outside Rotenburg. The aerodrome had been used as a base for fighter planes during the war, but runways, hangars and the office block had survived largely undamaged.

The following morning Erika and I cycled out to work and met our new boss. Major Waring was a very big man with a handlebar moustache; he had a somewhat gruff manner, but was not unfriendly. Wasting no time he handed us over to Mr Wallwork, the office manager. Mr Wallwork was another man with a moustache; he was also tall, but rather reserved and I can't say that I ever warmed to him. Although he did not show it, I think he did not like Germans and I must have sensed this. Actually, all through my employment with the British Control Commission I came across many service personnel who looked on all German men as bearing guilt for National-Socialism while considering all German women to be innocent. This was clearly a male bias and therefore natural, but it often annoyed me.

Our duties, as explained to us by Mr Wallwork, were twofold. Most of our time was to be taken up with translating letters, documents, discussion notes, details of agreements, etc., but we would also be asked to do a lot of translating at meetings between British staff and German spokesmen for townships and the business sector. A fair amount of travelling could be involved in the area between Hannover, Bremen and

Hamburg. A big bonus in our job was that we would get lunch in the officers' canteen which meant a saving on our precious ration cards. By this, Mrs Gerkens would also benefit. All in all, Erika and I could be well pleased with the arrangements and it looked as if the work might also be very interesting.

What I enjoyed most about my work were the trips on which I acted as interpreter. The subjects discussed almost invariably dealt with getting industry going again, rebuilding the infrastructure and assessing the immediate needs in various districts. This meant meeting important people and getting an insight into the workings of civic authorities and business generally. One other advantage of these trips was that I usually accompanied officers of a much higher rank than I associated with in my office job and they did not seem to have any anti-German bias.

As soon as Erika and I had settled into our jobs we set about our aim to get back to Ireland quickly. Germans had no regular way of communicating with the outside world, so we had to find another way of getting a message to our parents. Making enquiries around the office building, we came across an officer who came from Dublin, a Captain Mulholland. We put our problem to him and he promised to contact our parents when he went over on leave in a week's time.

Our big difficulty was that it would not be easy to get permission to leave Germany; as Germans we had no rights. We thought of claiming that we were "Displaced Persons," which was not strictly accurate, but we hoped the umbrella organisation might take up our case. With this in mind we took a train to Bremen on our first week-end off and placed an application with the relevant authorities. While in Bremen we also visited the Red Cross on the off-chance that they could help us, but they said they had no responsibility for us. Satisfied that we still had two irons in the fire, Erika and I returned to Rotenburg to await developments.

Our problems aside, we were extremely lucky to be where we were. With six million refugees from the East looking for housing and work, we had both.

A few weeks after our arrival in Rotenburg we had a minor set-back when we got a letter saying that we did not qualify as Displaced Persons. As Germans living in Germany we were not reckoned to be displaced, even if our home was in Ireland. Towards the end of June we got some good news and some bad news. One Saturday afternoon we had a surprise visitor called Sean Twomey who was a private in the British army and came from Mallow, where my parents lived. They (my parents) had been told about us by Captain Mulholland and had managed to get in touch with a soldier on leave who was stationed in Hamburg, only a short train journey from Rotenburg. He had very kindly brought us letters from our parents as well as clothes, but the bad news was that our parents could do nothing to get us back home. We had to achieve that ourselves, but they would meanwhile keep on trying through diplomatic channels. We gave Sean Twomey letters for him to post on to our parents and he promised to see us again after his next visit to Ireland and to act as a postal service for us. Sean Twomey's news from our parents put an end to our schemes for getting home quickly, so we had to think of something new.

Ever since 5 June, four Control Commissions, British, French, American and Russian, had been formally set up to assume overall control of the four zones of occupation in Germany. Erika and I decided to approach the British Control Commission with the claim that we had been born in Czechoslovakia and that a special case should be made to allow us to leave Germany. This turned out to be a catastrophic idea which could have cost me my life.

One day a sergeant from British Military Security came to my office and questioned me in detail about my background and also my army service. I gave him all the information quite frankly; how I was sent to school in Germany and got caught up in the war. The sergeant, called Levy, took down copious notes before he left.

Three days later, Sergeant Levy returned when I was at work in the office and arrested me. He said I would be sent to a prisoner-of-war camp with the recommendation that I be deported to Czechoslovakia in order to stand trial as a traitor to the country of my birth! It was a patently monstrous accusation, but it spelt major trouble for me. It was as much as I could do to persuade Sergeant Levy to let me tell Erika what had happened and to also go back to the farm to get a tooth-brush and a few things I would need. Poor Erika was quite shattered by my news and promised to contact Major Carver right away to see if he could help.

What happened next was quite ridiculous. Sergeant Levy called in two soldiers who, with rifles at the ready, marched me to a jeep. He himself sat in front with the driver and I sat in the back between the two soldiers who still held their rifles ready for action. We drove to the farmhouse where one soldier was put guarding the front door pointing the rifle at the entrance and the other soldier was sent to do the same at the back. Then I was allowed to go into the house and the sergeant, pistol in hand, walked behind me taking all the professional precautions as if I was James Bond personified.

This ludicrous performance did not bother me, but I felt for the embarrassment of my host whose neighbours had witnessed this undignified spectacle. When I had put a few things together, I was marched back to the jeep and the same precautions were again taken as we drove off. Our destination was the town of Munster about thirty miles east of Rotenburg and there I was handed over at a prisoner-of-war camp. Sergeant Levy gave the authorities a copy of my interrogation report and also gave me a copy for myself.

The first thing I did was to read the report. It contained a lot of wrong details, not important as such, but inexcusably erroneous all the same. What was more serious was a vicious bias with which he sought to misinterpret the motives behind my going to school in Germany and volunteering to join the Division Hermann Göring. His concluding recommendation that I should be handed over to the Czechoslovakian authorities could turn out to be the last nail in my coffin. After all I had gone through in the past year, the problem of survival had come back to haunt me.

I had arrived at the camp at midday and by four o'clock I began to feel the psychological pressure caused by my confinement. The effect on me of being surrounded by barbed wire was something that I had not anticipated and made me take a desperate action which seemed foolhardy in the extreme. When an NCO made the rounds some time later calling out, "Are there any foreigners here, the Camp Commander wants to see anybody who is not German," I was on my feet in an instant calling back, "Can I see him, I am Czechoslovakian."

I clearly remember my feelings when I threw all caution to the winds. It was partly that I already sensed the spirit-breaking effect of incarceration and could not remain inactive any longer. What also influenced me was the childhood bond with English people which had survived recent negative experiences. I was convinced that I would not so soon come up against another man like Levy.

My request to meet the Officer-in-Charge was allowed and moments later I found myself in the presence of Major Bilsland. I immediately admitted that I was not a Czechoslovakian and said that I had been brought into the camp with a damning report containing completely distorted information about me. I quickly went on to tell the major about myself, since he would not yet have seen the report, and then I handed him my copy. When the major finished reading, I saw the trace of a wry smile cross his face and he remarked quietly, "Yes, I think the sergeant is a keen man." He went on to say, "I will look into this," and he gave me such a kind smile that I was sure everything would be all right. I returned to my view of barbed wire, but now felt happier and I breathed a sigh of relief that my impetuous action had not catastrophically back-fired. The following morning I was called to the camp office at eight o'clock; my discharge papers had been signed and I was free to collect my belongings and leave. It was yet like another miracle.

As soon as I left the camp, I did a strange thing. There was a rail connection to Rotenburg, but I decided to walk the thirty miles without even considering looking at a time-table. I think the reason was that my sudden confinement had shaken my confidence. I did not want to be cooped up in a train or to meet uniformed railway officials and I just wanted to shun all human contact. Walking along the road restored my self-confidence; seeing woods and undergrowth reminded me that there I could seek safety from human beings. Thinking back on my disturbing experience has made me realise that I can have had only the most minute concept of the effect of long-term imprisonment.

I left the camp shortly after eight o'clock and I set myself a cracking pace as if pursued by devils. I ate nothing on the way and hardly allowed myself a breather, so it was just after five o'clock in the evening when I arrived back in Rotenburg. I had covered the thirty miles in only nine hours! There was nobody at the farm when I got back and sank exhausted into a chair. Minutes later I heard Erika returning from work. A look of utter disbelief crossed her face when she saw me sitting there in the bedroom. She and all the Gerkens were delighted at my good fortune, as was Major Carver, when we phoned him from the office in the morning.

Once again we began searching for an avenue which might help us to emigrate, but this time it had to be a safer way. We next tried UNRRA, the United Nations Relief and Rehabilitation Administration. This was an organisation operated by forty-four nations during the Second World War and was the precursor of the International Refugee

Organisation, a specialised agency set up after the creation of the United Nations in 1951. Unfortunately, after waiting for weeks, we again drew a blank. The problem seemed to be that until there was a greater normalising of conditions, there was absolutely no mechanism available to us.

To while away the time I began to visit friends I had made in the Hermann Lietz schools. Many of my friends were still in prisoner-of-war camps and others were reported missing, so I was delighted when I was able to renew some of my contacts. One day in early September we had a visitor, Nurse Mary Walsh from County Cork. Private Twomey had been suddenly transferred to a more distant location and, good man that he was, he had quickly found somebody to take his place. Nurse Walsh worked in a hospital in Bremen, which was even nearer to us than Hamburg. Once again there were presents for us, and also for the Gerkens.

In early October I was transferred to another job which was also on the aerodrome. I was told that a decreased demand for translating and interpreting no longer justified the employment of two people. This seemed a reasonable explanation and I fully accepted it. What did not seem logical to me was being told that I could no longer get lunch in the officers' canteen and would have to look after my own requirements. It was a pity about the lunches, but Mrs Gerkens was feeding me well and my new job was challenging in a new and interesting way.

I was now working on Nr 350 CEVP which stood for Captured Enemy Vehicle Park. Some 2,000 German ex-Army vehicles of every description were parked on the runways. There were cars of German, French, Italian, English and American make; there were vans, trucks, ambulances, fire-brigades and a whole range of motor-cycles up to heavy side-car outfits. The disused aeroplane hangars were used as workshops and a gang of fifteen Germans worked as mechanics overhauling the vehicles. None of the fitting staff were qualified motor-mechanics; they were all just people, with some knowledge of cars, who needed work.

My job was that of clerk and general administrator. More vehicles arrived every day which had to be assessed and overhauled for issue on licence to civic authorities, industry and doctors. My immediate boss, Sergeant Robinson, was in overall charge, but when he saw how I was handling things he let me get on with it and never interfered. It suited me because I enjoyed having full responsibility.

My new job brought me a bonus which was a welcome compensation for the loss of my lunches. I was allowed the use of any car within the boundary of the aerodrome. I made it my business to drive a different car or lorry each day, so that I soon had experience of driving almost every vehicle in existence. Strangely enough, I got on very well with Sergeant Robinson even though he was fiercely anti-German. "Robby," as he allowed me to call him, was a cockney and quite a rough diamond. Sometimes, when customers arrived bringing their small children, I could see Robby glaring at them and heard him snarling "Little Hitlers" under his breath. Over the weeks an amazing change came over Robby and he began to love German children and always had little presents for them when they came. Robby was a Jew and a very simple, uneducated person, but he had a heart of gold. I think it was when he began to forget the propaganda and learned that average Germans are like anybody else that he began to overcome his bias and his true nature asserted itself.

The months went by, autumn changed to winter and Mary Walsh still faithfully came to visit us. Ireland was as far away as ever and Mrs Gerkens must have been thoroughly fed up with us although she did everything to make us feel welcome. By paying more rent Erika and I hoped to compensate partly for the inconvenience we were causing. Christmas came with some festive snow and it was wonderful to celebrate again as a civilian, even if it was not in my own home.

In the New Year my parents applied to the Irish Department of External Affairs for certificates of naturalisation. In the aftermath of the war all Germans had been expelled from Czechoslovakia and their property and assets were confiscated. Since my parents had lost their home in Czechoslovakia and they liked Ireland, they decided that this was where our future would lie.

Towards the end of January, the stock of vehicles began to dwindle. Back in November there had been a peak of over 3,000, but then fewer came in for repair and the number of irreparable, cannibalised vehicles grew steadily. In February scrap dealers began to haul away the wrecks and by the beginning of March my staff was down to two mechanics. I began to wind down the whole operation and my last day of work on the aerodrome was on 13 March, 1946, but I had already found a new job with the local German police and started working for them on 15 March.

In my new job I worked in the criminal investigation section and my boss was Polizei-Hauptmann (Police Captain) Klein. He was a small, roundish man, full of fun, and I enjoyed working in his section. Most of my work was clerical, but there was also a certain amount of translating in cases where complaints had been made about the occupation forces.

Some weeks earlier, on 16 February, my parents had been granted Irish citizenship. In the hope that this might also speed our return home they had made an open-ended advance booking with the American Airline TWA for two flight tickets from Paris to Rineanna, as Shannon was then called. These tickets were deposited with the Irish Legation in Paris where it shared premises with the British Embassy. There were no direct commercial air-routes between Germany and Ireland and the airport nearest to Germany from which we could have flown home was Paris. So now Erika and I had to set our aim at getting to Paris. At about this time my parents had moved to Dublin from Mallow which had the advantage of giving them a more direct contact with the diplomatic services.

Once again the weeks dragged on - we had been almost a year in Rotenburg and it was no easier to get to Paris than to Ireland. When Erika and I got home from work in the evening of 27 April, we found a letter waiting for us from the French Vice-Consul in Hamburg asking us to call to his office urgently in connection with our application to travel to Ireland. This was quite out of the blue and it looked as if things had suddenly started moving.

On arrival at the Chancellery we were told that we had been granted transit visas which permitted us to enter France. We were also told that we would be travelling on a train from Frankfurt reserved for members of diplomatic services and that we should keep this information strictly to ourselves. The train was due to leave Frankfurt on 2 May at six in the evening. Apparently, this was the only way for us to leave Germany; no other travel arrangements were possible. It was amazing that even at this stage our emigration was accompanied by such complications. We were given our documentation and also special tickets for the train.

We arrived back in Rotenburg in a state of euphoria. It seemed impossible that the miracle had finally happened and that we would be in Ireland in a week's time. Our news brought the Gerkens delight, and relief that they would have their house to themselves again.

There was much leave-taking to be done in the final days; friends and neighbours had all been so kind, just as if we were all members of one large family. We also gave a special thanks to Major Carver who was a characteristic English gentleman. Our last day in Rotenburg came and went and then we were ready to leave.

19

HOMEWARD BOUND

On 2 May Erika and I picked a train that would get us to Frankfurt in good time for our connection to Paris. Herr and Frau Gerkens said good-bye to us at the farm and seemed quite moved by our departure - I also felt sad at parting from these very kind people. Willi and Ilse walked us to the station and then waited on the platform till the train came and whisked us out of sight.

When we arrived at Frankfurt and went to the Paris train, our travel-documents were given a particularly careful scrutiny because we would be leaving Germany. We must have looked unusual since we had not been able to buy suit-cases in Rotenburg and, though we were not badly dressed, our luggage consisted of cardboard boxes tied together with string; we did not exactly look like diplomatic staff. A railway-official brought us to the last carriage of the train and then he did a strange thing. After asking Erika and me to get into a compartment, he apologised profusely and said that he had orders to lock the door behind us. I got the impression that our trip was not quite legal and that we were more or less being smuggled out of Germany, protected by diplomatic immunity. The official went on to assure us that, once the train had crossed the French border, our door would be unlocked.

Well, that was nothing to upset us. We would be crossing the border in a few hours and we had come well provided with food for the journey. The train pulled out of the station on time and Erika and I relaxed while we watched the countryside pass by. Soon we were travelling upstream beside the Rhine, but it was not long before the train turned westwards and began to cross the higher ground of the Palatinate with its large expanse of woods.

We had a long trip ahead of us and would have to sleep on the seats in the compartment, but they were well upholstered and would give us a good night's rest. Later on we ate some sandwiches, but had to delay going to sleep until we had gone through the border checkpoint. Shortly before midnight we stopped at the town of Forbach on the river Moselle near Saarbrücken and our entry into France was stamped on our transit visas. With a sigh of relief I sank onto my makeshift bed and within minutes I was asleep.

I woke early in the morning and gazed out at the French landscape. What I saw was not remarkable, but it represented an end to our problems and that gave it a special aura of magic. When the train pulled into Paris, Erika and I went into the station restaurant to refresh ourselves with a warming cup of coffee and to make further plans.

It was still fairly early, so we decided to take our time and walk to the British embassy. It was wonderful to just stroll along the Paris boulevards and soak up our impressions; it was so hard to believe that we had really achieved our freedom. The Irish consul saw us immediately and straight away rang TWA Airlines. We were in luck, because he managed to book us on a Dublin flight departing late that evening.

After we left the Irish Consulate, Erika cut open a seam in the lining of her coat and took out some pound notes that our parents had sent us some time ago. Having exchanged them for French money at a bank we now felt quite rich and first went to a hairdresser's to get spruced up. I think events must have left me quite bewildered, because I remember so little of our day in Paris. I do recall our having a celebratory lunch in an exclusive restaurant, but I must have gone through the rest of the day in a trance.

When Erika and I arrived at Orly Airport that night all formalities went without a hitch. I was very much impressed by our plane, which was one of the large and beautifully designed American Constellations with the characteristic three vertical tail-fins. It was pitch dark when we took off, but the darkness allowed me one of the most beautiful sights I have ever seen. The whole centre of Paris was ablaze with lights. The Champs-Élysées and all other roads radiating from the Arc de Triomphe could be seen like a lit-up star and I craned my neck to enjoy this magnificent spectacle for as long as possible. Once the Paris lights disappeared from view, pitch darkness took over and I settled down for a snooze during the two-and-a-half-hour flight to Ireland.

It was close to midnight when we touched down at Rineanna and a light meal was offered to all passengers. We were served so much meat that Erika asked the waiter whether all the meat on her plate was for her. After the meal an airline bus brought us to the National Hotel in Pery's Square in Limerick where we had been booked in for the night. Tired as I was, I found it impossible to get off to sleep. Maybe the journey had created a lot of tension in me and I was not as relaxed as I had expected to be. What certainly did not help was the Tait's clock-tower in the square beside the hotel which struck every quarter of an hour.

One of the first things we did after getting up was to contact our parents and to give them the good news of our safe arrival. After so many years of separation I was conscious of a slight awkwardness when speaking with my father, but it soon passed and we got down to discussing our travel arrangements to Dublin.

The luxury of my first breakfast in Ireland provided proof that I was still quite disoriented. When the waitress reeled off the list of all that was on offer I asked her what I could get without food coupons. The poor girl looked at me blankly, so I told her that I unfortunately did not yet have my ration cards. Luckily, Erika had her wits about her and whispered to me, "We probably do not need any," which was indeed the case.

Soon afterwards Erika and I were enjoying the pleasure of travelling to Dublin on an uncrowded train; how different this was after our wartime and post-war experiences in Germany. The Irish countryside was still just as I remembered it and it seemed strange to hear only Irish accents from all the other passengers. Erika and I slipped into conversation with our co-travellers as if we had never been gone, while Germany now seemed to have receded a million miles away. It was a slow journey to Dublin, but now there was nothing more to go wrong and we could indulge in the joyous anticipation of soon being reunited with our parents.

The time was coming up to half past one when our train steamed into Kingsbridge Station, as it was then called. Leaning out of the window we could make out our parents from afar waving to us. We were home at last.

EPILOGUE

Sixty-five years have elapsed since I was on the Russian Front and over the years people have asked me what effect living in war-time Germany, and then serving as a soldier, has had on me and my life. This question has also interested me, but it is difficult to be completely objective, because who can tell how one would have developed if certain factors had not been part of one's life.

First of all, being stranded in Germany as a teenager was not as hard to bear as others might think. I loved the life in my two boarding schools and I had a wonderful time during all my holidays. Relatives and friends went to great trouble to make me feel at home and provided me with all sorts of treats. Another factor must be that I had had plenty of practice in learning to settle down in a new environment, so I must have already been a fairly independent person.

I think the war made me very critical of waste and I will always remember my experience of living with rationing over many years. A further lasting memory has been of people exchanging essential food rations for cigarettes. This has left me with a resolve never to become prey to such dependence.

Fortunately, I did not get caught in a city during an air-raid, nor was my battery ever attacked directly during my service as a Luftwaffen-auxiliary, so it was not until I joined the army, and became more directly involved in the horrors of war, that I experienced acute personal danger and severe hardships.

When I was on the Front, I was extremely lucky to have suffered from nothing worse than acid burns and the conditions of extreme cold. It becomes more difficult when trying to assess whether I suffered so-called mental scars. I think there are two reasons why I did not suffer from severe post-war trauma, as happened to many ex-soldiers.

In the first case, I never found myself in a position where I had to cold-bloodedly take human life or cause personal injury. In the second case, and this is something which has always amazed me, soldiers never seemed to get killed or injured within my sight. I remember only one exception, and that was when our ammunition train got blown up and some of us were hit by shrapnel fragments.

This brings me to the only problem of a psychological nature that I had. It first hit me about a month after the war was over. One night I had been fast asleep in bed on the farm in Rotenburg when I awoke with a start and was struck by the unnerving conviction that I must have been killed on the Russian Front. My mind flew back, darting from event to event, when unbelievable luck saved me every time and I argued that to think I had survived was absurd. The only explanation that made sense to me just then was that when a person is dead, the mind continues to function and to throw up images as if one continued to live out one's expected existence.

Over the course of time these doubts returned, but with an ever-decreasing frequency. I soon learned to apply self-control and to switch my thoughts to other matters so that I was no longer troubled after the first few weeks. When I began to write my narrative, I wondered whether this would cause my doubts to re-surface. In actual fact my memory has only been jogged about this experience of long ago and I have had no trouble setting down a dispassionate record of these recollections.

After my personal experience of tight discipline in the German army, revelations about the policy of extermination in concentration camps came as a great shock to me. That the excesses of a well-organized minority in power can inflict so much lasting damage on mankind must be a grim warning to us all and to future generations.

I have at no time felt any bitterness that I was unfortunate enough to get stuck in war-time Germany when I could have enjoyed an almost peace-time existence in Ireland. By the same token I have never thought of blaming my parents for sending me to Germany. Of course, a loss which can never be made good is the seven years during which I grew to adulthood without seeing them.

At the same time, my life has been enriched by the years spent in Germany and army service has given me a greater self-confidence than I would otherwise have had. I have often felt that if I could survive the Russian Front then I could survive anything. Though I lost much by my parents' decision to send me to Germany, I also gained a lot in other areas and this included meeting the girl who later became my wife. In whatever way my life might have been different, this is how it turned out and I am well content.

In writing these memoirs I have fulfilled a long-time ambition of wanting to record my service on the Russian Front. While doing this I was constantly reminded of the terrible tragedy of the death of millions of young soldiers on all sides whom I would nowadays look on as being hardly more than boys. Next, it awoke memories of the horrendous fate suffered by German refugees from the eastern provinces. Another reminder was of the total destruction of old European cities with so much loss of life and of irreplaceable art treasures. What a terrible waste it had all been!

It was a great sadness for me to be reminded of the friends in the Lietz schools who had been killed on the Front, or were listed as missing and never heard from again. So many young gifted people, full of life and with high hopes for their future, were lost to their families.

I did not, of course, have the same ties with the men in my division whom I knew only fleetingly, but I was nevertheless deeply shocked to discover from military archives that so few had survived death, or capture by the Russians. In a tragic ending for the Hermann Göring Divisions, nearly all of the surviving units became encircled by the advancing Russian forces at some stage during the final days of the war. Soldiers of the last units to surrender became prisoners-of-war near the town of Geising one day after Germany surrendered and less than twenty-four hours after I had passed along that same road. Very few soldiers managed to break out of the ring and then still elude Czechoslovakian partisans before surrendering to American troops.

Although I was never enthusiastic about being a soldier, I cannot but feel deeply saddened by the fate of my army-corps. I had known it when it was at full strength, I had respected it for the exemplary discipline that was maintained whatever the situation and I had never known any units or individual soldiers to be guilty of dishonourable behaviour. That I was one of the very few to escape unscathed was just my good luck.

Both Heinelt twins survived the war and fulfilled their ambition to become doctors. Sadly, Günther developed multiple sclerosis in his early thirties and both he and Heinz died in their fifties. Willi Gerkens settled down in his home town of Rotenburg, but he also died in his fifties. I never discovered the fate of any other of my mates in the Division Göring.

Hertha's brother, Adolf, returned to Döllnitz after Germany became reunited. Under the conditions of unification, no claim for repossession of the family farm was possible and re-purchase was also not permitted. Adolf rents part of the land and farms it organically. His brother, Georg went into publishing and lives in Stuttgart. Over the years Georg and I have spent many a time hiking in the southern German Alps.

My guardian, Uncle Oskar, survived the war and was soon reunited with his wife and baby. Aunt Hella was evicted from her house in Karlsbad, but she managed to build a new life in

Munich. In her typically enterprising way she took up horse-riding and painting when in her sixties.

My sister, Erika, married an Irishman in 1954 and emigrated to Canada. They live near Toronto and have two children and five grandchildren.

My in-laws, the Goedeckes, were dispossessed of their farm in 1945 and first settled in West Germany. In 1953 I arranged for Mr. Goedecke to get a position as a farm manager near Carlow and he and his wife lived in Ireland until 1967. They loved Ireland, but returned to Germany because they were getting on in years and missed their many relatives.

Erika and I had no problem adjusting to life in Ireland. Although it did not strike me at the time, I think my parents must have found it very hard to suddenly have two adults in the family, when they last knew them as children. To have been deprived of witnessing seven years of one's children's lives must have been very sad and a great loss to them.

I took an engineering and science degree in University College Dublin and spent my professional life working for the Electricity Supply Board. I became involved in running the first turf-burning power-stations in Portarlington and Allenwood and also worked in Cork and Dublin power-stations.

Since my retirement I have visited many scenes from my early years. Annual class re-unions in Haubinda and holidays in Karlsbad have been particularly poignant.

I am very grateful that Hertha's and my children have been able to grow up in a time of peace in this part of Europe. They are long since happily married and we now have four grandchildren.

Though my family and all our relatives were displaced from the land of their birth as a result of the war, we were more fortunate than others and, maybe, of us all, it was I who received the greatest share of luck.

Army-Corps	Group of two to four divisions
Army-Group	Group of two to four armies
Bannführer	Senior leader of a Hitler Youth group
Battalion	Unit composed of 500 - 1,000 men
Bazooka	Hand-held rocket launcher
BDM (Bund Deutscher Mädchen)	Association of German Girls
Division	Unit composed of 4,000 - 20,000 men
Elite Division	Division made up of soldiers with superior training and equipment
Feldmarschall	Field Marshal
Festung	A city which is defended to the end and becomes part of the war-zone
FLAK (Fliegerabwehrkanone)	Anti-aircraft gun
Gauleiter	High-ranking SS official, with wide-ranging powers, in charge of a province or zone
Gefreiter	Private, first class
Gun	Description of all types of canon, as against rifles or pistols
Generaloberst	Highest rank of a General
Hauptmann	Captain
Hauptwachtmeister	Staff sergeant in FLAK unit
Helper	Schoolboy drafted for service in an anti-aircraft battery
Herrenrasse	Master race
Hitler Jugend	Hitler Youth
Jungvolk	Junior section of the Hitler Youth
Kanonier	Private in a FLAK unit
Katjuscha	Russian multiple rocket launcher
Labour Service	Prescribed period in which young

	Germans had to do unskilled labouring work
Luftwaffen Helfer	Luftwaffe helper, or auxiliary
NCO	Non-commissioned officer
Oberst	Colonel
OC	Officer-in-charge
Panzer	Tank
RAD (Reichs Arbeits Dienst)	Labour Service
Realgymnasium	Grammar School
Sapper	Member of a special task force: building pontoon bridges, dynamiting and using flame throwers
Self-propelled gun	Gun mounted on tank-type tracked undercarriage
Skat	Popular card game for three players, similar to 'Solo'
SS (Schutzstaffel)	Private army of elite guards
Sudetenland	German-speaking areas of Czechoslovakia
Volkssturm	Type of Home Guard Militia created in September 1944
Wachtmeister	Sergeant in FLAK unit
Waffen SS	Military arm of the political SS
Wehrmacht	German Land Forces

AVERAGE STRUCTURE OF GERMAN LAND FORCES

Each army-group has 2 to 4 armies of approx. 200,000 men
Each army has 2 to 4 army-corps of 40,000 to 80,000 men
Each army-corps has 2 to 4 divisions of 4,000 to 20,000 men
Each division has 4 to 6 regiments of 1,000 to 4,000 men
Each regiment has 2 battalions of 500 to 1,000 men
Note: Germany had a peak of 27 armies in action during the war, comprising over 6 million men.

Equipment of Panzer-Corps Hermann Göring

FLAK guns	216
Tanks	190
Self-propelled artillery	66
Anti-tank guns	73
Mortars	74
Rocket launchers	206
Machine-guns	1,270
Flame throwers	18
Armoured reconnaissance vehicles	36
Armoured personnel carriers	56
Aeroplanes	2

Added to this there were vehicles and equipment associated with: sappers, supplies, communications, medical services, workshops and repair units, catering, military police and administration staff.

FLAK-gun equipment of Panzer-Corps Göring in January 1945

20-millimetre single-barrel guns	82
20-millimetre four-barrel guns	12
37-millimetre guns	44
88-millimetre guns	78

Total manpower of Panzer-Corps was 12,000 men.

20-millimetre self-propelled FLAK-gun

Theoretical firing rate 180 - 200 rounds per minute. Range 4,800 metres. Ceiling 1,070 metres. Muzzle velocity 800 - 900 metres per second. Eight shells per magazine. Net weight of shell 115 - 148 grams. Gun mounted on half-tracked modified Panzer 4 tank propulsion system.

37-millimetre self-propelled FLAK-gun

Theoretical firing rate 150 rounds per minute. Range 6,500 metres. Ceiling 1,525 metres. Muzzle velocity 840 metres per second. Eight shells per magazine. Net weight of shell 635 -700 grams. Gun mounting same as above.

88-millimetre FLAK-gun

Firing rate twenty rounds per minute. Range 19,700 metres. Ceiling 14,930 metres. Muzzle velocity 1,020 metres per second. Net weight of shell 9 - 9.5 kilograms.

105-millimetre FLAK-gun

Firing rate ten to fifteen rounds per minute. Range 17,300 metres. Ceiling 10,500 metres. Muzzle velocity 900 metres per second. Net weight of shell 15.9 kilograms.

T - 34

Medium Russian tank. Crew of four. 500 horse-power engine. Weight 26.3 tons. Armour plating 75 millimetres. Max. speed 53 km/hour. Range 400 km. One 76.2 millimetre gun and two 7.6 millimetre machine-guns. Most commonly used Russian medium tank. Excellent in difficult terrain such as sand, swamps and snow. Very reliable.

T - 75 "Joseph Stalin"
Heavy Russian tank. Crew of four. 513 horse-power engine. Weight 45 tons. Armour plating maximum 120 millimetres. Max. speed 37 km/hour. Range 240 km. One 122 millimetre gun and three 7.6 millimetre machine-guns. Heavy Russian tank. Good manoeuvrability for its size.

"Tiger"
Heavy German tank. Crew of five. 700 horse-power engine. Weight 50 tons. Armour plating 110 millimetres. Max. speed 38 km/hour. Range 100 km. One 88-millimetre gun and two 7.92-millimetre machine-guns. Superior to all opposition, but lacked manoeuvrability. 1,350 tanks built.

"Königstiger"
German "super tank." Crew of five. 700 horse-power engine. Weight 68.6 tons. Armour plating maximum 150 millimetres. Max. speed 38 km/hour. Range 110 km. One 88-millimetre gun and two 7.92-millimetre machine-guns. Most powerful of any tank in 1944. Exceptionally heavy armour. Mechanically unreliable. 485 tanks built.

"Panther"
Heavy German tank. Crew of five. 700 horse-power engine. Weight 44.1 tons. Armour plating 80 - 120 millimetres. Max. speed 45 km/hour. Range 176 km. One 75-millimetre gun and two 7.92-millimetre machine-guns. Overall one of the best tanks built in World War Two.

Ilyuschin Il-2 "Stormovik" or "Black Death"
Russian two-seater fighter-bomber. Single 1,600 horse power engine. Max. speed 411 km/hour. Range 600 km. Ceiling 4,160 metres. Two 37-millimetre cannons, three 7.6-millimetre machine-guns and eight 25-kilogramme rockets or 600 kilogrammes of bombs. Special feature was its armour plating, up to 81 millimetres thick. 42,330 planes built.

Junkers Ju-87 "Stuka"
German two-seater dive-bomber. Single 1,210 horse-power engine. Max. Speed 400 km/hour. Range 800 km. Ceiling 6,730 metres. Three 7.92 machine-guns and 690 kilogrammes of bombs. 4,880 planes were built. The 'Stukas' dived at an angle of 70 to 80 degrees whereby air-brakes were used to limit the speed to 710 km/hour. A screaming siren operated during diving.

Bazooka "Panzerfaust" (Tank fist)
German hand-held rocket-launcher used against tanks. Weight 6.1 kilogrammes. Length one metre. Diameter five centimetres. Range 80 metres. Able to penetrate 200 millimetres of steel.

MG - 42
Highly successful German 7.92-millimetre machine-gun. Weight 11.6 kilogrammes. Length 1.22 metres. 1,500 rounds per minute. Range 3,500 metres.

V - 1
German long-range rocket. Weight 2.14 tons. Length twenty-five feet. Speed 660 km/hour. Range 370 kilometres. Carried 0.82 tons of explosives. 10,500 rockets were built. Rocket flew on a pre-determined course. Descent was activated by a propeller-driven timing device.

V - 2
German long-range rocket. Weight 12.9 tons. Length 12.2 metres. Diameter 1.4 metres. Speed 5,760 km/hour. Range 360 kilometres. Ceiling 185 kilometres. Carried one ton of explosives. Rocket was propelled by four tons of liquid-alcohol fuel together with five tons of liquid oxygen for combustion. Flight controlled by an electric guiding beam. Rocket travelled through the stratosphere.

Katyusha "Stalin Organ"
Russian rocket launcher. 48 projectiles dispatched within seconds. Range, according to model, 2.5 to 8.2 kilometres. It achieved a strong psychological effect due to howling noise of rockets during flight.

BIBLIOGRAPHY

Braun, G.: Der Fallschirmjäger. (Verlag) Karlsruhe, Articles contributed between 1959 and 1980 by:
   Dinger, Ludwig:
   Der Wandernde Kessel, 1960.
   Die Winterschlacht beginnt, 1959.
   Tollhaus - Steinau Brückenkopf, 1959.
   Versprengt, 1960.
   Dittrich, Heinz.
   Die letzten Kriegswochen im Osten, 1967.
   Otte, Alfred:
   Das Fallschirmkorps in Ostpreussen, 1968/69.
   Das war das stärkste Flakregiment, 1976
   Der neue Panzer-Grossverband 1972/73.
   Die Schlacht an der Neisse, 1969.
   Sie erlagen der Übermacht, 1980.
   Unser Einsatz an der Weichsel, 1970/71.
   Von Utrecht nach Graudenz, 1972/73

Ellis, John: The Sharp End of War, David & Charles, London, 1980.

Guderian, Heinz: Panzerleader. Holles Street Press Ltd., Slough, Jan 1952.

Haupt, Werner: Das Ende im Osten. Podzun Verlag,Dorheim, 1970. (Later Podzun-Pallas, Friedberg).

Magenheimer, Heinz: Abwehrschlacht and der Weichsel 1945, Verlag Rombach, Freiburg 1976.

Michaelis, Prof. Dr. Herbert, et al.: Der Zweite Weltkrieg Bilder Daten Dokumente. C. Bertelsmann, München. 1983.

Nehring, Walther K.: Der 'Wandernde Kessel.' Deutsches Soldatenjahrbuch, compiled by Helmut Dameran Schild Verlag, München, 1976.

Niepold, Gerd: Mittlere Ostfront Juni '44. Mittler Verlag, Bonn, 1985.

Otte, Alfred: Die Weissen Spiegel, Vom Regiment zum Fallschirm-Panzerkorps. Podzun-Pallas, Bad Nauheim, 1989.

Snyder, Louis L.: Encyclopaedia of the Third Reich. McGraw Hill, 1976.

Überreiter, Carl: Die Zertrümmerung der Ostfront 1944. Zeitschrift für die Ausbildung im Bundesheer, Verlag Carl Überreiter, Wien, 1969.

White, B.T.: Tanks and other Armoured Fighting Vehicles of the World. New Orchard Editions Ltd., 1988.

Zentner, Kurt: Illustrierte Geschichte des Zweiten Weltkrieges. Südwestverlag, München, 1963.

Map 3 produced with acknowledgements to;

Zentner, Christian, Lexikon des Zweiten Weltkrieges. Jahrverlag KG, Hamburg, 1977

41540569R00183

Made in the USA
San Bernardino, CA
04 July 2019